From Union Stars to Top Hat

From
Union Stars
to Top Hat

a biography of the
extraordinary General
James Harrison Wilson

by Edward G. Longacre

Stackpole Books

FROM UNION STARS TO TOP HAT
Copyright © 1972 by

THE STACKPOLE COMPANY

Published by
STACKPOLE BOOKS
Cameron and Kelker Streets
Harrisburg, Pa. 17105

Printed in U.S.A.

Library of Congress Cataloging in Publication Data

Longacre, Edward G   1946-
    From Union stars to top hat.

    Bibliography: p.
    1. Wilson, James Harrison, 1837-1925. I. Title.
E467.1.W74L6   355.3'31'0924 [B]   72-7401
ISBN 0-8117-0697-4

for
JILL

Contents

List of Illustrations and Maps

Preface

When civil war came upon America in 1861, the federal government was caught very much by surprise. The small peacetime force which had served the nation for so many years was swelled by an influx of raw recruits; and high-rank commissions were doled out to almost anyone, it seemed, who showed promise of leadership. Inevitably the burden of high command fell to the lot of graduates of the United States Military Academy, including those who completed their education shortly before and during the conflict. These "boy generals" soon became one of the most remarkable phenomena of the war.

With the possible exception of George Armstrong Custer (who is represented by a body of literature extensive enough to stock a small library), James Harrison Wilson was the most distinguished of these young commanders. In many facets of generalship Wilson was superior to Custer, for he possessed greater tactical and strategic ability. He also attained higher rank during the conflict and achieved more dramatic victories. In fact, he was the only general, Federal or Confederate, to command almost 15,000 mounted soldiers during independent campaigning—campaigning which made Wilson, at the ripe old age of twenty-seven, the country's most successful cavalry leader.

Both Custer and Wilson were glory-hunters of the first magnitude. Yet at the present time, almost everyone who knows anything at all about American history has heard of George Custer (though it is true that much of his fame derives from his dramatic death in 1876 at the Little Bighorn), while Wilson remains, to most, an unknown figure. Given Wilson's impressive war record (a record further embellished by his services during the Spanish-American War in 1898 and the Boxer Rebellion of 1900), this seems paradoxical indeed.

To understand the paradox is to understand Wilson's problems in personal relationships. He was often imperious and outspoken, to the extent that he alienated fully as many people as he attracted. He made friends with many who later, for one reason or another, became his bitter enemies. Such a man was Ulysses S. Grant, who sought revenge by writing off many of Wilson's war achievements as minor deeds and by failing to note others at all, when he published his memoirs in 1885. Other enemies sought to tarnish Wilson's Civil War reputation in published works, influencing later historians to disregard his services.

A major reason why Wilson's single greatest military achievement—his 1865 Selma campaign—attracted little notice at the time it occurred, was the absence of newsmen from the Federal columns during the expedition. Journalists foresaw that the trip would prove too dangerous for their comfort, and so were not on hand to publicize its dramatic results immediately after its close. And when it finally began to circulate in June 1865, news of the campaign was overshadowed by the more momentous stories that had broken a short time previously, including Lee's surrender at Appomattox and Lincoln's assassination.

Furthermore—and most tragically—Wilson outlived his era of glory. When he died in 1925 at the age of eighty-seven, very few of those who had fought the tragic conflict were still living. Thus no close associates could be spurred by Wilson's death into considering his military contributions and according them the importance to which they were entitled. Fresher in the minds of the nation were Wilson's services in Cuba and China, but these could not compare with the caliber of his accomplishments in the Civil War. Thus Wilson passed away in an age whose people could not recall his great efforts, nor even his name.

James Harrison Wilson does not deserve to be so neglected. The primary purpose of this book—the first full-length biography of his life—is to resurrect his image, so as to give deserved consideration to one of the most distinguished military careers in American history. Hopefully it will offer insight into the personality of a man who often epitomized the qualities found in every great soldier—energy, determination, intelligence, resourcefulness—and stimulate appreciation of a general whose contributions to military science were not restricted to application during his own era but which have significant implications for modern-day warfare.

Secondly, the book attempts to illustrate how a man of strong character, great self-confidence, and solid organizational talent can triumph over certain qualities of personality which in other men would pose severe difficulties. For Wilson was also egotistical, blatantly ambitious, dedicated to succeeding at almost any cost; and he did not go out of his way to win popularity among his associates when he perceived that such behavior would not necessarily advance his career. At no point in his life, either in or out of uniform, was Wilson saintly. Rather, he was merely a man who knew exactly what he wanted from life and believed he knew how to go about attaining it. Sometimes he did not succeed, but he succeeded more often than he failed, and his successes are still worthy of note today.

This book chiefly concerns Wilson's Civil War career, in which he performed most of the deeds which solidified his reputation. However, it also gives due consideration to his postwar business life, during which he manifested many of the same traits which had won him high rank and notability on the battlefields. Finally, it describes his services in later wars and throughout his long and productive political/commercial career, which extended to the time of his death.

It is hoped that the story thus presented will suffice to generate renewed interest in Wilson's life and bring about a greater appreciation of his many accomplishments during six decades of public service. Such a story has remained untold for too many years.

Acknowledgments

The author is deeply indebted to several libraries, historical societies, and individuals for assistance in the preparation of this book. Those most deserving of formal notice are here listed.

Mr. Roy P. Basler and his staff of the Manuscript Division, Library of Congress, were most helpful in supplying the papers of General Wilson and those of his Civil War associates. Many of the illustrations for this book were obtained through the assistance of Le Roy Bellamy, of the Library's Prints and Photographs Division.

Mr. Jack Best, of the Old Military Records Division, National Archives, went out of his way to furnish obscure facts from Wilson's personnel file and from War Department archives. Also helpful in the Old Army Division was Dale Floyd; and Gary Morgan, of the Cartographic Division, made available numerous topographical maps, some drawn by Wilson, others prepared under his supervision.

The author wishes to express his thanks to *Civil War Times Illustrated* for permission to reproduce the maps of the Wilson-Kautz raid, the routes of the Union and Confederate forces in the Spring Hill-Franklin Campaign, and the routes of the Union and Confederate forces during Wilson's Selma raid, which originally appeared in the May 1970, December 1964, and January 1963 issues of the magazine, respectively. The map showing the Virginia Wilderness battle terrain is one of the many excellent maps compiled by Edward Steere and Colonel W. S. Nye for Mr. Steere's book, *The Wilderness Campaign*.

Mr. Kenneth W. Rapp, Assistant Archivist, United States Military Academy Archives, provided useful information about Wilson's academic record at West Point, and furnished some photographs of the Academy as it appeared in the 1850s.

The staff of the Historical Society of Delaware (Wilmington) made available the valuable diaries of Wilson and his wife, as well as other research tools.

The War Library and Museum of the Military Order of the Loyal Legion of the United States, Pennsylvania Commandery (Philadelphia) provided a staggering array of Civil War literature, including many rare volumes. Personnel of particular assistance were Mrs. Sara Moore and Mr. Henry Warrington.

The numerous volumes which comprise the Official Records of the Union and Confederate Armies were efficiently furnished by the Public Documents Department of the Philadelphia Free Library.

Other institutions which provided valuable assistance include:

The Gallatin County (Illinois) Historical Society; The Nebraska State Historical Society; the interlibrary loan desks at both the University of Nebraska Library and the Library of La Salle College; The Historical Society of Pennsylvania; Fort Vancouver National Historic Site; McKendree College (Lebanon, Illinois); and the Haddonfield (New Jersey) Public Library.

The author also wishes to express his gratitude for aid furnished by the following individuals:

Professor James A. Rawley, History Department, University of Nebraska, who made helpful suggestions pertaining to Civil War research; Mr. Thomas Robson Hay of Locust Valley, New York, for his interesting impressions of General Wilson, whom he had the privilege of knowing personally fifty years ago; Mr. Samuel W. Newman of Waco, Texas, who probably has accumulated more facts about Wilson's post-Civil War career than anyone else alive; Mr. Jerry Keenan of Thornton, Colorado, who supplied an index to the Wilson Papers in the

Library of Congress and gave other valuable assistance; Mr. Bruce Catton, Senior Editor of the American Heritage Publishing Company and the nation's most esteemed Civil War scholar, who offered some intriguing opinions about the Wilson-Grant association; Mrs. Jess Ann Logsdon of Shawneetown, Illinois, who supplied needed facts about the village in which Wilson was born; Mr. John Wagstaffe of Omaha, Nebraska, for sharing some perceptive observations on Wilson's character and personality; and—last but by no means least—Mr. Edgar Thorp Longacre, the author's father, for all manner of editorial assistance.

★ I ★

I Must Succeed,
for It Is My Only
Alternative

On the morning of July 23, 1861 the transport *Cortez* put out into the Columbia River from the harbor at Portland, and steamed westward toward the Pacific Ocean. With varying degrees of reluctance, her passengers left behind the small frontier settlement and the nearby United States Army outpost at Fort Vancouver, District of Oregon. In a matter of minutes the vast expanse of the Pacific swallowed up both town and fort.

At least one passenger had few regrets about departing. For twenty-three-year-old James Harrison Wilson, second lieutenant of topographical engineers, the outpost had been the scene of a long period of unrewarding activity. He had served at Fort Vancouver for the past nine months, engaged in unimaginative and sometimes trivial work.

Under normal circumstances, young Wilson might have tolerated such a life. A realist, he had no illusions about serving an exciting tour of duty in the peacetime army, whose ranks he had joined the year before. But by this midmonth of 1861 he was no longer in the peacetime army. Two months ago, the tensions which had charged the national atmosphere for so long had been ignited by violence at Fort Sumter, South Carolina. Time-worn sectional quarrels had at last exploded into full-scale civil war.

The national crisis had quickly fed Wilson's determination to leave Fort Vancouver. He felt that no worthy cause bound him to service in the wilderness while, almost 3,000 miles away, soldiers of the Federal Union battled warriors of the newly established Confederate States Army in a struggle which was to decide whether the country would remain united or would dissolve forever.

Wilson was determined to support the cause of union and to defeat the unconstitutional evil of secession. Shortly before the opening guns had fired, he had declared in a letter to his family: "As for me, I owe all allegiance and 'true faith to the United States of America.' They have given me my education and I have solemnly sworn more than once to defend them 'against all their enemies and opposers whomsoever.' My duty and that of every officer of the army is too plain to be mistaken, and in the hour of danger I only hope my performance of it may be as honest and fearless as my conception of it is clear and decided. . . ."

He was well suited to defend his country. A year ago he had graduated from the United States Military Academy in the top seventh of his class. Throughout his West Point career he had displayed keen talents for both military and civil pursuits, as well as a robust physique. Energetic, dedicated to the soldier's life, and as patriotic as any officer in the army, he had also impressed his superiors at Fort Vancouver, who marked him as a soldier with a bright future.

Wilson was a brash and impatient young man who had a lofty opinion of his own capabilities. Unwilling to sit along the fringes of the war, he had wasted little time in going through the usual channels to secure an assignment in an active theater. Once war came, he wrote directly to influential congressmen, asking their help in furthering his ambitions. His perseverance had recently been rewarded by the arrival of orders: Second Lieutenant Wilson was to proceed at once to Washington City to report for assignment to the chief of the Topographical Engineer Corps. Hence this shipboard departure from his first tour of active duty.

Aboard the *Cortez*, Wilson anxiously gazed over the Pacific, trying to glimpse the distant smudge of land which indicated his first port of call. Six days before, he had started on this same journey, with unhappy results. After saying farewell to friends at the outpost, he had steamed away aboard a ship which soon ran into a huge rock; he had been obliged to return to Fort Vancouver on a rescue ship, for a second attempt at leaving Oregon. Now he was more eager than ever to leave the region's mountains and timberlands. A long and monotonous voyage lay before him—down the Pacific coast to southern Mexico, across that country by rail, and, finally, aboard another ship from the Gulf of Mexico up the eastern shore of the United States. But he was prepared to endure the trip, for this was the most practicable route to his destination.

The lieutenant traveled with several companions in uniform, most of them bound for the war. And after reaching San Francisco, he resumed his voyage on July 26 aboard the *Golden Gate* and found himself in the company of still other soldiers, who had been stationed at the local military installation, the Presidio.

One of these was a charming, good-natured captain in the construction engineers, named James B. McPherson. He and Wilson became acquainted as the *Golden Gate* left California, and their friendship grew stronger with each passing league. McPherson was nine years Wilson's senior, a graduate of the West Point class of 1853; he was a couple of inches taller than Wilson's five feet, ten inches and somewhat stockier than Wilson's medium build.

Their friendship was destined to endure for three years, until McPherson's death as a major general in battle near Atlanta. For Wilson, his company was the single rewarding feature of this Pacific voyage. They sought out each other to discuss the present national crisis, to match recollections of Academy life, and to speak of their hopes for their careers.

McPherson also provided Wilson with the first opportunity to promote his wartime career. The captain had recently been offered a commission in one of the engineer regiments recruiting in the East. When he arrived in Washington he might be eligible to lead a company of sappers and miners, the highest command a captain in the construction engineers could attain. However, McPherson openly wondered if such a position might not be beyond his grasp. Wilson was impressed with McPherson's good fortune, and no doubt a bit jealous as well, for envy was a vice which Wilson often indulged. Congratulating McPherson on his great opportunity, he encouraged him to exert every effort to secure the post. In turn, McPherson was pleased that his companion should express such an interest in his career, and vowed that if he received the command, he would tender Wilson a first lieutenancy in it.

A few months later, this enterprise would reveal itself to be a modest prospect for both officers. But at the time it was presented, the venture enthused Wilson, for he had no definite prospect of vital employment elsewhere. Consideration of it helped sustain him throughout the journey.

Even so, his impatience to reach the States bedeviled him time and again. His military career was the consideration always uppermost in his mind, and he simply could not tolerate delays, necessary or avoidable, which slowed its progress. Late in August he noted in his diary that he was "disgusted with our long voyage." A contributing factor to his displeasure was the news he had by then received about the first large-scale land battle of the war, which had taken place near Manassas Junction, Virginia and a stream named Bull Run.

First accounts of the fighting had come from the *New York Herald*; the United States consul at Acapulco, Mexico had brought copies of the paper aboard ship when the *Golden Gate* arrived there on August 9. By that time the news was nearly three weeks stale. Even so, the dispatches covered only the opening phases of the battle. To Northerners, including most of the travelers in Wilson's party, the news was glorious.

Because Wilson possessed a clear speaking voice, the passengers prevailed upon him to mount a chair in the main cabin and read the reports aloud. As he did so, he was carried away by excitement and joy. During a series of skirmishes in upper Virginia, Brigadier General Irvin McDowell's army had swept the Confederates from its path. Surely McDowell had broken the spine of the rebellion; surely the hostilities were coming to a rapid close. The ship's company cheered the news wildly, for it carried not so much as a hint of Federal difficulties in the field.

When the ship was again under way that evening, however, Lieutenant Wilson and Captain McPherson found themselves mulling over the same thoughts. If the great battle had already been won and the war was approaching its finale, they had traveled a long distance for nothing. Wilson also confessed to being more than a little disappointed that the Union had triumphed without requiring his assistance. These were hardly admirable feelings, but they reflected a state of mind which would characterize Wilson throughout his career. Often his vision of military service narrowed too severely. His attention would focus first upon what advantages were offered for his personal advancement and gain and only afterward upon what was best for the country as a whole.

On April 15, Wilson's chagrin fled. That day the *Golden Gate* arrived at another Mexican port and diplomatic officials again provided New York papers for the passengers. This time the war news was not at all sanguine.

As before, Wilson used a chair as a speaker's platform and read the latest dispatches to his companions. Curiously, the battle of Bull Run had changed from a glorious victory to a shameful defeat, even a disaster. The Confederates had rallied and sent the Federals stumbling northward toward Washington. The officials of the government feared that Rebel troops might follow up their victory by taking the capital by storm.

The news distressed most of the ship's company. Wilson and Mc-Pherson shared their gloom, but, being professional soldiers, also experienced a sense of relief. Later Wilson perceived that their reaction was not wholly commendable, given the amount of human suffering which would result from the prolongation of the conflict; it was, he wrote, "strangely at variance with our patriotism."

So the war was not over after all; it was, in fact, only beginning. Should the sappers and miners venture fail to materialize, there still would be important work for him to do. He would now be permitted to make his contribution to the war effort.

Evidence of this came vividly to hand on August 30, when Wilson's ship berthed in New York harbor, ending his month-long journey from Oregon. Disembarking, he found Staten Island crowded with army tents and dotted by parade grounds and flagpoles from which the Stars and Stripes waved in the breeze. Though he had arrived on the scene late, the war had waited for him.

JAMES HARRISON WILSON WAS BORN ON September 2, 1837 on a large farm outside Shawneetown, Illinois, a bustling village on the Ohio River just across the border from Kentucky. The son of Harrison and Katharine Wilson, he could trace his lineage through past centuries to Northumberland, part of ancient Bernicia, from which his ancestors had migrated to North America. The Wilsons had originally located in Virginia in the seventeenth century and had intermarried with the leading families of that state. From the Tidewater region they later crossed the Blue Ridge Mountains into the western part of the Old Dominion, from there moving on to Kentucky, and finally as far as the Ohio.

James's grandfather had brought the family from Kentucky to Illinois. Alexander Wilson established a farm near an Ohio River shipping center named Raleigh, a few miles below the mouth of the Wabash River. He made a modest living at first, and saw it substantially increased when the owners of the Illinois salines laid out a community, Shawneetown, which they designated the landing for the nearby salt works. In short order the settlement grew into the region's most important village, and through a kinsman who became governor of the territory Alexander Wilson obtained a grant to operate a ferry across the Ohio to and from Shawneetown.

The income from this enterprise made Alexander one of the most prosperous settlers in the territory. In time he also became one of its most distinguished lawmakers. In 1812 he was elected a member of the first American legislature ever convened in Illinois. In this capacity he exercised considerable influence on all local ordinances, and when he died the following year he was recognized as a leading figure in the establishment of the state.

Alexander's son, Harrison, polished the lustrous name the family had acquired. Intelligent and energetic, he extended the Wilson enterprises to include stock raising and trading, and also served with distinction in political and military positions. He was county treasurer and sheriff, an ensign and then a captain of frontier riflemen during the War of 1812, and an officer of Illinois mounted volunteers in the Black Hawk War of 1832. In the latter conflict he commanded some of Gallatin County's leading citizens and made the acquaintance of soldiers who would later win national fame, including Zachary Taylor, Jefferson Davis, and Abraham Lincoln.

When his military career closed, Harrison Wilson returned comfortably to private life. He lived quietly in Shawneetown with his second wife, the former Katharine Schneyder, the daughter of a veteran of the Napoleonic wars who, after serving as mayor of a village in Rhenish Alsace, had come to America in 1818. By Katharine, Harrison had seven children, four of whom reached adulthood. His eldest surviving son, born at home, was James Harrison Wilson. James grew up in Shawneetown with one sister, Lucy, and two brothers, Henry and Bluford.

The Shawneetown of the 1840s, in which James spent his boyhood, had changed substantially from the village his father and grandfather had known. Although a small town still (its population remained less than 1,000), it had become a point of special vantage for the penetration of interior districts by incoming settlers. It was now also a thriving commercial center which provided for the exchange of farm products for the finished output of the factory, and ranked with larger Ohio River ports such as Cincinnati and Louisville in the volume of goods shipped and traded. For a boy such as James, it was an exciting place in which to grow.

After the Mexican War of 1846–48, the salt works closed, but Shawneetown continued to expand. By 1850 it had almost twice as many inhabitants as ten years previously. But its growth—the result of a great influx of immigrants from Kentucky and Tennessee—brought a multiplicity of problems. Rowdyism began to plague the community, and gambling, drunkenness, and other vices ran rife. Local vigilante groups known as Regulators quelled the troubles which the established authorities could not handle. At first the vigilantes rendered valuable service, but later they grew corrupt and terrorized law-abiding citizens and criminals alike.

Another fact of life ,for Shawneetown in the 1840s and 1850s was the growing debate over slavery. Proslavery influences came with the droves of southern immigrants who swelled the town to such a size as to make it the seat of Gallatin County. Quite naturally, the village became a Democratic stronghold and in national and local elections gave a wide majority of support to candidates who upheld that party's conservative policies.

When they came to Illinois early in the nineteenth century, the Wilsons brought slaves. In later years, however, they came to oppose slavery; by 1850 they retained Negroes only as servants. Influenced by his family's views, James came to believe that slavery was morally wrong, although he felt that every state in the Union should be permitted to decide its own position as to the legality of the practice. And despite his antipathy to the "peculiar institution," he could not see the Negro as the white man's equal, and felt that a white society would forever rule America.

James's father died in 1852 at the age of sixty-three, bequeathing to his family several financially successful enterprises and an untarnished reputation. Despite the prominence he had gained in Shawneetown, however, Harrison Wilson had not amassed a fortune. In fact, toward the close of the 1850s, when the tide of national settlement began to sweep farther westward, bypassing Shawneetown and causing its decline as a population and commercial center, the Wilsons had to work strenuously to secure their economic future.

The weight of this burden fell primarily upon James, who, at fourteen, became the oldest male in the household. Because his father and grandfather had been imaginative, energetic men successful at almost all of their endeavors, James found it difficult to countenance the idea of failure. He worked extremely hard operating the family farm and doling out work to the hired help. With a keen mind for economics and mathematics, he efficiently managed the family budget. Strong and vigorous, he worked in the fields and in the stock pens, and later at a variety of outside jobs which raised additional money for his family.

His role as breadwinner made him, in quick time, mature and independent. Since his enterprise usually yielded gratifying results, he began to consider himself the equal of his forebears, capable of handling any situation he might encounter. He assumed an almost parental relationship with his brothers and strove to make certain that his mother and sister would want for nothing.

His family had always held a high regard for education—something which James and his brothers saw they would have to provide for themselves. At an early age both James and Henry decided they wished to study at the United States Military Academy, where tuition was free and the academic program of a high caliber. James considered himself physically and mentally qualified to pursue the soldier's life, and in so doing would follow, to some extent, in his father's footsteps. He fully approved of the strict discipline and exacting standards which military service demanded.

Until age fifteen James received his formal education in the common schools near his home. Afterward he worked part time in a general store as well as in his uncle's produce business to earn one year's tuition at McKendree College in Saint Clair County. Endowed with considerable foresight, he realized that a term there would provide study experience which would prove valuable at West Point. In the fall of 1854 he left home for the first time and traveled northwestward to school.

McKendree College was an enjoyable experience; it posed few problems for him. From the outset he was a conscientious and methodical student, carefully budgeting his time to permit sufficient concentration on his studies. He worked diligently at mental philosophy, geometry, Latin, Greek, algebra, trigonometry, and logic, and displayed an aptitude for the mathematics courses. Because his family had held the acquisition of knowledge in such esteem, he had been a voracious reader for many years; now, whenever the opportunity arose, he poured over such diverse works as Shakespeare, Blackstone, and the Book of Mormon. Often he preferred to spend even his Sundays with his books rather than attend church services. Fiercely independent, he rarely stayed longer than five minutes when he did attend church, and disliked the emphasis McKendree put on organized religion because "I am opposed to being driven at anything. . . ."

Much later in life he would come to embrace orthodox Protestant teachings, and would become a church member. But for many years he found it difficult to accept all the tenets of Christianity and reproached himself for being unable to enjoy an unwavering faith in the existence of a Supreme Creator.

Through the winter of 1854–55 he pursued the wide-ranging course of study which McKendree offered, and still found time for extracurricular activities such as debating. Then, as a smallpox epidemic ravaged the school, he left Saint Clair County for home. Late in March, back in Shawneetown, he again secured employment in his uncle's office, at a salary of twenty dollars a month, in order to collect spending money for his first term at West Point.

He was fortunate to have family friends with political influence. Through the efforts of his legal guardian, Major Samuel K. Casey, and two local congressmen, Willis Allen and Samuel Marshall, he was nominated for an Academy appointment on May 18. In due course he received word to report to West Point for the start of the summer encampment in June. Until that time came, he worked long hours in Shawneetown, remaining on his job till within an hour of his departure for the East.

By the time he again left home, he had been toughened by work and still felt the keen edge of his college training. He had learned to apply his methodical ways to the pursuit of education as well as to physical labor, and he had yet to fail signally at any endeavor. Armed with such confidence as this brought him, he said good-bye to his family at the local depot and boarded a train in company with several friends, including Major Casey.

After many days' journey, he and his companions arrived in Washington City. There, on June 9, he secured his cadet application. From the capital he traveled via Baltimore, Philadelphia, and New York City—which provided a fascinating sightseeing tour—and reached West Point at 10:30 on the morning of June 12. At that hour he had his first panoramic view of the school at which he was to spend the next five years of his life (Secretary of War Jefferson Davis had decreed an experimental five-year program for the incoming class).

Upon his arrival, he was assigned to quarters. Then he fell in for the first of numerous inspections he was to undergo during his term of study.

The first summer encampment set the standard for the whole of his West Point career. The early days of his life as a plebe were not easy, but neither were they tedious. He took part in seemingly endless drills, passed a battery of physical and mental examinations, won a number of friends, and fit comfortably into place in the corps of cadets. It was not long before his comrades began to call him by a nickname, "Harry."

By his tolerant acceptance of the hazing practices then in vogue, he won the high regard of older cadets as well as of other plebes. Strong and self-confident, sure of his ability to defend himself by physical force if necessary, he was able to regard hazing as beneficial, believing that it stimulated a man's curiosity and heightened his sense of awareness. Thus he met it with "good-natured resistance."

He demonstrated this on one occasion early in the encampment, when two older cadets invited him for a swim in the nearby Hudson River. Because swimming had long been a favorite diversion, Wilson accompanied them gladly. Not until they were all in the water, however, did he discover that his companions intended to give him a thorough ducking. When they came at him, he reacted swiftly. He turned the tables on one of them, and shoved him deep below the surface; by skillful maneuvering he gave the other cadet a sharp kick against his nose, which drew blood and ended the fracas. Surprised to find that a raw plebe could swim and defend himself so well, the older men decided they liked the young Illinoisan.

Wilson's class numbered 121 at the start of its course of study, but the rigorous work that lay ahead eventually caused two-thirds of them to leave the Academy. Till the end, nevertheless, the class remained a conglomerate of diverse heritages and backgrounds, comprising men of modest circumstances as well as those of high birth. Wilson's democratic spirit, the product of his frontier-settlement heritage, led him to approve of this commingling of doctors' sons, mechanics' sons, and the sons of farmers and statesmen: "All were equal, and nothing counted but character and brains."

Wilson did not lack either quality; yet he moved off to a slow start academically. No doubt it was a consequence of trying to gain a footing in the unfamiliar territory of a large eastern academy. For a time, this must have raised the specter of impending failure and the attendant concern of having to leave West Point and return home in disgrace. By

West Point, as It Appeared in 1855—*Engraving courtesy West Point Archives*

this time, he seemed almost obsessed with the fear of failure. He had
planned his life and career most carefully, and thus far his plans
seemed to be bearing fruit. Any setback at this stage was a horror to
contemplate. Shortly after beginning his studies at the Academy, he
noted this fear: "I must succeed, for it is my only alternative, to succeed or be dishonored and this I could not bear. . . ."

As months passed, his classwork began to improve, he grew accustomed to daily routine at the Academy, and his crisis period passed.
His upbringing in Illinois enabled him to excel at many of the skills a
soldier must master; he was physically fit, a superb horseman, and a
fine marksman. In time he also came to relish his textbook studies, and
soon won high grades in drawing, chemistry, natural and experimental
philosophy, ethics, grammar, and geography. In marked contrast to his
mathematical proficiency at McKendree College, he achieved his highest Academy grades in geology, languages, and English studies.

When he became accustomed to West Point life, he was able to
dispose of his studies and still have free time for reading and other
recreations. He haunted the 20,000-volume library, attended dancing
classes (an innovation at the Academy), and sometimes took pleasure
trips off the grounds to go swimming, riding, and, occasionally, party-
ing at nearby taverns. But he never touched spirituous liquors or engaged in unlawful carousing, though more than a few of his classmates
did so.

As his schooling progressed, he grew more regular in his chapel
attendance, came to enjoy the Sunday sermons, and continually gave
thought to the serious issues of the day, particularly to the growing
threat to national union. In a short period of time he developed a
strong interest in Constitutional law, which buttressed his belief in the
sovereignty of the federal government and caused him to dread the
concept of secession. To other cadets he spoke his belief that no state,
northern or southern, had the right to declare itself divorced from the
rest of the country; if it did, anarchy would result. He expressed similar
opinions to his professors when he wrote classroom themes such as
"The Sectional Feeling Between the North and the South." On another
great national question, slavery, he remained a moderate. Though he
still considered the institution a moral disgrace, his reading of national
law convinced him that the Constitution provided sanctions for its
continuance. Above all else, Wilson respected the articles of that great
legislative document.

When he spoke out on such topics, Wilson—a very earnest young
man who took himself quite seriously—often became dogmatic. Be-

cause he had done considerable study in formulating his beliefs and ideals, he felt they had the natural ring of truth. Therefore, people who disagreed with him were wrong. That is, those who went against his beliefs set themselves against the Constitution as well. Because Wilson held the Constitution infallible, the logical assumption was that his opponents were hideously in error. Coupled with his vast personal ambition and his lack of a strong sense of humor, this characteristic caused him a great deal of trouble at West Point, particularly during his first two years of study.

Such an attitude resulted in a violent fistfight with another cadet in the middle of Wilson's fourth-class year—his second year of study. By that time his high grades in tactics and on the drill field had won him a cadet sergeant's stripes. Ostensibly the fight occurred because at artillery drill one morning First Sergeant Wilson was unreasonably impatient with one of his squad members, Cadet William McCreery of Virginia. But the true cause was the hostility which McCreery felt toward Wilson's upbringing and his widely publicized remarks about union and secession.

The confrontation was symptomatic of a problem which affected the cadet corps as a whole. A select society representative of the nation, the corps reflected divergent political attitudes. As the country slid inexorably toward civil war in the late 1850s, the sectional antagonisms among the Academy men intensified. Inevitably, marked lines were drawn and observed. Few cadets could maintain neutrality; most had to declare themselves relative to states' rights and slavery.

Wilson battled McCreery only when he saw he could not avoid it. He and his antagonist chose their seconds as though about to fight a duel in the grand style. Wilson picked a northern friend named Bob Hall, while McCreery chose Wade Gibbes, a fire-eating secessionist from South Carolina. The news of the impending fight drew a crowd of onlookers, but the combatants avoided them by going to neighboring Fort Clinton, where they could thrash each other in privacy. There, at a signal, punches were thrown and blood began to flow. The fight was short and vicious. Wilson won decisively, and thereafter he was not challenged by McCreery or any other southerner.

In later years at West Point, Wilson's rigid demeanor relaxed. Because he had proven his physical prowess, he could afford to mingle with his classmates with less tension and anxiety than previously. In his last two years of study, he permitted himself to take part in sectional clashes which were little more than youthful pranks. On several of these outings he teamed with a pair of roughnecks, his classmate Alanson M. Randol of New Jersey, and Ohio cadet George Armstrong Custer (class of June, 1861).

An incident of this nature which he recalled vividly in old age involved a Texan, Thomas Rosser—later a noted Confederate general —whom many of the northerners felt to be insufferably conceited. One rainy night Wilson, Randol, and other northern friends pounced on Rosser, asleep in his field tent, took hold of him bodily, and dragged him by his heels through every mud puddle they could find. They then turned the furious Texan over to the officer of the guard and escaped, chuckling, to their own quarters.

Rosser's humiliation angered many of his southern-born comrades. A group of them met and voted to pit the husky Texas cadet against Randol, who they agreed was the antagonist most deserving of punishment. The northerners responded enthusiastically to the idea of a fight, and Wilson, perceiving another chance to humble the fire-eaters, trained and managed Randol. His work must have been skillful, for although Rosser outweighed his opponent, Randol was able to salvage a bloody draw.

For the most part, notwithstanding such pranks, Harry Wilson lived the life of a dedicated and thorough soldier. His firmness in command showed clearly when he led units on the drill field. He displayed a knack for making others obey his orders with alacrity and precision, and remained coolly in command during any situation which arose. Not even embarrassing moments could harm his poise for long. One afternoon, while drilling a squad of cadets under the stern scrutiny of William J. Hardee, commandant of cadets, he slipped on some paving stones and fell over backward, causing everyone in ranks to burst out laughing. Springing to his feet, he was chagrined to find that not even Lieutenant Colonel Hardee had suppressed a smile. This was most painful, for, above all, Wilson prized dignity and decorum, and from early youth had entertained fears of being made to look awkward or ridiculous before those elders or superiors he wished to favorably impress. To kill his embarrassment, he marched his squad at the double-quick twice around the drill plain. At the end of the mile-and-a-half jaunt he was as fatigued as his men, but would not permit himself to display weariness. In a loud voice he inquired whether the cadets would be able to witness a future incident of the sort without laughing. Almost overcome by exhaustion, his men could barely shout, "Yes!"

Wilson served as a cadet sergeant for two years, the second and third of his term at the Academy. He lost his stripes at the close of that period when he unwisely permitted his company clerk to allow first classmen to forgo sentry duty. This was a common if clandestine practice, for most cadets at that stage of their education considered such work "undignified." But the Academy officials did not agree, and Wilson deliberately compromised his integrity by concealing his actions from them, no doubt wishing to retain the friendship of his peers. Thus, when his company commander somehow learned of the rules violation, Wilson and all other sergeants were reprimanded. Colonel Hardee assembled them in his office and patiently asked for explanations. None of the culprits attempted to defend themselves—except Wilson. By now he had rationalized his actions by dwelling on the fact that the practice, a minor infraction, was widely followed and "unofficially" approved. Embarrassed too by being called to account, he loudly remarked that he felt he had exercised "proper discretion" in following the lead of other sergeants. Quite possibly, he spoke too vehemently. Colonel Hardee considered his answer brash, verging on insubordination, and flew into a rage. He sent all the sergeants to their quarters in arrest, reduced them to the ranks, and confined them to camp until they completed ten extra rounds of guard duty themselves.

Characteristically, Wilson worked off his punishment in twelve consecutive days, so as to be done with it as quickly as possible. While he made his rounds, he had considerable time to regret that he had never cultivated a prudent temper. Quite often he tended to overreact when superiors questioned his actions or his motivations; he felt too eager to speak up in the face of authority, to proclaim that he was not cowed by rank or position alone. Yet, if he wished to become a model soldier, he would have to alter his style.

Despite the loss of his stripes, Wilson immensely enjoyed his Academy years and came to regard the period as the "golden age" of West Point. On July 1, 1860 he graduated sixth among a class of forty-one, attaining his highest grades in geology, ordnance and gunnery, and cavalry tactics—the latter a particularly favorite subject. Though a distinguished student, his record of demerits kept him from advancing a further place or two in class standing. He had accumulated 325 of these black marks, a prodigious sum, largely due to his involvement in pranks and to his outspokenness of opinion, which had antagonized some of his professors.

Even so, his academic record was impressive enough to win him a brevet commission in the most highly esteemed branch of the service, the Topographical Engineers. Since military drawing was one of his strong points, he looked forward to duty as mapmaker as well as road builder, surveyor, and communications officer.

When leaving the Academy upon his graduation, he was forced to consider the possibility that he would wage war against some of his classmates in the future. The thought pained him; he dreaded the consequences of a fratricidal war. Yet he tried to put the worry out of his mind when he traveled home to Shawneetown.

His three months at home, prior to his departure for his first stretch of active duty, must have chagrined him. He was a professional soldier now and ready to take the field. But his friends and acquaintances in Shawneetown seemed unable to appreciate the training he had received and the new concepts he had assimilated during his Academy career. He had matured in ways alien to them, and no longer held much common ground with them.

His leave ended in late September. Again boarding a train, he journeyed back to New York and there took ship for Fort Vancouver, headquarters of the District of Oregon. He did not relish the thought of serving at an isolated wilderness outpost, yet hoped that such duty would somehow provide a propitious start to his Army career.

The first stage of his ocean voyage—the longest he had ever made —was rough. Because the Atlantic was choppy, he fell violently seasick. Only when his ship at last moved up the California coast and left the Pacific for the smoother Columbia River, could he find full relief from his discomfort. After a month of travel, he landed at Portland and then moved north to the scene of his first active duty.

He found the frontier fort to be small and without a stockade, and its garrison tiny. Soon he also discovered that its few topographical engineers took on the labors of construction engineer officers by building works and bridges, in addition to surveying and reconnaissance chores. But if such a circumstance would bring him a rewarding career, Wilson decided he would not mind the hard work.

At first, he liked the way of life at Fort Vancouver. He came to enjoy the company of the garrison, became close friends with some of the officers, and fell into a smooth relationship with his superiors. He found particularly agreeable the absence of violent temperaments among the soldiers. The majority were northern-born and the few from southern states were not radical secessionists.

In time, however, he became vividly aware of those drawbacks common to outpost duty. Isolated from the mainstream of civilization, located near villages scarcely more than sawmill centers, the fort provided little excitement, and recreational facilities were scarce and crude. Since mail from the States made irregular appearances, news drifted slowly into the region. But most depressing was the scarcity of

Fort Vancouver in the Late 1850s—*Drawing courtesy Mrs. George Donough*

work readily available to him. His new engineer chief, Captain George Thom, had, as Wilson later recalled, "no professional work for himself or for anyone else." In fact, the only immediate advice Thom could give his young subordinate was that he acquaint himself with the few unmarried ladies at the outpost.

The winter of 1860–61 was an especially trying period for Lieutenant Wilson. Although at intervals he was sent to reconnoiter for the construction of military roads, the work did not satisfy his inherent craving for adventure. Once bad weather prevented outdoor activity, he was assigned routine tasks such as tracing maps and winding chronometers—jobs which his superior tried in vain to depict as vitally important. Not even a few expeditions into the towns of Portland and Olympia relieved his boredom.

To escape the monotony of outpost life, he corresponded with his family and a host of friends, and expressed great disappointment whenever the mail failed to bring quick letters in reply. He wrote with particular diligence to his brothers, in whose fortunes he was deeply concerned. Still serving as the father-surrogate, he eagerly followed the academic career of Henry, who had begun study at West Point during James's final year there. He was disappointed when his brother was eventually compelled to leave the Academy for scholastic deficiencies. But Bluford, as he proudly learned, was progressing admirably at McKendree College. In his correspondence, James also sent money to his mother—as much as he could spare—and was scrupulous in repaying debts he had contracted from friends like Major Casey. He hated to be in anyone's debt, even when indebtedness seemed unavoidable or desirable, for it did not fit in with his desire to become independent, to be his own man.

At Fort Vancouver he became more conscientious in his moral outlook than he had been at either McKendree College or West Point. He felt himself drawn closer to the concepts of orthodox Christianity and regularly attended Methodist services. He also read inspiring books such as *Napoleonic Ideas*, and avoided the company of carousers and hard drinkers. He had grown up to be a zealous cold-water man, no doubt as the result of strict parental guidance, perhaps reinforced by his reactions to the sight of drunken rowdies stumping about Shawneetown. In this frontier garrison where a bottle often seemed a man's only amusement, he had ample opportunity to put his principles on public display. His belief in temperance never wavered, and in his diary he made disparaging references to drinking men. On the first day of 1861, for instance, he passed the afternoon "in making New Year's calls and the night in seeing how foolishly full grown men can act. . . ."

In the months which followed, he became increasingly attuned to a greater menace, the long-lived threat of national disunion. News of the great sectional quarrel, by this time deeply volatile, had spread to the West. Reading newspaper reports of impassioned oratory by northern and southern politicians also heightened Wilson's sense of isolation and intensified his disenchantment with his situation. As an officer in the United States Army, he felt a natural desire to serve in a vital capacity. But should open war flame forth, his location and duty status would provide no such opportunity.

Entries in his diary for this period reveal his increasing concern for the country's plight. "Every one filled with fear for the fate of our republic," he wrote on January 5. Less than a month later, having learned of South Carolina's defection from the Union, he noted, a bit prematurely: "Highly inflammable news from 'States'—Secession—rebellion—Civil War. . . ." And on March 23, after the failure of an eleventh-hour peace conference in Washington, he wrote: "The last hope gone!"

Short days before Confederate guns bombarded Fort Sumter, he wrote a long letter to his brothers, in which he forcefully stated his views on union and rebellion. The letter displayed his thorough knowledge of the Constitutional issues and opened by echoing the words of one of Wilson's heroes, Daniel Webster: "I am for the Union, one and inseparable, now and forever, as a blessing paramount to all others known to the American people. . . . The 'right of secession' is a transparent inconsistency, totally inadmissible and at variance with the first idea of stable government. But there is even a stronger reason for denying its validity. The Constitution (Art. I, Sec. X, par. 1 and 2) specially provides that 'No state shall enter into any treaty, alliance or confederation,' and the tone of that whole instrument is opposed to the idea of secession. . . ."

But his words could not silence those of politicians or counteract the force of popular opinion. War commenced in mid-April, and soon afterward the southern-born soldiers left Fort Vancouver and returned to their native states, unable to comply with a government order requiring all soldiers to take anew the oath of allegiance to the Federal Union. Wilson's fears had been realized; the nation had been torn apart by violence.

He was at his post late that month when he learned that President

Abraham Lincoln had issued a call for 75,000 volunteers to put down the rebellion. By now the full-scale war had wholly captured Wilson's imagination and determination. At all costs, he vowed, he would participate in it, to protect the strength of his country and in the process give impetus to his military career.

Discovering that requests for a transfer brought no immediate word from his departmental superiors, he decided to write to any Illinois officeholders who might be willing to help the son of Harrison Wilson secure reassignment to the East. Recipients of these letters included Congressmen John McClernand, a family friend, and John A. Logan. In his letters Wilson begged that he not be shelved in a remote corner of the country while fighting raged elsewhere. Surely in this time of crisis, the nation needed the services of every loyal soldier.

When this tactic yielded no prompt result, he revealed the extent of his impatience by addressing a letter to Secretary of War Simon Cameron, and persuading Congressman Logan to deliver it. Wilson did not worry that this measure might be considered brash and impetuous as well as unorthodox; he could think only of starting a wartime career. But even so dramatic a gesture as this brought no success.

Meanwhile, he busied himself about Fort Vancouver as best he could. In addition to his regular duties, he voluntarily assumed those of post adjutant and carried the burden of administrative responsibilities to the end of his tour of duty. The increased work load helped to some extent to divert his thoughts from the war.

On the tenth of June he was elevated to the full rank of second lieutenant; now, at last, he was formally considered a commissioned officer in the Army of the United States. But the news was less exciting than the order, received three days later, which directed him to report to the chief of his corps in Washington.

He never discovered which of his letters had brought about the transfer, and so felt equally grateful to each of the officials he had contacted. And he could take pride in another personal achievement. Once again he had succeeded in his designs; his self-confidence and self-esteem continued to grow.

Transferring his duties to other officers, he left the fort on the seventeenth, was forced to return after being shipwrecked, and departed again—for the final time—six days later.

All things considered, his feeling of relief in being able to leave the wilderness must have been quite deep. At last he was off to war, ready to join in the effort to unmask the "transparent inconsistency" of secession.

★II★

I Do Myself
and the Country
an Injustice
by Staying Here Idle

Second Lieutenant Wilson began his war service on a rather distressing note. En route from New York to Washington in company with Captain McPherson, he fell ill of "cholera morbus" and on August 24 had to stop over alone in Wilmington, Delaware. There, after receiving medical attention, he sought to convalesce at the home of his West Point roommate, John Andrews. The young man was not at home but Wilson was warmly received by his family, particularly by John N. Andrews, Sr., the newly elected colonel of the First Delaware Volunteer Infantry.

Despite his illness, the period was a rewarding experience for Wilson, for it gave him the opportunity to renew his acquaintance with Colonel Andrews's daughter, Ella, whom he had first met on a vacation visit three years before. Dark-haired, dark-eyed, and vivacious, Ella seemed much more mature than her age—thirteen—might have indicated. Although ten years her senior, Wilson was attracted by her beauty and her lively personality. In the past few years he had had few opportunities to be in the company of young women—sometimes there seemed but little place for them in the life of a professional soldier— and Ella's presence at his side was most agreeable.

When fully recovered, he promised to return on another visit as soon as he had the chance. Then, thanking his hosts for their gracious hospitality, he resumed his train trip to Washington City. He arrived there early on the twenty-seventh and at once reported for duty to the office of the Topographical Engineer Corps in the War Department.

He had supposed that some assignment was awaiting him, but now he was quickly disillusioned. Because of its unexpected defeats in the early fighting, the federal government had yet to adopt a firm course in prosecution of the war. Reflecting this general state of affairs, Wilson's corps was disorganized. Instead of offering him an opportunity for active service, his superior suggested he look about the capital for a few days and make up his own mind as to how and where he might wish to serve. Such vague and casual advice frustrated him; after his initial conference he noted in his diary that he was "disgusted" with his chief's "want of vigor." He had not traveled cross-country merely to watch his superior scratch his head in bewilderment.

But he did take the officer's suggestion. Almost aimlessly he walked through the capital, hoping for a golden opportunity to materialize. In the course of his wanderings, however, he had a brainstorm, and at once acted upon it. Once again he sought to go directly to the top, by paying his first courtesy call on the nation's most honored soldier, General-in-Chief Winfield Scott. Perhaps if he could arrest the general's attention with some well-chosen words uttered in the proper key. . . .

To Wilson's delight, the octogenarian hero of the War of 1812 and the Mexican conflict received him warmly. They chatted in Scott's office for a long time, Wilson patiently awaiting an opportunity to mention his duty status. Before one occurred, however, General Scott unexpectedly turned melancholy and began to lament the dire times the nation had fallen upon. Years later Wilson recalled (with an unknown degree of accuracy) that Scott mourned the loss of such great soldiers as Robert E. Lee and Pierre G. T. Beauregard, who had resigned from the Army to join the Confederate forces: "How we shall make head against them, or how it will all end I dare not say, but my heart is full of doubt and sorrow!"

Curiously enough, Scott's despair helped dispel his visitor's gloom. Feeling a great surge of passionate energy—and as though reading a well-researched treatise to a West Point professor—Wilson began to refute the general-in-chief's assertions. He recited the names of soldiers who had not gone south and thus far had played prominent roles in the Federal war effort. These generals about whom Wilson had read or had heard fine things included George B. McClellan (who soon would replace Scott in chief command) and General Irvin McDowell, whom most observers considered a capable leader despite his ill fortune at Bull Run. In the end, Wilson recollected, the elderly hero saw the light and smiled with renewed hope.

But the only offer of service which the interview produced concerned a possible teaching position at the Military Academy—a prospect which made Wilson shudder. He spent the remainder of his stay in Washington with Captain McPherson. They visited nearby camps, watched raw recruits strive to master the essentials of soldiering, inquired unsuccessfully after employment, and made new acquaintances as well as renewed old ones in the officer corps. One afternoon they lunched with Irvin McDowell, whom Wilson had so heartily recommended to General Scott. Wilson entertained second thoughts when he watched McDowell ravenously devour every dish within his reach, topping off the meal with a whole watermelon.

A few days later Wilson again reported to his corps chief. He found, to his surprise, that now he could nearly write his own orders. Since Captain McPherson enjoyed a similar privilege, they talked matters over and then applied jointly for permission to implement plans they had made aboard ship during their voyage east. They wished to form an engineer unit, with recruiting headquarters in Boston. After some slight delay the necessary orders came through, and Wilson started north on September 6.

En route he made a return visit to the Andrews's home just outside Wilmington. He went riding with the family through the countryside, admired the pleasant autumn weather, and found young Ella charmingly embarrassed by his attentions. He was "much pleased" to see her again, he wrote in his diary.

He arrived in Boston on the ninth, where he remained for almost five weeks. The time passed more slowly there than it had at Fort Vancouver after the outbreak of war. Not even the news of his appointment to the rank of first lieutenant, which reached him during this period, could greatly cheer him.

His disappointment was caused by what he considered "an unseemly squabble between the veteran chiefs of the two corps of engineers." These difficulties prevented McPherson and him from cooperating in their venture. Wilson, in fact, was never granted formal authority to enlist a single recruit. On his own he selected a promising candidate for first sergeant, "but that was as far as I ever got."

At the same time, he was forced to turn down a major's commission in an Illinois cavalry regiment, secured for him by friends back home. This was a painful necessity, for the lure of high rank was powerful, the prospect of at last seeing field service was inviting, and he had long entertained a desire to test his talents as a cavalryman. But to gain a commission in the volunteer service—usually awarded by a state government, to expire upon the conclusion of hostilities—a soldier in the Regular Army had to obtain a leave of absence from such duties as had previously been assigned him; and Wilson knew that at present the Army would grant no leaves unless at least a colonelcy was offered in the volunteer ranks.

His agonizing wait was finally ended on October 14. That afternoon unexpected orders arrived for him to report to Annapolis, Maryland for reassignment. A specific post would be given him: he was to be named chief topographical engineer on the staff of Brigadier General Thomas West Sherman, who, as Wilson learned in due course, was preparing a massive Army-Navy expedition to strike enemy positions along the Atlantic coast.

This time, active service definitely awaited him. Wilson bade Mc-Pherson farewell, packed his belongings, and left Boston in lofty spirits.

"TIM" SHERMAN WAS A SOLDIER OF impressive appearance. Tall, robust and pale-eyed, he wore his hair long and bushy and kept his jowls clean-shaven. Born in Rhode Island in 1813, a West Pointer and a veteran of twenty-five years' active service, he had been among the first group of professional soldiers to be appointed volunteer generals by President Lincoln. The upcoming expedition was to be his first independent command of the war.

When he reported for duty at Sherman's Maryland headquarters, Wilson found him a remarkable-looking man but also terse, austere, even distant. These impressions deepened when on October 29 Wilson and 12,650 other soldiers set sail in Sherman's fleet. At the start of the voyage, Wilson learned that the general would not divulge the destination of the expedition or its precise nature. At first shipboard speculation centered on the Confederate stronghold at Savannah as the focal point of the operation and its landing site. Finally, on November 3, it became clear that the fleet would try to force its way into Port Royal harbor, South Carolina.

The next day Sherman's thirty-odd transports, convoyed by a 5,000-hand, 17-cruiser squadron under Flag Officer Samuel F. Du Pont, anchored at the mouth of the Carolina harbor and confronted the heavy guns emplaced there. Aboard Sherman's flagship, Lieutenant Wilson waited anxiously for his baptism of battle. He grew quite impatient when he heard that Sherman planned a tedious series of reconnaissances preceding his movement into the harbor channel. The rumor was true; for three full days Sherman gathered intelligence and mustered the determination to make his move.

On the morning of the seventh he moved at last. At Sherman's command, Flag Officer Du Pont sent his men-of-war against the enemy batteries and opened fire. Wilson watched spellbound as the squadron exchanged screaming shell-blasts with the Confederate cannon, gradually pounding the harbor works into rubble. By half-past two in the afternoon, the might of Du Pont's guns had ended the contest. Sherman's fleet then entered the harbor and Wilson, still suffering the effects of another bout with seasickness, was in one of the first landing parties to touch Hilton Head Island. For the first time in the war, Federal troops had gained a foothold on the Rebel coast.

As soon as his position at Hilton Head was secure, Sherman occupied all nearby islands and settled down to grapple with administrative problems. In so doing, he again tried Wilson's patience. The lieutenant could not understand why most of the army had to remain idle. He believed Sherman ought to move inland at once and capture enemy positions and destroy vital transportation lines. This would keep the Rebels, now scattered over the islands, from communicating with one another, regrouping, and hindering the Federals' movements.

But when Tim Sherman returned his attention to offensive operations, he studied a matter he considered of greater import. This was Fort Pulaski, a pentagonal brick stronghold on an island eighteen miles below Georgia's greatest seaport, Savannah, where it commanded the entrance to the Savannah River.

Capture of the positions at Port Royal had resulted in the Rebels' abandonment of all coastal towns south of Charleston except Savannah, which Pulaski defended. Sherman had already turned the fortress from the north during the Port Royal engagement; if now he could isolate it and force its surrender he believed he could navigate the river and capture Savannah with a minimum of effort.

Once he determined to move against the island stronghold, Sherman commenced massive preliminary operations. As his topographical engineer, Wilson was called on to conduct land and water surveys under the direct supervision of Captain Quincy Gillmore, chief engineer on the expedition and erstwhile instructor at West Point. Commandeering a swift rowboat and Negro oarsmen from local plantations, Wilson paddled in all directions along the intricate network of waterways above the mouth of the Savannah, and on foot explored the colorfully named landfalls in the area. He later reported: "Before ten days had passed I had been into every creek between Pull-and-be-damned, behind Dawfuskie, through Calibogue Sound and the back passages to North Edisto. . . ."

On his explorations he sometimes passed within a few yards of sentries patrolling the islands, but usually avoided detection because of the dense marsh grass and the muffled, almost noiseless oars wielded by his boatmen. On a few occasions the enemy noted his movements but did not oppose his passage. On a reconnaissance late in November a sizable picket force of Confederate horsemen near a ferry crossing spied his boat. The cavalry might have offered trouble but, fortunately, they quickly scattered, perhaps believing that Wilson's presence heralded the coming of a large water expedition.

Wilson's explorations were most successful, for he possessed stealth, keen eyesight, and an ability to digest and evaluate intelligence. To Sherman he accurately reported the distances between various land and water sites, the location of terrain features such as marshes and quicksand, and valuable information about whether the areas inspected would accommodate the passage of warships or columns of soldiers. The general was pleased by the thoroughness with which his topographical engineer conducted his surveys.

Wilson's activities were not limited to reconnaissance chores. When Lieutenant Horace Porter fell ill in November, Wilson took on some of his duties as Sherman's assistant ordnance chief. Porter, the sergeant-major of the cadet corps during part of Wilson's term at West Point, had been engaged in mounting, moving, and remounting cannon to fortify Sherman's main line of defense at Hilton Head. Soon, therefore, Wilson was hard at work directing the positioning of heavy guns, often working beside the soldiers he supervised.

Sherman spent months reinforcing his base and putting the finishing touches on plans for an assault on Fort Pulaski. Supply-laden ships continually steamed into Port Royal harbor, some carrying various types of ordnance with which the Federal commander planned to shatter the garrison. Wilson was kept furiously busy during this period;

nevertheless, he was disappointed that the prelude to action must be so methodical and slow.

One unusual assignment given him at this time came personally from Sherman. On a particular morning the general called Wilson to his headquarters tent and inquired how long he felt it might take to load a steamship with enough supplies to outfit a nearby Federal garrison. Without experience in such business, Wilson could not say. But he did not wish to show his ignorance to his superior officer; impulsively he replied that four or five hours would probably suffice. Sherman began to rant and rave. His quartermasters had informed him that three days' time, which he considered excessive, would be required to load a ship then in the harbor. Now Sherman ordered Wilson to handle the job, expecting him to complete it within five hours.

Wilson might well have recalled his West Point encounter with Colonel Hardee regarding his "proper discretion" as cadet sergeant. Realizing that once again he had voiced an imprudent opinion, he went down to the docks, where he found two regiments of infantrymen at his disposal. Studying the ship in question, he tried to remember how Ohio River roustabouts, whom he had observed several times as a boy, had handled such work. Fortunately, he could think quickly under pressure. Telling the ship's captain to stand ready to receive freight as quickly as it could be brought aboard, he parceled out work as he thought best.

For two hours one regiment labored at top speed, carting boxes, barrels, and bales from the harbor warehouses onto the deck of the steamer. Then, at Wilson's command, the men of the second regiment replaced those of the first. The work continued at a furious pace for two and a half hours, by which time, amazingly, the ship was fully loaded. Highly impressed by his dramatic success, Wilson watched the steamer put to sea. He then strode in triumph to Sherman's tent and reported his mission accomplished. A little surprised and much pleased, Sherman offered him congratulations and a glass of champagne to celebrate the occasion. Praise was something Wilson never rejected, but he gave his commander exclusive title to the wine.

Late in December, Wilson was again given work which satisfied his thirst for activity of consequence. On another reconnaissance he rowed up the Savannah River via three water routes to a point a few miles inside Fort Pulaski. When he returned to Sherman he stated the opinion he had formed on the mission, that an important passageway to the Savannah, Wall's Cut, could easily be cleared of a sunken hulk and other obstructions placed in it by the enemy. He believed that with the cut cleared, light gunboats could squeeze through New, Wright, and

Mud rivers and reach the Savannah west of the fortress. Then, also, gun batteries could be placed along the river to prevent ships from running supplies and reinforcements to the garrison.

Although Sherman was enthusiastic about Wilson's plan, two weeks were spent removing the obstructions from Wall's Cut. In his impatience to get the job done, Wilson had minimized the extent of the work involved. During this period he continued his rowboat surveys, running up New River to a site opposite the lower section of Savannah. On this mission he saved the life of a civilian friend.

The friend, an aide to Captain Gillmore, was a *New York Express* reporter named Adam Badeau. Slight and bespectacled, red-haired and of delicate features, Badeau had come south to cover the Port Royal operations for his paper and had ingratiated himself with Sherman, Gillmore, Wilson, and other officers. Wilson and he would remain close for several years.

On a morning in January, 1862, the two, accompanied by five enlisted men, rowed to an isolated section of an island which Wilson was to reconnoiter. Leaving their boat in a run by its landing spot, the party waded three miles across a shallow marsh to a vantage point from which Wilson could study the work of Confederate engineers, who were erecting a line of coastal defenses across the river.

After several hours' observation, the group turned back to their boat, only to discover that flood tide had added several feet to the level of the marsh water. Progress during the return was wearisome, then dangerous. Midway through the trip, an exhausted Badeau gave way, no longer able to slosh through the water. When it became necessary that everyone start swimming or risk drowning, Badeau begged Wilson to leave him and save himself.

Wilson would not hear of it. With the enlisted men's help he held Badeau's head above water and carefully maneuvered him across the deep rivulets, paddling furiously. In this way they managed to return the reporter to the boat, in which they quickly sailed to a safe shore.

In later weeks, Wilson concentrated on promoting his plan for an attack on Savannah via the routes he had explored. In the middle of January he attempted to sell his project to the proper authorities, the naval commanders who had come south with Sherman. One foggy night he accompanied Captain John Rodgers, U.S.N., and some of Rodgers's subordinates through the several waterways. Visibility was so poor that the journey almost ended in shipwreck, but finally the route was explored, and Wilson believed he had amply demonstrated that it was practicable for the passage of gunboats and transports. But when they reported back to General Sherman, Rodgers expressed a substantial reservation: he remarked that, even if the ships could get through the waterways without damage, they would be destroyed when grounding at high water within range of Fort Pulaski's guns.

Wilson was furious. Apparently Rodgers had given no indication of his feelings until he spoke to Sherman. What Wilson found most galling was that anyone should object to his plan in any detail. No doubt Rodgers's reason for submitting an adverse report was strong— after all, he was skilled in such operations, while Wilson could hardly be called a seafaring man—but Wilson considered Rodgers's report a personal blow to his pride and esteem. Rodgers had made him look bad in the eyes of their common superior, Sherman, and this was something Wilson could not bear. Thus he rationalized his bad fortune when he noted in his diary that Rodgers had "talked incoherently of difficulties" to Sherman. He added: "The Navy are determined not to go in; why I can hardly say; but probably it is the old fable: 'a herd of Lions led by a deer'. . . ."

Wilson's plan rejected, Sherman directed all his energy and attention to the work of reducing Fort Pulaski. In conjunction with siege operations, Wilson returned to ordnance duties. But he still clung to the hope that his project to reach the great river could win out. Early in February he tried to salvage a part of the plan by volunteering to direct a team of workmen in navigating Wall's Cut (now free of obstructions) and erecting a battery on the Savannah above the garrison. When Sherman adopted the idea, Wilson found that the work involved was frustrating and difficult. Cannon had to be moved from shipboard and placed in position on a salt marsh known as Venus Point by means of a pine-plank causeway. The planking had to be continually dismantled and its pieces moved forward to permit the movement of the guns. For four days and nights the soldiers sweated and cursed their way through the operation. Their patience was frayed time after time when cannon slipped off the causeway, sank in the slimy gumbo, and had to be hoisted back into place.

The incredibly strenuous work ended on February 14. The next day the workmen had the satisfaction of watching the unsuspecting enemy come under a bombardment. That morning a fleet of ships ran down from Savannah, carrying supplies to the fort. Lieutenant Porter, who had helped erect the battery, later wrote his family that under the cannonade the five ships "were driven back, and the Commodore's vessel so disabled as to have to be towed off by another boat."

Thus, thanks largely to Wilson, supply lines to the fortress no longer existed. In consequence, Sherman moved his base of operations to Tybee Island, along the southern shore of the Savannah and directly across from Cockspur Island, where the fort stood. There he began to build a long line of coastal batteries facing the stronghold.

But Sherman could not witness the fruition of his labors. In the midst of his operations, on March 31, he was transferred to the western theater of the war. By this time he had come to fully appreciate the abilities of his topographical engineer, and sought permission for Wilson to accompany him. The War Department said no, that Wilson was more urgently needed in his present location.

Major General David Hunter replaced Sherman as commander of the newly formed Department of the South. An old veteran of dragoon service, with unkempt black hair and a perpetual squint, Hunter saw that he had become the beneficiary of a campaign which seemed to assure great success. He made no radical changes in Sherman's procedures, allowing work on the batteries to continue under the immediate supervision of chief engineer Gillmore, whom Sherman had appointed an "acting" brigadier.

After long weeks of back-breaking toil, eleven batteries arose on the marshy expanse of Tybee Island, their gun barrels trained on Fort Pulaski. Arranged in emplacements named for Union heroes such as Lincoln, Scott, McClellan, and General Ulysses S. Grant, they boasted thirty-six heavy pieces, including mortars, siege cannon, and rifled ordnance.

Although sanguine about success, General Hunter had to admit that never in American history had cannon been able to reduce a brick fortress at such long range—more than 2,000 yards. Then too, Pulaski was a formidable stronghold, its walls seven and a half feet thick and twenty-five feet above high water. It mounted two tiers of cannon, forty-eight in all, of which twenty bore on the batteries along Tybee Island.

At sunrise on April 10 Hunter dispatched Lieutenant Wilson in a rowboat to deliver a surrender demand to the fort's commander, Colonel Charles H. Olmstead. The honor was strictly in keeping with Wilson's desire to be involved in important, dramatic events. The enemy received him with great courtesy; and Colonel Olmstead, a bearded, dignified officer, carefully read the message he carried. It warned him: "The number, caliber, and completeness of the batteries surrounding you leave no doubt as to what must result in case of your refusal. . . ."

Olmstead did not agree. He felt that he could rely upon his thick, casemated walls to withstand a bombardment, though he was not so confident about being able to endure a subsequent siege. He gravely informed Wilson that he had been ordered to "defend the fort, not to surrender it."

Hunter must secretly have been glad that Olmstead refused his demand; if he had surrendered so quickly, all the hard work on Tybee Island would have been unnecessary. Soon after receiving Olmstead's reply, the general turned to engineer Gillmore and casually informed him that he could commence firing whenever he pleased.

A rather comic event attended Gillmore's subsequent command. For some reason, Adam Badeau was chosen to carry the order to the nearest guns, commanded by Lieutenant Porter. Badeau was less than an accomplished horseman; when he arrived at Porter's position, he almost fell from the saddle while dismounting. Then, wobbling forward on stumpy legs, he cried in a shrill voice: "Commence firing!" At first, Porter's men found it hard to keep straight faces, but when the lieutenant repeated the command they grimly set about to obey.

They launched the first shell a minute later with a blast that shook the earth like a volcano. "The shell rose gracefully like a black moon on its course," Wilson remembered, "followed by a series of discharges from the other mortars, Columbiads, and breaching guns, and pandemonium seemed to have broken loose."

From the outset a thin fog settled over Tybee Island as the heavy guns coughed fire and an overwhelming volume of sound. Across the river Fort Pulaski and Cockspur Island were dotted by clouds of smoke as the enemy replied with their twenty cannon. For thirty hours the blast of battle rolled on, occasionally dwindling to a dull roar and then quickly regaining its full fury.

Long before the finale, however, the Federals sensed ultimate victory. Colonel Olmstead had been wrong; his walls offered little protection against Hunter's shells. Although the Federal mortars proved ineffective, the heavy cannon, particularly the long-range rifled guns, battered the stronghold at will, opening a breach along two casemates to an aggregate width of thirty feet, shattering adjacent walls and threatening to collapse them.

At 2 P.M. on April 11—by which time more than 5,200 shells had hurtled toward the fort—Olmstead ran up a white flag. Shortly afterward, Wilson and a party of men rowed out to receive the surrender of the 400-man garrison. General Hunter had reaped the rewards of a campaign which Tim Sherman had so long and so thoroughly prepared.

Because Pulaski's surrender opened the river to Federal shipping, Wilson hoped that Hunter would cooperate with the Navy in attacking Georgia's seacoast citadel. But after making only a token effort to move against Savannah and for a variety of reasons, most of which concerned the fact that the operation was too formidable to approach with haste, Hunter ceased offensive operations for an indefinite period. His thinking may well have been sound, but it angered Wilson. Wilson's remedy for almost any situation was to move swiftly and decisively no matter what troubles seemed to lie ahead. It was hardly a prudent philosophy, and before his career ended it would cause him a great deal of grief as well as win him much success. But he would never abandon it.

A WEEK AFTER FORT PULASKI FELL, Hunter sent Wilson, accompanied by several companies of a Michigan infantry regiment, to survey Wilmington Island, which lay several hundred yards west of Tybee. On this assignment the lieutenant sampled hand-to-hand fighting for the first time.

On Wilmington Island the reconnaissance party encountered, quite unexpectedly, a large force of Rebel infantrymen. When shooting broke out, the Michigan soldiers beat a hasty and embarrassing retreat. Against his will, Wilson was forced to flee with them to better positions. Finally he and some regimental officers found an opportunity to steady and re-deploy some of the Michigan men. Calling upon his West Point training, Wilson directed a detachment in receiving and repelling another enemy charge, and, when the Rebels drew off, he led the Michigan soldiers forward. In the swirl of fighting that resulted, an infantry officer was shot through the skull, spattering blood across Wilson's face and uniform. To the end of his days, Wilson would recall the incident vividly. Nor would he ever forget his first bullet wound—a stinging blow by a spent bullet which was deflected by his boot top. After both forces had suffered many casualties, the Federals managed to keep their opponents at bay until they made their way back to General Hunter's base camp.

At first the skirmish had gone very badly for the Federals; the enemy had made them look like frightened rabbits. Wilson feared that somehow guilt might attach itself to him as well as to the foot soldiers. He wished to prove his abilities as a fighter as well as an engineer, and hated the thought that Generals Hunter or Gillmore might think he was in any way to blame for the retreat. Therefore, when he saw them he sought—and won—exoneration of any possible blame.

A determination to absolve himself of every vestige of responsibility for a flawed or questionable performance in command was one of

Wilson's most enduring traits. To an extent this showed the influence of the Army system, whereby an officer covered himself, as a matter of course, from a superior's blame. As a professional soldier, albeit a young one, Wilson realized the necessity for doing this. However, the roots of this characteristic were probably connected to his early years. Perhaps as a boy in wide-open Shawneetown he had had boisterous friends who had given him, by association, an undeserved reputation for recklessness which he disliked. Without doubt, at West Point (and also at McKendree College) he had teamed with rowdy students who, either unwittingly or through a desire to "get" him for being rather snobbish, had tarnished Wilson's reputation in the minds of professors. There was, for example, the incident involving first classmen and sentry duty. Wilson must have felt himself wrongly blamed, since he had merely helped perpetuate a practice initiated by other cadets more culpable than he. By 1862 he was determined not to be charged with any act of omission or commission not wholly his fault. Now and again his boundless desire to advance his own good name and to promote his career would cause him to carry this desire to obsessive lengths, as on the present occasion. His concern about being blamed for the Michiganders' retreat was unfounded, for he had not been the ranking officer during the reconnaissance; yet the mere possibility that he would receive such a stigma made him feel threatened and vastly self-protective.

Back at headquarters, Wilson found no immediate work of consequence. This put him in a black mood, and before long he was taking his complaint directly to General Hunter. But when he asked that he be relieved and sent to Washington for reassignment, Hunter only nodded and smiled sympathetically. Wilson was forced to rage in silence—something he did quite well.

As spring came in, the war for the Union began to expand in other theaters. General McClellan made plans to launch a campaign to take Richmond (a campaign he would later regret). In the West, Major General Grant drove down the Tennessee and Cumberland rivers, capturing Rebel forts. But in South Carolina and Georgia, things remained quiet.

As the weeks dragged by, Wilson grew quite depressed. He remarked in his diary that his life had become "horribly dull; waiting for something to turn up. No news. . . ." Finally he came to regard himself maliciously held inactive by the Army. He held his military talents in high esteem and believed they would greatly aid the nation if properly utilized—if utilized at all. He wrote: "Have become thoroughly convinced that nothing is to be done in this department and that I do myself and the country an injustice by staying here idle. . . ."

He tried to lessen the tedium of his free time by various methods, chiefly by carrying on an extensive correspondence. Through the summer of 1862 he wrote religiously to family and friends, including West Point classmates, companions in the Engineer Corps, and to more than one young lady. Already, however, his interest had begun to focus upon the girl whom he had met in Wilmington and with whom he had gone riding so many months ago.

Blessed release from boredom came at last on August 26, when he received orders to report to Washington. Four days later he took leave of General Hunter, whose attempts to exploit his foothold on the Rebel coast continued to advance slowly, and sailed north aboard a battered tub of a transport which enabled him to reach his destination on September 5.

In the capital he found himself without an assignment for the second time in his budding career. Neither his corps superior nor the army's newly appointed general-in-chief, Major General Henry W. Halleck, whom he successfully importuned for an interview, could provide him with immediate employment. But his superior did sound an optimistic note: because of a general scarcity of qualified topographical engineers, he soon ought to find a position somewhere, possibly in the western theater. When Wilson expressed interest in that prospect, noting that he would enjoy the chance to serve near his brothers, both of whom had become volunteer officers in the West, the corps chief promised to work hard to obtain transfer papers for him.

In the meantime, still restless, Wilson cast about for a temporary position on active service. Fortunately, his West Point career had acquainted him with many officers in high positions throughout the War Department. Ever quick to seize opportunity, he would utilize this advantage to its full extent throughout his military life. After only a few days of searching, he was aided by a friend in the adjutant general's office, who provided him with an assignment as assistant engineer and volunteer aide-de-camp on the staff of General McClellan.

Upon being turned back from Richmond in June by General Robert E. Lee's Confederates, McClellan had relinquished control over the Army of the Potomac to Major General John Pope. Pope had wasted no time in sending the Federal forces to the slaughter in the Second Battle of Bull Run, in August. Now the remnants of the army were racing northward after the victorious enemy, attempting to check their invasion of Maryland. Once again the Federals had been placed under

"Little Mac," whom they loved and admired with a zeal rather surprising in view of his uneven combat record.

On September 8 Wilson reported for duty at McClellan's headquarters at Rockville, Maryland, twelve miles from Washington. He was most impressed with the general, who was handsome and sartorially splendid and who displayed to him the charm and sophistication which had become his hallmarks. McClellan put his aide to work at once. Wilson and two West Point classmates, Lieutenants George Custer and James P. Martin, carried dispatches to various units of the army, reporting back to them at regular intervals to certify that subordinate commanders obeyed Little Mac's orders.

A few days later McClellan sent Wilson as his personal representative to an infantry column which at South Mountain on the fourteenth waged a bitter fight against a portion of Lee's army. After other limited engagements were fought, the rival armies clashed in force along the banks of a stream known as Antietam Creek and on the seventeenth waged the deadliest single day's fighting in American history.

On that morning Wilson rode north along the battle line to observe the activity of Major General Edwin V. Sumner's army corps, which held the Federal center. This was the first time Wilson had taken part in a full-sized battle, and he made a fine showing. Ignoring the ubiquitous cannon and rifle fire, he jumped his horse over fences, fallen trees, and streams to complete his errand.

When he reached Sumner's headquarters, he found the elderly general filled with despair and obsessed with the fear that his ranks were being sliced to pieces. But Wilson relayed an order from McClellan, that Sumner hold his position with his command. With that, Sumner pointed toward his near-distant battle line, now obscured by cannon smoke and surrounded by rocking sound, and shouted: "Go back, young man, and tell General McClellan that I *have* no command!"

Sumner was exaggerating his condition, but it was true that up and down the line the Rebels were battering the Army of the Potomac with savagery. Yet both McClellan and Wilson perceived that the army might triumph if Major General Ambrose E. Burnside pushed his corps across the Antietam at the southern tip of the Federal line and crumpled the enemy's right flank and rear.

In later months Ambrose Burnside would win McClellan's job and would smash the Army of the Potomac nearly to bits attacking impregnable enemy positions at Fredericksburg, Virginia. At Antietam, he displayed this same quality of perverse obstinance. He threw his men at

the Confederate positions across the river, but although he outnumbered his opponents by a wide margin he failed to plan his assault
properly and saw his drive stalled time and again. It was not until
midafternoon that he could finally cross a stone bridge and carry his
objective. But his slowness in attack had enabled Confederate reinforcements to arrive on the scene, neutralizing his success and saving a
stalemate for General Lee.

After the fighting ceased and the Rebels drew off, nonetheless,
Lieutenant Wilson saw that McClellan had been as much to blame for
the outcome as had Burnside or any other subordinate. Little Mac had
launched a slow and uncoordinated attack against both flanks of Lee's
outnumbered army, had kept 36,000 troops out of the fighting, and had
failed to pursue the weary enemy after the battle. While he still admired
McClellan the man, Wilson no longer accepted the view of many observers, who felt he was an excellent strategist and tactician.

Ten days after the battle Wilson was allowed to rejoin his corps.
He was so anxious to escape the scene of wasted opportunities that he
covered the distance to Washington—seventy-five miles—by an all-
night ride.

He did not remain long in the capital. Soon after arriving, he
learned that he must return to the army to appear as a witness at a
court-martial. But before that time came, he had the chance to meet a
very interesting man and to hear an inviting prospect for active service.

The man was Major General John A. McClernand, a short,
swarthy gentleman with a thick beard, bushy eyebrows, and a knack for
exploiting any opportunity to advance his personal standing. The last
trait made him a kindred spirit to Wilson. For many years a leading
figure in Illinois politics, he had received one of the letters Wilson
wrote from Fort Vancouver asking help in securing a transfer east.
McClernand had been a close friend of Wilson's father, and late in
1861, prior to the Port Royal expedition, had tried unsuccessfully to
attach Wilson to his own staff. Now, meeting the young lieutenant in
Washington, he spoke of renewing his request. If his current plans
materialized, he would need a trustworthy aide.

His latest scheme concerned an expedition to capture the Mississippi Valley for the Union by seizing the great enemy stronghold,
Vicksburg, then by operating eastward into the interior of the Confederacy. A staunch Democrat who had aided the Republican administration's war effort by contributing funds, recruits, and political goodwill,
McClernand wielded strong bargaining power with the president. Lin-

Major General John A. McClernand—*Photograph courtesy Library of Congress*

coln had already given initial approval to his project, and McClernand hoped to receive formal and final authority very soon. When such authority came, he would win the right to campaign independently of his former superior in the West, General Grant, whom he disliked and distrusted.

Wilson was not so confident that McClernand would gain independent command, for he possessed no formal military training. But he understood the man's ambition and admired his energy, foresight, and self-assurance. Accordingly, he agreed to deliver a message from him to General McClellan, whom rumor had on the verge of again being relieved of command of the Army of the Potomac.

Soon afterward Wilson returned to Maryland, testified at the court-martial, and then encountered Little Mac and secured an audience with him. Seated inside McClellan's headquarters tent, he relayed General McClernand's suggestion that Little Mac seek the united command in the Mississippi Valley.

Wilson understood McClernand's reasoning, and believed that his host did also. As a figure of national prominence, McClellan stood a chance of winning such a promotion more easily than McClernand could. If the Illinois politician offered him help in attaining that goal, McClellan might be so grateful as to tender him a command higher than any he could secure on his own.

When Wilson finished speaking, General McClellan candidly admitted the probability of his impending relief. But he dismissed McClernand's suggestion with a wave of his hand. He was so attached to the officers and men of "his" Army of the Potomac that if denied authority over them he could not even consider accepting another command.

This evidence of McClellan's unwillingness to subordinate personal considerations to the greater concept of the nation's well-being dismayed Wilson. Of course, Wilson had himself displayed the same tendency on a number of occasions, such as in 1861 when he had feared missing out on the fighting, barely considering that a short war might be best for the country. In later campaigns—and later wars—he was to demonstrate the same characteristic more than once, when jockeying for command positions he favored, disregarding what the War Department or the White House wished for him. The ambitious man often decries unenviable qualities in others without recognizing their presence in himself. And to Wilson, evidence of personal ambition in so prominent a hero as McClellan would have seemed more shocking than the thought of so much ambition in a mere lieutenant such as himself.

In any case, he took it upon himself to deliver a fervent little lecture about the course which he felt McClellan ought to pursue. In later years he recollected that he said: "Pardon me, General, if I add— if they don't give you an army, you should take an army corps or even a division. If they will not give you a division, were I in your place, I should ask for a brigade. If they deny that, I should resign and go back to my state and raise a regiment. If I couldn't get a colonelcy, I should take on any position open to me, and failing a commission, I should take my musket and go out as a private soldier!"

Strange advice for a junior lieutenant to give a major general and army commander. But it was a right-minded suggestion. McClellan apparently took no offense at his outburst. He remarked, however, that no one had ever spoken to him in such a manner. Yet when he said he would think over Wilson's advice, he smiled meaninglessly. Seeing that his words had not produced the desired effect, Wilson sadly left the tent, remounted, and started back to Washington.

In the capital, he gave John McClernand the gloomy news. Learning that final authority for the Mississippi project was still lacking, Wilson then packed his bags and prepared to head west. His own plans had materialized, though McClernand's had not; the War Department had approved his transfer to Grant's army.

He went to Tennessee via a roundabout route which ran through Delaware and New York. In Wilmington he again saw Ella and her family and again rode about the city in the Andrews's carriage. The next day he went to Manhattan, where he made a courtesy call at the home of Lieutenant Colonel Richard Delafield, the superintendent of West Point during Wilson's term there. The visit included some hours spent with the colonel's daughter, Laura, with whom Wilson had been corresponding for months. He recorded no specific indication of his feelings toward the young lady, but they were destined to exchange letters for a long period.

Before leaving Washington, he had been "informally authorized" to seek a commission in the New York Volunteers. After visiting the Delafields he stopped at the Astor House, where he called on Thurlow Weed, one of the Empire State's most powerful political bosses. Their conversation was cordial, but Weed played deaf when Wilson requested a colonelcy in an infantry or cavalry regiment. Finally the politician admitted that only natives of New York could be considered for such high rank. Since Weed's visitor could not afford to negotiate for a lower position, their talk proved beneficial to Wilson in but two regards: it showed him the cynical methods by which state commissions were awarded, and made him resolve to seek further promotions on the basis of merit as a soldier, not through political maneuvering.

Finally he boarded a train for Tennessee. As it carried him westward, he considered his situation, and grew depressed. A welcome change of scenery was upcoming, and all the activity and adventure he ever hoped to experience might lie only miles ahead. But the unpleasant truth was that after a year and a half of war he was still a junior lieutenant, and as a lieutenant he would join Grant's army.

Better Send Wilson;
He Belongs to
the Get-There Gang

The trip west was uncomfortable and tedious, pro-longed by worn trackage and overage trains. But Wilson's patience was eventually rewarded; one of the first persons he met in Tennessee was his brother Henry, who after leaving West Point had helped recruit an infantry regiment and was now a captain and staff officer. A genuine hero, he had served with gallantry and distinction in the Battle of Shiloh and during the campaign to capture Forts Henry and Donelson, and had been twice wounded. James envied his reputation and must have been somewhat chagrined to find that Henry, who possessed neither Academy diploma nor Regular Army commission, outranked him.

On November 8, one day after meeting his brother in the village of Jackson, Wilson reported to Grant's headquarters at La Grange. There too he saw familiar faces, those of hometown friends now on Grant's staff. And before meeting Grant himself, he had the chance to speak to another native of Illinois, Major John A. Rawlins, adjutant to the commanding general.

Although not an acquaintance of Wilson, Major Rawlins had known Wilson's maternal grandfather, who had located in Galena, Rawlins's home village, late in life. However, at thirty-one Rawlins was only six years older than his visitor, and in temperament was much akin to him. A few inches shorter than Wilson, he was black-haired, brown-eyed, and luxuriantly bearded.

An intense and earnest man, Rawlins was apt to use explicit words whenever vexed. He was vexed on this day, as was reflected by his manner of greeting Wilson: "I am glad to see you, lieutenant; damned glad to see you. . . . I want to be friends with you. Indeed, I want to form an alliance, offensive and defensive, with you."

Rawlins's anxiety had reference to his self-adopted role as General Grant's watchdog. Since the outbreak of war, Grant, one of the most successful Federal commanders, had been plagued by a plethora of nagging problems, which Rawlins constantly helped him fight. These included jealous subordinates, such as McClernand, equally envious superiors, such as General Halleck, angry politicians who favored personal friends and constituents over Grant, and an array of social weaknesses. Prominent among the latter were an occasional fondness for liquor and for the company of intemperate friends. Thus far, he had been able to surmount these obstacles, thanks largely to his adjutant's solicitude.

Rawlins had the ability to win fast friends and made quick enemies. He saw a fast friend in Wilson. Rawlins had already heard reports about Wilson's talents and his blameless personal life. Having now the chance to see and to speak with the man, Rawlins realized that the reports must be true. At once, as he had implied in his welcoming speech, he perceived in Wilson a valuable ally in the fight to keep Grant's name pristine.

In turn, Wilson was impressed by Rawlins's desire to aid the Federal cause by making smooth the ways of one of its greatest soldiers. He was also pleased by Rawlins's frankness. He had come west influenced by reports of his own, about Grant's drinking problems. He was interested to hear Rawlins admit that such problems did exist. The adjutant added, however, that Grant's overindulgence was largely the result of his fraternizing with irresponsible staff officers who deserved to be dismissed from their posts. And Rawlins was just as candid when pointing out that Grant possessed solid virtues as well as considerable military ability.

General Grant and Staff—*Photograph courtesy of Library of Congress*

Standing, left to right: Captain Henry W. Janes, headquarters quartermaster; General Grant; Major Michael Morgan, chief of commissary; and Captain Peter Hudson, aide-de-camp. *Seated, left to right:* Brigadier General John A. Rawlins (temporarily beardless), assistant adjutant general and chief of staff; Lieutenant Colonel Cyrus B. Comstock, aide-de-camp; Lieutenant Frederick Grant (Grant's eldest son), aide-de-camp; Lieutenant Colonel Orville Babcock, aide-de-camp; and Captain Ely S. Parker, Grant's military secretary.

After conferring with the adjutant, Wilson met the major general himself. Grant turned out to be something of a disappointment; in the flesh, he was anything but imposing. He was short and stubby, dark-bearded, and casual in dress and demeanor; Wilson would always remember his first sight of Grant's "simple and unmilitary bearing." But though he fell far below a man like General McClellan in martial grandeur, Grant soon appeared to Wilson as intelligent and interesting, rather reserved and soft-spoken, but articulate in a direct, uncomplicated manner.

For much of that afternoon, Grant chatted with his newest officer in his tent. They discussed the war in Virginia and in the West and the political climate in Washington, as well as less significant matters. Grant seemed pleased to at last have found a chief topographical engineer, West Point-trained. At the same time, Wilson expressed himself as fortunate to have won a position under so renowned a general.

Wilson was in fact much pleased. Grant was unpretentious and kindly; he encouraged Wilson's friendship and by his self-assurance won Wilson's confidence. After only one session in his company, the lieutenant realized that his transfer west had been a stroke of good luck.

IN THIS AUTUMN OF 1862 GRANT'S Army of the Tennessee was moving south through the corridor of land in central Mississippi in the hope of taking Vicksburg. If Grant could accomplish this, the Federal forces would control the Mississippi River from source to mouth, cutting the Confederacy in two—a blow which might prove fatal.

The movement had begun on November 4. The army was now advancing slowly toward the line of the Mississippi Central Railroad; from there it would move to Jackson, the state capital. As the Federals marched, the Confederate army in this theater, under Lieutenant General John C. Pemberton, fell back steadily, eventually moving as far south as Grenada, about 100 miles above Jackson.

Two days after arriving at Grant's headquarters, Wilson went to Bolivar, Tennessee, where he was assigned to the right wing of the army, under his old shipboard acquaintance and recruiting colleague in Boston, James B. McPherson. Having a year ago come west and accepted a commission in the volunteer ranks, McPherson was now a major general and one of Grant's most trusted subordinates.

On his first active assignments, Wilson could make little use of his engineering training. He accompanied advance cavalry units on patrol through northern Mississippi. On November 17 the force with which he rode reached the fringes of Grenada and exchanged pistol shots with Rebel horsemen. Wilson proved alert and quick in his first mounted skirmish. When the enemy finally broke and fled, the Federals pursued; and, being a superior horseman, the lieutenant outraced his companions and captured a prisoner.

When he returned to McPherson's main force and accompanied it southward, Wilson had an ample opportunity to renew and bolster his friendship with its commander. This pleased him, but soon he grew dispirited about the slowness of McPherson's advance and that of the other Federal columns, as well as by the bleakness of the surrounding country. He wrote in his diary of the "desolate appearance of the farms" and the "extreme ignorance of the people."

Grant's advance troops moved so sluggishly that by December 5 his main body had not yet reached Grenada, and thus the enemy had not been seriously harried. In fact, perhaps the only beneficial result of the operation thus far was the neutralization of General McClernand's threat to Grant's power. McClernand had raised a large expeditionary force by recruiting thousands of soldiers in the Northwest. While he remained in Washington, his levies were transported to Memphis to be organized. But General-in-Chief Halleck liked McClernand even less than Grant, and he informed Grant of the politician-general's intentions regarding an independent command. Early in December Grant decided to send one of his most reliable subordinates, Major General William T. Sherman, to Memphis. There Sherman sorted out the new recruits and without McClernand's knowledge removed them from his authority. Sherman then led them south to operate in concert with Grant's overland drive, but via a route which diverged from that taken by the main army. Grant planned to have Sherman launch an amphibious operation against Vicksburg while the bulk of the army struck Jackson and Vicksburg on land.

Grant's plans for his campaign, however, were foiled late that month, when a large band of Confederate cavalry, under Major General Earl Van Dorn, cut around the Federals' left flank and destroyed their supply base at Holly Springs, Mississippi. The raiders wrecked a million dollars' worth of matériel and influenced Grant to pull back to Memphis, abandoning all hope of continuing on to Vicksburg.

But General Sherman did not conform to the withdrawal and on the twenty-sixth attacked Confederate positions near the stronghold, though he lacked support. After suffering a bloody repulse on treacherous ground, he returned his troops northward.

Sherman's severe defeat at Chickasaw Bayou seemed to indicate that an overland campaign would not succeed. Wilson fully approved of Grant's decision to call off such a drive. In addition to the fact that an operation of that nature exposed the army's supply lines, Wilson felt that McPherson's troubles with bad roads and inclement weather demonstrated that any offensive on land, especially in winter, was doomed to failure. Early in January, when he returned to army headquarters from McPherson's column, Wilson tried to convince Grant and Rawlins that "the Mississippi River itself was the true, central, and only feasible line of operations and supply for an army large enough for the task of taking Vicksburg."

He reinforced his argument by stressing the danger in McClernand's efforts to gain an independent command. If the army did not operate according to a feasible plan, McClernand might use its lack of success to Grant's detriment.

By now Wilson felt solicitous of his new superior's well-being and regarded McClernand as a meddling outsider. In part this was because Wilson became firmly attached to anyone who seemed influential enough to advance his career. He doubted that McClernand was enough of a soldier to win the renown and the power which Grant had attained. Furthermore, Wilson had come to share Rawlins's opinion about Grant's energy and skill. And, though McClernand was a family friend and had treated Wilson kindly enough, he seemed much less entitled to lead the great Federal army in the West.

Later events strengthened Wilson's close association with his commander. When the army pulled out of Mississippi to reorganize and refit, newspapers arrived in camp with an announcement that Wilson had been named lieutenant colonel on the staff of David Hunter, who was still in South Carolina, now as a corps commander. Wilson was rather pleased to learn that Hunter still held him in high regard. But the prospect of leaving Grant, Rawlins, and other new-won friends was painful.

Grant solved the dilemma in mid-January, 1863, during a trip south from his newly established headquarters at Memphis. Wilson and Rawlins (himself a new lieutenant colonel) accompanied the general on the four-day visit to that part of the army which had remained in camp farther down the Mississippi. During the inspection tour, Wilson grew even more closely acquainted with Grant, finding that "he acted throughout with a simplicity, modesty, and good fellowship that won my hearty admiration, friendship, and confidence."

He was particularly enthused—as well as surprised—when during the tour Grant went General Hunter "one better," by offering Wilson the prestigious post of assistant inspector general of the Army of the Tennessee, with rank of lieutenant colonel.

It was a flattering indication of Grant's high regard for Wilson's talents as a staff officer. During the short period he had been in the West, Wilson had turned in some highly creditable performances at surveying, reconnoitering, and mapmaking. Grant did not care to lose so valuable an officer to another general.

At once Wilson accepted the offer. Through Grant's efforts his position in the volunteer ranks and his appointment as inspector general were at first authorized on a tentative basis and finally, after some months, were confirmed by the War Department.

During the intervening months, while Wilson awaited the necessary authority to begin inspections, winter arrived in full fury. Until it passed and the army could resume offensive operations, the Federals lolled in their camps along the Tennessee-Mississippi border. Ice and snow curtailed much of the work of the headquarters staff, leaving Wilson and his companions a great deal of idle time.

Left to his own devices, Wilson engaged in a favorite pastime, military theorizing, and increasingly his thoughts focused on the formulation of a nationalized army. An old-line Regular at heart if not by length of service, he was convinced that such a force, divested of all political trappings, would solve all of the Union's military problems. He even jotted down a point-by-point system which he felt would properly employ and promote officers while weeding out political appointees.

He saw the need for such an army in the context of the total war effort. In the East, the situation was bleak for the Federal forces. In December General Burnside had brutally mismanaged the Army of the Potomac at Fredericksburg, and its disgruntled veterans were now retreating through the Virginia mud. Here in Tennessee, Grant was inactive, revamping his campaign plans. Elsewhere in the divided country, prospects of a Federal military success were slim. This current situation in the field, where clumsy prosecution of the war had dimmed so many Unionist hopes, made Wilson feel (as he wrote in his diary) like a man bound head and foot while all he cherished was sweeping toward destruction before his eyes.

But soon after noting his despair, the situation in lower Tennessee began to improve. Though he admitted that bad weather made large-scale offensive activity impracticable, Grant adopted a plan for waging a limited campaign. His idea was sound for several reasons. For one, McClernand had at last come west and had angrily regained control of his so-called Army of the Mississippi. With General Halleck's aid Grant had been able to subordinate McClernand to the position of corps commander under his authority, but McClernand might find this only a temporary setback. Grant wished to give him no time to improve his situation. Then, too, Grant realized that if his soldiers were allowed to remain inactive through the winter, discord and dissension might result. It was painfully obvious that thus far operations to gain control of the Mississippi had failed. If the men had time to brood about this, and if the often hostile press jumped on the bandwagon, Grant's position in command might become tenuous in the extreme.

Therefore, though entertaining little hope of success, Grant launched a number of projects aimed at reaching the high ground east and south of Vicksburg. He directed some of his engineers to build a canal to divert the Mississippi and leave the stronghold high and dry. Other troops spent weeks trying to cut a water route from Lake Providence south to the Red River, to permit gunboats and transports to move below the fortress without having to run the heavy batteries which protected it on the Mississippi shore. Ultimately, these ventures failed, but they did put thousands of men to work at time-consuming, muscle-building labor. Come spring, the army would find itself in no better strategic position, but at least it would be fit for active campaigning.

One of these projects was predicated upon the possibility that troops might move south by encircling Vicksburg's right flank across the upper Yazoo Delta country. Because Grant so highly regarded Wilson's talents, he sent his newly minted lieutenant colonel to oversee the operation.

The Yazoo Delta was an area of drowned forest, swampland, and cotton plantations northeast of the enemy fortress and was streaked by a network of small streams, canals, and crisscrossing bayous. Wilson's project involved cutting the long levee opposite and below the Federal-held town of Helena, Arkansas, to flood an adjacent cotton canal known as the Yazoo Pass. That done, Grant could send an amphibious expedition across the northern part of the Delta and down the Yazoo River to dry ground above Vicksburg, the proper site from which to launch an assault. It was also hoped that ships and troops could sail through the broken levee to destroy neighboring railroad bridges, sink enemy steamboats in the Yazoo River, and stop the flow of cattle and grain from the Yazoo district into Vicksburg.

It was a formidable undertaking, but Wilson saw it as his first opportunity to win renown on an independent mission. On January 29, pursuant to orders, he went to Helena by boat. There he called on the city commander, Brigadier General Willis A. Gorman, and from him received a fatigue party of 500 soldiers to help him reopen the Yazoo Pass. The next day, accompanied by part of this force, Wilson boarded a tin-clad warship and sailed toward the entrance to the Pass. The rest of the detail followed aboard two steamers.

On its way to its destination, the small fleet encountered Rebel cavalry pickets on shore at the lower end of Helena. The enemy opened fire, and the soldiers aboard Wilson's ship, the *Forest Rose*, replied in kind. Wilson himself took up a rifle and set his sights on the pickets, who already had begun to scatter. He fired, and a Confederate, shot through the body, fell from his horse.

At noon on February 2 the fleet reached the Yazoo Pass. Carefully the soldiers examined the levee which years before the state of Mississippi had thrown up to block access to the old, abandoned waterway. Reconnoitering, Wilson grew hopeful of success, noting that the channel leading to the levee seemed clear of major obstructions. "The stream looks quite navigable," he later wrote Rawlins, "and I am sure will allow the boats now here to navigate it without difficulty. . . ."

By 2 P.M. Wilson's crew was hard at work, chopping away at the embankment to allow the Mississippi to flow through the Pass and flood the backcountry. By late afternoon on the third, the pioneers had cut two ditches through the levee. They stood aside as other soldiers then buried a keg with fifty pounds of powder under the dike near one of the ditches.

At 7 P.M. the mine was detonated. Wilson watched from a safe distance as an immense spray of earth and rock shot into the air and a torrent of water rushed through the gap. He quickly engineered the planting and exploding of three other mines, which completely shattered the levee. By the next morning the Pass had been opened to a width of seventy-five yards, and as he told Rawlins, the water was flooding through "like nothing else I ever saw except Niagara Falls. Logs, trees, and great masses of earth were torn away with the greatest ease."

When Grant heard of Wilson's success, he wired General Halleck in Washington, expressing confidence that his soldiers would soon accomplish the first of their objectives, the sinking of all Rebel transports in the Yazoo tributaries. This job he entrusted to Admiral David Dixon Porter, commander of the Mississippi Squadron, which was operating in concert with the Army of the Tennessee. If Porter handled his assigned work properly, the path to Vicksburg would also lie clear.

When Porter—one of the most experienced and most efficient Federal naval leaders—was briefed about Grant's plan, he gave the immediate task of destroying Yazoo shipping to Lieutenant Commander Watson Smith. This was unfortunate, for although Smith was a competent seaman he was advanced in age and was inclined to act in slow stages.

But Smith readily agreed to follow Porter's instructions—that is, to enter the cut with a shipboard contingent of 700 soldiers, move eastward toward the Tallahatchie River and wreck neighboring bridges, proceed to the Yalobusha River and, finally, 250 miles later, to the all-important Yazoo River.

Even before the naval commander reached Wilson, however, the enemy set to work to complicate matters for them. Having learned of operations along the levee, the Confederates felled trees across Yazoo Pass for a twenty-mile stretch between its junction with the Coldwater River, far to the east, and a site not far from the broken levee.

On February 7 and 8, Wilson accompanied Acting Master George W. Brown aboard the *Forest Rose* to survey the extent of the enemy's interference. They discovered about forty felled trees in the pass, but Wilson wrote Rawlins that "in no place had it obstructed the channel so as to resist or prevent the passage of boats. . . . no one here entertains a doubt of our being able to work through." In the same dispatch, however, he noted that General Gorman at Helena had ordered 1,500 men to aid in removal efforts and to chop down trees which overhung the river and menaced navigation.

This contingent of laborers, under Major General C. C. Washburn, set to work on the morning of the tenth. The soldiers stripped to their waists and rolled up their trouser legs so they could slosh through the deep water. In details of several hundred, they attached steamboat hawsers to the butts of the logs and by sheer force dragged them out of the water. Although some of the felled sycamores and cottonwoods weighed several tons, the laborers wielded fantastic strength. "Seeing such an exhibition," Wilson later recalled, ". . . it is easy enough to understand how the Egyptians moved the great stones, columns, and slabs from the quarries to their temples and pyramids."

The work was grueling, the conditions harsh, and progress agonizingly slow. But Wilson remained confident of ultimate success and repeated his expectation in numerous letters to Rawlins.

By the middle of February, Grant was sufficiently impressed with Wilson's progress to order 4,500 soldiers under Brigadier General Leonard F. Ross to proceed from Helena through the Pass, aboard Commander Smith's division of light-draught ships. On the twentieth Smith began to move his flotilla from the Mississippi toward the Pass.

Wilson completed his removal work on the twenty-first and so informed Grant, in laconic triumph: "I have to report, for the information of the major-general commanding, that Yazoo Pass is now open for navigation." He admitted that a few overhanging trees which could not be cut down for fear of again clogging the river, still posed some difficulties for Smith's fleet. But he felt that recent events confirmed "the practicability of this route, during proper stages of water, as a line of military operations."

As was his style, Commander Smith moved slowly, and was not in position to utilize the new water route until the twenty-fifth. When the fleet finally reached the cut, Wilson was impressed neither by its ships —many of which were obviously unseaworthy—nor by their commander. Thereafter he grumbled about delays caused by snags and swift currents, which kept the fleet from reaching a point near the town of Greenwood until March 11, some days behind schedule. And Wilson's temper boiled when the flotilla encountered the Confederate garrison at Fort Pemberton, at the head of the Yazoo River.

Smith had heard rumors that local Rebels were gathering at a makeshift defensive position on an island enclosed by a loop of the Tallahatchie five miles above Greenwood. He ought to have paid them close heed. Yet not until the evening of the tenth had he and Wilson learned from reliable informants that the rumors were well founded. On the morning of the twelfth, with General Ross, they boarded an ironclad, the *Chillicothe*, and steamed south. At 10:15, rounding a bend in the river, they found the fort 800 yards dead ahead.

At first sight Fort Pemberton seemed extremely vulnerable. It was an earthwork with cotton-bale parapets reinforced with sandbags, and was surrounded by a slimy bog. Confident he could blast it into surrendering, Commander Smith opened with his guns as soon as he came into range. To his shock, he found that the work was manned by several thousand defenders and was protected by some long-range guns, including a heavy 32-pounder rifle, which had only recently been mounted. Confederate shells struck the *Chillicothe* twice in her port

side, inflicting fourteen casualties among her crew. Ordering a withdrawal, Smith steamed upstream, out of range.

The Federals spent the next several hours reconnoitering the fort,
while the rest of the flotilla—one ironclad, two steam rams, and six
light-draught gunboats—sailed downstream. Finally all the ships tied
up at the east bank of the Tallahatchie but still several miles above the
garrison.

Wilson soon discovered that the bog around the fort prevented the
launching of a land attack. He and General Ross grew short-tempered
about the situation, and their mood did not improve when Smith manifested an apparent disregard for the necessity of speed. The commander
seemed in no hurry to confront the enemy again.

Smith's notion that the Confederates would soon abandon their
works in the face of such an awesome display of naval might finally
prompted him to make a second trip downriver. At 4:15 P.M. the
Chillicothe returned to Fort Pemberton, its captain ready to witness the
fort's evacuation.

But the enemy commander, Brigadier General Lloyd Tilghman,
had no such idea in mind. Thirteen months before, he had surrendered
Fort Henry to General Grant. It had been a painful and humiliating
experience, and now he hungered for revenge upon Grant's soldiers and
the naval force operating with them. For the second time that day,
Tilghman got his revenge. Seven minutes after his guns opened fire, the
Chillicothe again had to steam to safety.

Wilson raged. He had worked long and hard to cut the levee, to
remove obstructions from the waterway beyond—and to impress Grant
with his enterprise. Now, while standing on the threshold of full success
at the entrance to the Yazoo River, the passageway to Vicksburg, a
cotton-bale fort on a marshy wisp of land was threatening to foil his
plans. But Commander Smith gave him no comfort; he could merely
talk of another assault. Yet before Smith could act, Wilson was obliged
to report the situation to General Grant, remarking that "the rebel
position is a strong one by virtue of the difficulties of approach. . . ."

On the morning of March 13, the Federals tried again. This time
the *Chillicothe* was reinforced by the other ironclad, the *Baron De
Kalb*, and a mortar boat. The added strength meant little. Tilghman's
shells struck the *Chillicothe* thirty-eight times and forced her, once
more, to disengage. The *De Kalb* held her position 800 yards from the
fort, until nightfall, but this was at best a minor achievement, for not a
single gun within Fort Pemberton had been dismounted by a broadside.

This third defeat was almost the last straw for Wilson. He dashed off some blazing letters to Rawlins, decrying the navy's inability to use its firepower to effect: "I'm disgusted with 7, 9, 10 and 11 inch guns; to let one 6½-inch rifle stop our Navy. Bah!" He singled out Smith for particular abuse, laced with sarcasm: "I have no hope of anything great, considering the course followed by the naval forces under direction of their able and efficient Acting Rear-Admiral, Commodore, Captain, Lieutenant-Commander Smith." In one dispatch he added, unnecessarily, that "Smith, you doubtless have understood by this time, I don't regard as the equal of Lord Nelson." Perhaps Wilson's irritability was the result of constant work: "I've now been two days and entire nights without sleep, and am almost dead."

His criticisms of Smith were hardly fair. Despite his methodical style, Smith was intelligent and conscientious and was willing to work hard for success. He was in trouble because nothing in his education as a seaman had prepared him for a campaign in winding, tree-hung swamps; and already his ships had suffered damage from a treacherous current and other dangers. But Wilson grew impatient with anyone who seemed unable to give him the precise amount of cooperation and support he desired. Smith would not be the last colleague whom he would abruptly condemn on such grounds.

Spurred by Wilson's urgings, Smith agreed on the sixteenth to try once again to run past the fort. By this point Wilson had set up a small shore battery, comprising two 30-pounder Parrotts and one 8-inch ship howitzer, about 700 yards from the fort, to assist the Navy. Late that morning the battery began to pound away at Fort Pemberton and soon afterward Smith led his ironclads downriver, carrying some of Ross's infantrymen. But when within 1,100 yards of the Rebel works, the *Chillicothe* was struck several times and had her gun ports sealed shut. For the fourth time, Smith ordered a retrograde maneuver.

For several hours the shore guns traded shots with the enemy, but that evening Wilson had to inform Grant: "I am sorry to say we are no nearer the accomplishment of our object to-night than we were yesterday." In this letter he again went out of his way to cover his tracks and to shift the burden of blame for what was now shaping up to be a failure: "You will please remember, general, that I am not responsible for the defects in the organization of this expedition, neither directly nor indirectly. . . ." Again, too, he was patently unfair to his associates, who were giving as much effort toward the accomplishment of the mission as he was. In times of stress and ill fortune, when he perceived himself caught up in a debacle, Wilson's determination to succeed often carried him far beyond the limits of fair play. However, it is unlikely that he realized the extent of his cruelty. His primary concern—as it had been since the days of his youth—was for his own reputation, not that of others; and divesting himself of all responsibility for failure, when he did not consider such responsibility rightfully his, was his foremost aim.

On the day that Smith beat his fourth retreat, Wilson formulated a plan which he hoped would recoup his lost prestige. Noting that the ground under Fort Pemberton lay only a few feet above water level, he considered cutting the Yazoo levee near the entrance to the pass, to allow additional water to flow into the Tallahatchie and around the garrison. A four-foot rise, he believed, would compel its abandonment.

He took the plan to General Ross, who thought it had merit, and then wired it to Major General Benjamin M. Prentiss, the new commander at Helena. Prentiss endorsed Ross's opinion and immediately put soldiers to work cutting the levee at Austin, eighteen miles above the Arkansas stronghold.

The results were disappointing. The water level did rise but not sufficiently to send the Confederates scurrying to higher ground. Later Wilson came to feel that if Prentiss's men had broken the levee at a more strategic point and for a wider distance, at least a two-foot rise would have resulted. By then he had revised his estimate of the depth required to drive the Rebels out: "The enemy could not have withstood more than 12 inches."

Thus it seemed that the operation to open and navigate the long stretch of waterway across the Yazoo Delta had fizzled out. Wilson could never accept defeat stoically. "It's provoking beyond measure," he wrote Rawlins, "to think that everything we undertake must be marred by incompetence and stupidity! I am intensely disgusted. . . ."

On March 17 Commander Smith ordered a full withdrawal and took Ross's soldiers back up the Coldwater River. The next day the naval officer bowed out of combat service, having fallen ill from serving in the pestilential swamps of upper Mississippi. He later resigned his commission owing to "aberration of mind," and not long afterward died of the fever he had contracted.

Technically speaking, however, the campaign to exploit the Yazoo cut was not yet over. Though discouraged by Wilson's recent reports, Grant decided to make a final effort to force a passage. He sent reinforcements under Brigadier General Isaac F. Quinby to launch another amphibious expedition across the southern part of the Delta, and ordered Wilson to assist Quinby in any way possible. Quinby met Smith's flotilla on the Coldwater and made it retrace its path down the stream toward Fort Pemberton. Entertaining little hope of success, Wilson accompanied the new commander on a swampy twelve-day reconnaissance which succeeded only in forcing Quinby to agree with Commander Smith that the operation was not feasible. By then, Wilson was thoroughly willing to abandon the project.

When the fleet headed north for the final time, the soldiers aboard expressed the highest degree of disgust. For many weeks a large percentage of them had been shuttled back and forth through swamps and bayous, had been put to work at strenuous labor in deep, stagnant water, and had been forced to watch as their leaders made unsuccessful attempts to level a small enemy fort. After all of this, they were retreating ignominiously and, to add to their humiliation, were being pursued on land by bands of triumphant Confederates. It was too much for one Iowa infantryman, who jotted in his diary sentiments shared by many of his comrades: ". . . a disgraceful and disastrous retreat—no effort made to force a passage. Somebody in command to blame."

The Yazoo operation did signal a failure for Lieutenant Colonel Wilson in his first major independent assignment. However, he could hardly be considered the "somebody" deserving of all blame. He had worked long and carefully to assure its success, and could not have been called to account for the Navy's troubles with Fort Pemberton or for the enemy's determined, step-by-step resistance to the Federal drive. If his attitude about quick action had infected Commander Smith, it is even possible that the fleet would have reached the fort before the Confederates were able to gather there in force and to mount the long-range guns which proved the crucial factor in its successful defense.

When Wilson reached Tennessee and rejoined the main army, Grant welcomed him without a word of censure, glad to have him back at his side. Wilson's energetic campaign in the swamps had won him favorable publicity in camp, and his reputation as a multitalented aide had already begun to climb. Soon afterward, in fact, a popular expression, coined by Grant himself, began to circulate about headquarters. Whenever a particularly tough problem came to hand, requiring the services of a skillful troubleshooter, someone would advise: "Better send Wilson; he belongs to the get-there gang, and you won't have to explain!"

★IV★

*I Will Pull You off
That Horse and Beat
the Boots off of You!*

During Wilson's absence from Tennessee, the weather had begun to moderate, the high-rising Mississippi to recede, the roads to dry, and the army to flex its muscles in preparation for the coming campaign. Grant had made a new plan to take Vicksburg, had sent it to Halleck for his study, and had received permission to test it.

The final plan was similar to the one which Wilson had promoted shortly before being sent into the Yazoo area. It involved running the Vicksburg batteries with Admiral Porter's fleet of warships and transports while troops were moved in barges and small steamers as well as on foot down the bayou-infested territory west of the Mississippi and out of range of the guns. Once beyond the batteries, Porter's ships would sail to the western shore of the river and ferry the troops across, below Vicksburg. Then the army would be on the proper bank to launch an all-out campaign against the "Gibraltar of the West."

77

When this plan first came up for discussion in January, Generals McPherson and Sherman had argued against it. It would accomplish nothing, they believed, but the destruction of Porter's flotilla. Probably Wilson was not the first to consider the river campaign; however, he did supply Grant with arguments to use against his corps commanders. Perhaps his foremost argument was derived from his experience with naval operations of a similar nature. At Port Royal late in 1861 he had seen seemingly vulnerable warships challenge shore batteries without suffering serious damage; he doubted that the accuracy of Vicksburg's guns would prove a greater menace. Bolstered by Wilson's encouragement—having by now come to rely more heavily on his advice than upon that of any other staff officer—and with all attempts at canal-building having failed, Grant was prepared to handle any further skepticism.

Therefore, he ordered preliminary operations, including two diversionary movements. In mid-April he sent a cavalry brigade under Colonel Benjamin Grierson galloping through eastern Mississippi to destroy railroads and public property, as well as to divert attention from the movements of the main army. Grierson achieved great success, drawing after him thousands of Confederates who might otherwise have gone into battle against Grant. The other diversion, while not so dramatically triumphant, did considerable to mask Grant's intentions. A division of infantry under Major General Frederick Steele penetrated northwestern Mississippi and destroyed enemy supply areas, then fell back before the advance of a strong force sent out from Vicksburg. Steele's withdrawal led the Rebels to believe Grant was not going to come south in force at this time.

They were decidedly in error. With the advantage of surprise, the advance elements of the Army of the Tennessee began to trudge along southward-leading roads, their march spearheaded by McClernand's XIII Corps. Through the month of April the soldiers moved down the west bank of the great river afoot and aboard their troop ships, unbeknown to General Pemberton.

Grant had moved his headquarters to Milliken's Bend, Mississippi, only ten miles above Vicksburg, and there, on the evening of April 16, he boarded the *H. von Phul*, his command steamboat, for the run down the Mississippi. All told, Porter's fleet numbered thirty vessels—ironclads, rams, steamers, barges, and transports, including a ship laden with ammunition. Despite the possibility of danger, Grant allowed his wife and two of their children, who had been with him at headquarters, to accompany him aboard ship. Also on the hurricane deck of the *von Phul* as she moved south on the dark river were Wilson, Rawlins, and other staff officers, plus several high-ranking commanders including Major Generals McPherson and John A. Logan.

Grant was so confident in his belief in a safe voyage that when his ship anchored just beyond the range of Vicksburg's guns, he sat on deck and observed the progress of the rest of the fleet with an untroubled air. His youngest son, however, did not share his father's composure. Seated in Wilson's lap, the boy buried his head against the lieutenant colonel's chest with each roar of cannon fire from the batteries. Yet Grant and Wilson saw their judgment fully vindicated; the ships ran the gauntlet of shell fire without serious damage.

By April 30, the run completed, Grant ferried McClernand's and then McPherson's corps across the Mississippi to the landing at Bruinsburg, sixty-five miles below the fortress. Sherman, with the XV Corps, was still at Young's Point, below the jumping-off site of the expedition, where he intended to make some feinting maneuvers on the Yazoo River to keep part of Pemberton's army in place.

From Bruinsburg Grant's soldiers quickly moved inland. On Nelly, his sprightly little mare, Wilson accompanied the troops over roads south of Bayou Pierre toward the small village of Port Gibson. From there a system of roads led to larger and more strategic locations, including Vicksburg and, farther east, Grand Gulf and Jackson.

En route to Grand Gulf, McClernand's men encountered a large contingent of Confederates whom Pemberton, finally perceiving the Federals' presence, had dispatched to halt them. A mile west of Port Gibson the first extensive fighting of the campaign broke out. Thanks to help from McPherson's corps, General McClernand routed the enemy and forced them to retreat over Bayou Pierre toward Vicksburg, burning three bridges as they went.

On May 2 Grant moved through Port Gibson to the south fork of the Bayou Pierre and there confronted the ruined bridges. He called immediately for Wilson, who by now had built more than a half-dozen spans during the expedition. Today a plentiful supply of timber, in the form of deserted houses near the river, was available to him.

He outdid his previous efforts. Given a brigade-size detail, he set about creating a raft bridge 166 feet long and 12 feet wide. The span was composed of three rows of large millbeams stripped from the houses, with buoyant timber from nearby trees filling the gaps between the beams. The structure was firmly bound together by a cross-floor of materials two inches thick. Wilson also constructed a timber roadway approaching the span and added side rails to the bridge to prevent men and wagons from slipping into the five-foot-deep water.

The project consumed four hours; by late afternoon Grant's troops were moving across the bridge. The commanding general commended Wilson for his enterprise, and was particularly impressed that his chief topographical engineer had gone into the water to work beside the enlisted men.

Wilson pushed on with a small escort and a team of local guides, searching for another bridge to rebuild. He found one on the north fork of the bayou. Early that evening, working without respite, he supervised another crew in building a new bridge floor atop the remains of the old one, which had been damaged by fire. The army was moving over the repaired structure before 5:30 the next morning, finding that it remained sturdy throughout their crossing.

Soon afterward, Grant decided to cut loose from his long and unreliable line of supply and hurry into the interior of Mississippi with his 34,000 soldiers. He pushed eastward with McClernand and McPherson, as well as with Sherman, whose men had come south and then crossed the Mississippi to join the main army. On May 11 the Federal advance tangled with a much smaller force of Confederates near the town of Raymond, almost thirty miles southeast of Vicksburg. After fighting desperately and stalling Grant's drive for half a day, the Rebels withdrew. Grant then collected his detachments and decided to push farther east and strike Jackson—a main objective of his abortive campaign the previous November—to scatter troops reportedly gathering there as reinforcements for General Pemberton. Once he did so, and destroyed Pemberton's rail and factory facilities in Jackson, Grant could concentrate on Vicksburg.

At this juncture an incident occurred which marked a temporary rift in Wilson's relationship with his old friend McPherson. Following the success at Raymond, Grant sent Wilson, now serving as an all-purpose aide, to direct McPherson to push on to the railroad leading into Jackson at an early hour on May 13. But when he reached McPherson and relayed the order, Wilson received an unexpected reply. As Wilson later recalled: "Much to my surprise he said pointblank he would be damned if he'd do any such thing," explaining that his corps had been worn thin by the day's fighting and could not make such an early movement in force.

To Wilson's strict sense of military propriety, this smacked of insubordination. As though personally offended by the reply, he repeated Grant's order with cold formality and then gave McPherson a lecture on the penalty for refusing to obey. This was characteristic of Wilson in his now settled position as Grant's man, determined to do his commander's bidding and to tolerate neither disrespect nor disobedience in his name. Quickly riding back to headquarters, he secured a written copy of the order and with rather perverse delight delivered it to McPherson at midnight. This time the corps commander, who had recovered from his fatigue-induced irritability, made no outburst. Nevertheless, to Wilson's great displeasure, McPherson did not begin his march till 9 A.M.

Despite McPherson's deliberation, the Federals had a relatively simple task in capturing Jackson. There General Joseph E. Johnston, the ranking Confederate commander in the western theater, had assembled some 6,000 men; but upon Grant's approach he withdrew most of them north of the city. The small force that lingered till Grant's arrival offered resistance for three hours before evacuating Jackson. Grant was able to move in and wreck the city's military potential with ease.

While in Jackson, Grant learned that Pemberton had moved out of Vicksburg and was marching in his direction, seeking to link with General Johnston. Gathering its full strength, the Army of the Tennessee turned about and proceeded to thrash Pemberton's force at a site known as Champion Hill on May 16 and the next day near the Big Black River, on the road to Vicksburg. Recoiling from the shock of these defeats, Pemberton beat a hasty retreat to his fortress, aware that Grant would follow him.

Grant did, and by the nineteenth was in position to strike the river stronghold. Hoping to extend his run of success, he launched attacks against Vicksburg that day and again on the twenty-second. Both failed. Then he decided to settle back and starve the garrison into submission.

Lieutenant Colonel Wilson (now also a captain in the Regular service, his promotion having come through during the first week in May) was kept furiously busy during the operations preceding the siege. He carried orders to numerous units and personally led some forces into assigned positions about Vicksburg; he supervised the reconstruction of local bridges and the corduroying of muddy roads; and in general he acted effectively as a liaison officer between Grant and his corps, division, and brigade leaders.

The latter task was not always easy. When he served as go-between for Grant and General McClernand, it was, in fact, supremely impossible. This became evident when, shortly after the May 22 assault, Wilson had a confrontation with McClernand which in some respects mirrored his unpleasant encounter with McPherson ten days before.

Since coming west, the politician-general had been a thorn in Grant's side and, by association, a thorn in Wilson's side as well. However, though McClernand often sought to conspire against his commander and usually doubted the feasibility of Grant's plans, he did possess some soldierly qualities and led a hard-fighting corps. Consequently he had done well on a number of occasions, such as at Port Gibson and on the Big Black. On May 22 he had made the strongest effort of the corps commanders involved in the second Vicksburg attack. A handful of his men had actually penetrated the Rebel defenses at two points before being compelled to fall back for lack of reinforcements—an outcome for which he angrily and unjustly blamed Grant.

The encounter between Wilson and McClernand, one of the most curious incidents in Wilson's career, took place when the corps chief was smoldering over his near-success at Vicksburg. When Wilson relayed Grant's order to send some troops to guard crossings of the Big Black River, McClernand took the opportunity to vent his anger and disgust. "I'll be God damned if I'll do it!" he thundered, as the two men faced one another on their horses. "I am tired of being dictated to—I won't stand it any longer, and you can go back and tell General Grant!"

As if the outburst were not offensive enough to provoke Wilson, McClernand appended a series of oaths which Wilson took as a personal affront. He expressed shock at McClernand's attitude and said he believed McClernand had cursed him as well as their common superior. Then, reining his horse close to the corps chief, he said: "If this is so, although you are a major general, while I am only a lieutenant colonel, I will pull you off that horse and beat the boots off of you!"

McClernand was stunned, then sobered. Apologetically, he replied, "I am not cursing you. I could not do that. Your father was my friend and I am yours. I was simply expressing my intense vehemence on the subject matter, sir, and I beg your pardon!"

Wilson was only partially mollified. He rode to headquarters and reported the incident to Grant and Rawlins. Both agreed that at the first opportunity, McClernand would have to go.

That opportunity came sooner than any of them could have imagined, and when it did, Wilson was on the scene. Two weeks after the incident, McClernand printed a letter of congratulations to his soldiers, citing their valiant effort on May 22—and casting doubt on the tenacity of the rest of the army. This was bad enough, but when McClernand worked the letter into the newspapers the publicity drove Grant, Sherman, and McPherson into an unholy wrath. At once Grant wrote out an order cashiering McClernand for insubordination, and allowed Wilson to deliver it to the general's tent. This was the sort of revenge which Wilson cherished, and when he reached McClernand's headquarters he made a formal business of handing him the order.

McClernand's reaction must have warmed Wilson's heart. "Well, sir! I am relieved!" he cried, squirming in his camp chair. Then, as though addressing Grant, he added: "By God, sir, we are *both* relieved!"

But his influence in Washington did not save him. On June 18 McClernand was forced to leave the Army of the Tennessee. And despite his prediction, Ulysses Grant did not accompany him into eventual obscurity.

AFTER McCLERNAND'S DEPARTURE, GRANT was able to give his full attention to Vicksburg. He attempted no more assaults, content to wage a tight siege—a strategy which furnished prompt results. Pemberton's 25,000 soldiers had to subsist on dwindling rations and inadequate medical supplies, and the citizens of Vicksburg took to hillside caves to escape the shells continually fired into the town by the Federal artillery.

The greatest hardship, naturally, was the scarcity of food. By interrogating deserters and captives, Wilson learned that Vicksburg's commissary soon was issuing only one-quarter pound of beef and one-half pound of meal per man and that among the defenders there was a "good deal of grumbling." Toward the close of June, as he noted in a journal which he kept during the siege, even these meager supplies gave out, and mule meat became the garrison's daily fare.

In addition to interviewing enemy soldiers, Wilson performed a score of duties during the campaign. He designated troop positions, inspected units and reported their condition to Grant, kept subordinate commanders supplied with materials such as topographical maps, surveyed geographical locations, and assisted in constructing gun emplacements, roads, approaches, shelters, and parallels along the network of trenches which the Federals occupied. Such work crowded his schedule and the hot June weather discomfited him, but the conditions did not drain his enthusiasm. He felt that the siege was too languid, that limited attacks should be launched to further weaken the enemy.

His consistent display of energy came to the attention of a man with a deep interest in hard-working soldiers, Charles A. Dana. A forty-four-year-old former newspaper editor, Dana was the recently appointed assistant to Secretary of War Edwin McMasters Stanton. He had come west during the early stages of the Vicksburg campaign with instructions to keep the War Department posted on all important goings-on at Grant's headquarters. The circumstances of Dana's arrival, however, seemed to hint that Secretary Stanton did not entirely trust Grant, who had received some bad publicity thanks to McClernand and other antagonists. Consequently Grant's staff at first regarded Dana as a "genteel informer."

Their attitude soon changed. Dana, it became apparent, had not come to Mississippi to catch Grant at a bad moment. Instead he was merely acting as liaison between the Western army and the authorities in Washington. It was not long before Grant's military family accepted Dana as a brother, entrusting to him information of the highest priority, that he might redress the inaccurate image of Grant created by his detractors. Soon Dana was sending his superior reports which praised the general's character and skill and castigated those subordinates who sought to undermine his authority.

Wilson and he became close friends. They had much in common—a precise, systematic frame of mind, a great impatience with slow and incompetent officers, and a high degree of patriotism. Often they rode together to inspect guard details and troop locations, discussing strategy as they went. At other times they walked through the trenches and occasionally had to withstand enemy sharpshooter fire. Soon Dana was also wiring Stanton that the young lieutenant colonel was "unpopular among all who like to live with little work," adding that he "has remarkable talents and uncommon executive power, and will be heard from hereafter. . . ."

Both Wilson and Dana rejoiced when on July 3 the Confederates announced a desire to negotiate an armistice pending a full capitulation. The next day, after some haggling over terms, the opposing armies worked out surrender details, and the erstwhile defenders filed out of their fortress and turned their arms over to the Army of the Tennessee.

Wilson of course was on hand for the ceremonies, one facet of which later concerned him deeply. Although Grant had demanded an unconditional surrender, he had then decided to allow Pemberton's men to sign paroles and return to their homes so the army would not have to spend precious time and resources transporting them to far-off prison camps. In time Wilson came to see that Grant had made a serious mistake; many of the defenders violated their paroles and returned to combat against the Army of the Tennessee in subsequent months.

However, Vicksburg was so great a prize that the brilliance of its capture obscured widespread consideration of such an event. It also resulted in the quick capitulation of the only other Rebel stronghold on the Mississippi, Port Hudson, 110 miles downriver, and thus gave the Union complete control of the great waterway. Soon afterward President Lincoln exulted: "The father of waters rolls unvexed to the sea."

After the surrender, Wilson's duty schedule was much less crowded than previously. He even managed to find time for matters apart from the military. He was able to spend some time with his brothers—Henry, now a major, and Bluford, a captain of infantry who had seen his first action at Champion Hill. To them he expressed the hope that he would soon be able to go home to Shawneetown for a visit, a privilege both of his brothers had recently enjoyed.

He also visited with the fair sex, including a young Confederate widow, a Mrs. Moore, who lived within Grant's lines and with whom Wilson had become acquainted early in the campaign. Apparently she had no bias against receiving Federal officers in her home, and Wilson referred to her fondly as his "pretty Rebel." Although their friendship would endure for several months, it is likely that Wilson was more romantically disposed toward another young woman lodging in the vicinity, Mary Emma Hurlbut. But Miss Hurlbut, whom he characterized as of "very unusual beauty," was later wooed and won by the widower Rawlins and at Christmastime they were wed in her Connecticut hometown.

AFTER DISPOSING OF STAFF DUTIES at Vicksburg, Wilson made two journeys into Louisiana. During the first he supervised the return of 300 wounded and ill Confederates to their own lines; on the second, he accompanied Grant to New Orleans for a conference at the headquarters of Major General Nathaniel P. Banks, the besieger of Port Hudson. Upon his return to Mississippi, he had the opportunity to make yet another trip, which he had long anticipated. Six days after leaving Vicksburg, a steamboat deposited him upon the Shawneetown wharf, where he took the first look at his hometown in more than two years.

At first the homecoming depressed him. From the landing, the town looked bleak and empty, for many of its citizens had gone off to war. Not until he reached his house did he see a familiar face; his reunion with his mother was joyous.

The next day he visited other relatives and those friends still in the village, and spent a "pleasant" time with all. He must have much enjoyed the attention he commanded as General Ulysses Grant's most trusted assistant, for he thrived on notoriety and loved the adulation of both peers and elders.

At the end of his two-day visit, he boarded another steamer to commence a grand tour as Grant's inspector general. Instructions he had received before leaving Vicksburg directed him to travel through the Department of the Tennessee, inspecting and reporting on conditions at all important military outposts and districts.

The tour lasted more than a month and included stopovers at Paducah, Cairo, Columbus, Memphis, and various points in western Kentucky. While Wilson visited many districts in which affairs were proceeding smoothly under generals who made their headquarters among their troops, he also discovered a number of areas in which commanders concerned themselves with civil affairs to the neglect of their military duties. Although he left no specific record of his recommendations to Grant, he did send personal letters to his friend Rawlins, stating his belief that too many commanders headed departments, districts, and cities instead of restricting their attention to Army matters. "I tell you, sir," he wrote Rawlins, "the Government of the United States cannot be upheld in purity and honesty by hands that lay aside the sword for instruments of trade and peace. We want soldiers, not traders; generals, not governors and civil agents."

It is doubtful that General Grant could have changed such a state of affairs, for military-civil administration was a way of life in all areas in which citizens lived in close proximity to the war. Quite likely, Wilson realized this and merely wrote his letters to let off steam. He simply did not trust political intrusion upon what he rather narrowly conceived to be a purely military province, and he had no use for soldiers who thought of themselves solely as civic officials in uniform.

On September 21, convalescing after a battle with malaria and a fall from a skittish horse, he returned to Vicksburg, his tour completed. He found he had arrived just in time to participate in a sustained operation. Ten weeks of inactivity by the Army of the Tennessee came to an end the next day, when Washington directed Grant to send all available troops in Mississippi and western Tennessee to reinforce the other great Federal command in the West, Major General William S.

Rosecrans's Army of the Cumberland; additional reserves had already been dispatched from Virginia. Rosecrans's soldiers had recently been hammered into defeat at Chickamauga by the Confederate Army of Tennessee under General Braxton Bragg, and had been sent into a headlong retreat to Chattanooga, Tennessee, where they were now besieged. Capture of Rosecrans's men might result in disaster to the entire Federal war effort in the western theater; hence this plea to the victorious troops in Mississippi.

Soon after the momentous news arrived, Grant directed Wilson to Cairo, Illinois to sit at the terminus of the telegraph line and place the army in closer touch with the authorities in Washington. After a much interrupted journey he reached his destination on October 2, relayed a sheaf of telegrams Grant had entrusted to his care, then watched the instrument to make certain that all incoming dispatches reached Vicksburg swiftly. Thanks to his efforts, messages traveled to Grant via steamboat from Cairo in five or six days instead of the week to ten days which till then had been standard.

Wilson was at his post on the third, when he received the most important message thus far: "It is the wish of the Secretary of War that as soon as General Grant is able to take the field he will come to Cairo and report by telegraph." The order was of such moment that Wilson made the trip to Vicksburg and personally handed it to the general.

On the tenth, while Sherman collected four divisions at Memphis for the long trip, Grant, with Wilson and other staff members, left Vicksburg. His party reached Cairo six days later and Grant at once got in touch with Washington. Receiving word that a War Department official was on his way to Grant's side, the general then went to Indianapolis en route to Louisville, and in the Indiana capital was greeted on the eighteenth by Secretary Stanton himself, who had·come by train to meet Grant for the first time and to inform him that he had been named commander of all Federal-held territory between the Allegheny Mountains and the Mississippi River, with the exception of General Banks's enclave in Louisiana. Grant's new district of authority, to be known as the Military Division of the Mississippi, comprised the Armies of the Tennessee and the Cumberland, as well as a smaller command, the Army of the Ohio, plus a great many detached and garrison troops. The promotion thus gave him jurisdiction over more soldiers than had served under any other Federal field general.

Clothed in his new authority, Grant led his party along a circuitous route toward the Tennessee River and Chattanooga. Nearing his destination, he received word that the Army of the Cumberland, now led by Major General George H. Thomas, was in dire straits. Almost wholly cut off from supplies, Thomas's troops were gradually starving, just as Pemberton's men had starved in Vicksburg.

At Stevenson, Alabama, near the crossing of the Tennessee, Grant's band had a visitor—General Rosecrans, on his way north after having been relieved of his command. The once popular and successful general discussed the Chattanooga situation with Grant, under whose direct authority he had served earlier in the war. "The meeting," Wilson later wrote, "was brief and courteous but not effusive. They were far from sympathetic with each other."

Rosecrans proved more friendly toward Wilson, who was both surprised and pleased to learn that the general had recently applied for his services as acting commander of an engineer brigade in the Army of the Cumberland. Although he and Rosecrans had never before met, Wilson had been recommended by two members of Rosecrans's staff— his chief engineer, Brigadier General William Farrar ("Baldy") Smith, who had been one of Wilson's instructors at West Point and was still his close ally; and Rosecrans's chief of ordnance, Captain Horace Porter, Wilson's companion-in-arms during the campaign in South Carolina and Georgia.

Wilson left Grant and the main party at Stevenson, wishing to push on ahead so that he would "have at least one day in which to study the situation of the beleaguered army in its own camp and behind its own breastworks before Grant got there." Escorted by a company of cavalrymen and Assistant Secretary of War Dana (who only recently had returned from Chattanooga), Wilson struck out over a mountainside and through the wide Tennessee Valley. During rest stops along the way, Wilson and Dana dismounted, found a comfortable spot on the ground, and, to relieve the fatigue of the journey, discussed history and recited poetry. This was a favorite diversion for the well-read Wilson, who was rarely without a book or two in his saddlebags.

After a night's travel, during which they ran a gauntlet of rifle fire from Rebel pickets, the riders reached and entered the besieged city weary, hungry, and cold. But Wilson's spirits improved when he received food and warmth and held a pleasant reunion with his friend Porter.

The next afternoon, after several hours' sleep, he rode to General Thomas's headquarters to pay his respects and to herald Grant's coming. He was immediately struck by Thomas, whom he later described as "six feet tall, of Jove-like figure, impressive countenance, and lofty bearing." Wilson would have enjoyed serving under such a commander.

General George H. Thomas—*Photograph courtesy Library of Congress*

In fact, even from the time of this first meeting, he might have considered the prospect of such an opportunity.

After the audience, Wilson went out to inspect the local works, to study the situation in the field, and to see his friend "Baldy" Smith. At 9 P.M., when he returned to headquarters, he found that Grant, Rawlins, and the others had ridden in through a cold, driving rain. Upon arriving, Grant had come at once to see Thomas, another general with whom he had served earlier in the conflict.

The scene in the main room of Thomas's headquarters was strangely tense. Wilson recollected: "Grant was sitting on one side of the fire over a puddle of water that had run out of his clothes; Thomas, glum and silent, was sitting on the other, while Rawlins and the rest were scattered about in disorder."

He had no idea what had transpired since Grant's arrival, but evidently neither general had greeted the other effusively. Later Wilson suspected that since Thomas had virtually superseded Grant during the Shiloh-Corinth campaign he felt he should have retained his seniority and thus was miffed by the new command situation.

Wilson was brash enough for any situation and had no fear of speaking out in front of the brass. In a loud voice he called Thomas's attention to his lack of hospitality: "General Thomas, General Grant is wet and tired and ought to have some dry clothes, particularly a pair of socks and a pair of slippers. He is hungry, besides, and needs something to eat. Can't your officers attend to these matters for him?"

His words broke the uneasy silence which had crowded the room. Thomas at once bustled about to make Grant and his staff more comfortable. Perhaps until then, Wilson speculated, Thomas simply had not realized "that Grant was his guest as well as his commanding general."

Although the two commanders never became bosom friends, they teamed in subsequent weeks to engineer a masterful series of operations to thwart the enemy. Grant, of course, served as overall superior, giving immediate command of the Army of the Tennessee to Sherman, and allowing Thomas to continue to direct the Army of the Cumberland. In October and November they raised Bragg's siege, decisively defeated him in battle, and drove the Confederates from their positions along steep mountain ridges south and east of the city.

During the campaign, Wilson was kept quite busy. As an engineer he accompanied part of Thomas's army on various maneuvers. And in operations preparatory to lifting the siege, he assisted in the construction of defenses covering passes on the south side of the Tennessee

River, to deprive the enemy of access routes by which they might attack the main supply line into Chattanooga.

While the subsequent fighting at Lookout Mountain and Missionary Ridge raged, Wilson held a ringside seat. During the first battle, on November 24, he and a *New York Herald* correspondent, Sylvanus Cadwallader, mounted earthworks near General Thomas's field headquarters. From there they watched Federal troops charge up the mountain which anchored the left flank of Bragg's line and wage the fog-shrouded conflict which later won the name "Battle Above the Clouds." Wilson's front-line position was a focal point for Rebel bullets, but he and Cadwallader held their ground till the Federal advance pushed the Confederates eastward to Missionary Ridge. "We were stormed at, scolded, threatened, and repeatedly ordered down," Cadwallader later remembered, "but the fascination of the great battle wholly overcame all prudent considerations." Such a scene displayed one of Wilson's most visible characteristics. In the maelstrom of combat—whether he experienced it as a participant or an observer—his rapt attention to the details of battle seemed to diminish his awareness of fear.

The next day, Thomas's soldiers stormed the great ridge under a heavy fire and drove the Confederates in confusion from the summit. The Federals, who clambered up the mountainside in a frenzy which not even their commanders seemed able to control, sent Bragg on a retreat which carried him out of the campaign for good. Again watching from an exposed position in the rear of the attack columns, Wilson marveled at the power of the successful drive.

In the midst of this brilliant campaign to defeat Bragg, Lieutenant Colonel Wilson also performed service in a theater of action 100 miles northeast of Chattanooga. In many respects it was the most interesting assignment he handled during the war.

Soon after completing work on Thomas's supply line defenses, and before the Federal troops moved out to smite their enemy, Wilson received orders to travel to Knoxville, Tennessee, just above the Holston River, where for the first time since Antietam he was to call on Major General Ambrose Burnside.

After his almost criminal stubbornness at Fredericksburg, Burnside had been transferred west. Several months ago he had occupied Knoxville with the IX and XXIII Corps, known as the Army of the Ohio. Now a large part of Bragg's army, under Lieutenant General James Longstreet, was advancing on the city, threatening to bottle up Burnside's command. Since Burnside was in Grant's department, it seemed up to Grant to prevent a siege, save the hard-pressed corps, and protect Federal communication lines in eastern Tennessee.

On November 9, two weeks before the battles between Grant and Bragg, Grant sent Wilson to tell Burnside to hold his ground until the main army could detach forces to aid him. This was a direct response to a telegram Burnside had sent the commanding general on October 23, reporting himself low on rations and considering withdrawing from Knoxville or surrendering to Longstreet. Neither prospect pleased Grant.

To reach Burnside, Wilson made a roundabout 175-mile journey on horseback with fifteen cavalrymen and Dana, who went along as "the Eyes of the Government." For four days the party rode through valleys and across farmlands, steering clear of Confederate picket posts and bushwhackers, and seeking out stations manned by Federal soldiers. One night they bivouacked at such an outpost, and they spent another as guests of a Unionist farmer.

They reached Knoxville on the evening of the twelfth, before Longstreet had arrived. When Wilson and Dana sought out Burnside, however, they learned that the Rebels were moving on the city and that Knoxville, although fortified, might not be able to withstand an all-out attack. In fact, General Burnside had almost made up his mind to evacuate the city and save his army by retreating across a bridge he had constructed over the Holston. He claimed that by moving his troops southeast of the river into Blount County, he could support them for six to eight weeks and also harass Longstreet's communications. But he admitted that in doing so he could not prevent the enemy from taking Knoxville.

Not only Grant but also President Lincoln had specified that the city should be held at all costs, and Wilson and Dana reminded Burnside of this. Furthermore, they openly doubted that in the barren region south of the Holston an army could subsist for days, let alone weeks. Both visitors agreed that the general was unduly distraught, although rather eloquent in explaining his opinions. Dana later wrote that when Burnside spoke "you would think he had a great deal more intelligence than he really possessed."

Armed with discretionary authority to issue orders in Grant's name, Wilson and Dana told their host to gird his loins and wait for help, which was forthcoming. Burnside should contest the enemy's march with every means at his disposal and thus keep Longstreet in eastern Tennessee and unable to strengthen Bragg at Chattanooga.

It took many hours for them to persuade Burnside to adopt their advice, and they did not get to bed till midnight. Then, at three o'clock the next morning, Wilson and Dana had to get up, return to headquarters, and argue the matter all over again; Federal scouts now reported Longstreet's men in view, and a nervous Burnside had returned to his old plan.

At this point Wilson lost all patience and in plain language told the general that Grant's plans for the autumn campaign did not include the sacrifice of two army corps and the abandonment of a strategically important city. But even this had no effect, for Burnside was now obsessed with the idea of crossing the river.

The matter was finally settled by one of Burnside's engineer officers, Lieutenant Colonel Orville Babcock, another of Wilson's erstwhile Academy cronies. Disagreeing with his superior's plan, Babcock left headquarters and, while the argument raged on, destroyed the bridge which short days before he had helped build. After that, Burnside had to remain in the city and await Longstreet. At last Wilson and Dana could return to Chattanooga.

Skirting the head of Longstreet's column, they rejoined Grant on the seventeenth. They remained with him until Bragg was soundly whipped, and during that period learned that Burnside had been besieged but was holding his own.

When Bragg retreated, Wilson accompanied a force, led by Sherman, which Grant sent to Knoxville during the last week in November. En route, Wilson had to build another bridge, this over the Little Tennessee River fifteen miles from its juncture with the Holston. Frame houses near the river again yielded an abundant amount of timber, and within twelve hours labor crews had put together a 240-yard-long span sturdy enough to accommodate the weight of Sherman's command. The relief force then continued into Knoxville, dispersed the Rebels, rescued Burnside, and preserved the safety of Grant's communication lines.

Although Wilson went to Knoxville the first time as a lieutenant colonel, he wore a silver star on each shoulder when he returned there on December 5 as Sherman's chief engineer. Late in October Grant had sent to Washington a request that Wilson be promoted to brigadier general for the excellent service he had rendered to date. Grant specified that the Army should also place him in the cavalry service, for Wilson had maintained an interest in the mounted training he had received at West Point and could boast a solid knowledge of cavalry tactics. Dana had added his hearty endorsement, and in mid-November official notice of Wilson's appointment had come through.

It was, of course, a milestone in Wilson's early career, and indicated the attainment of a great personal goal. A year ago, he had been a junior lieutenant, with no prospect of a great future. All of that had changed, and swiftly. Now, at twenty-six, he was a brigadier in the volunteer ranks, and suddenly his future seemed assured.

★V★

I Want You to Reorganize the Business, Drive the Rascals Out

Almost from the moment he became a general, Wilson's career was linked with the fortunes of the cavalry. Grant assured this by recommending specific employment for him.

Grant had several reasons for making his request particular. Wilson had excelled in cavalry studies at West Point. Among headquarters personnel, he was the acknowledged expert in horsemanship. And he had had some experience with that arm of the service already. During the retreat from Mississippi following Van Dorn's raid in December, 1862, he had served as an aide in a cavalry command under Colonel T. L. Dickey, the same unit in which he had been offered a commission late in 1861. In later campaigning, too, he had handled paper work for Grant's cavalry, and as inspector general took particular pains in reviewing the condition of mounted regiments. By the close of 1863, in fact, Grant thought so highly of Wilson's achievements in cavalry affairs that he had seriously considered placing him in charge of a mounted raid into South Carolina, aimed at destroying enemy communications. For several reasons, however, the expedition had been scrapped.

Under these circumstances, it came as no surprise to Grant and his staff when Wilson was selected for a cavalry administration post soon after he was appointed brigadier.

The men most responsible for the assignment were Dana and Stanton. Late in the year Dana left Tennessee and returned to Washington for a conference at the War Department. At his urging, a plan soon evolved in which Wilson was to play a prominent role—a plan for reorganizing one of the Department's more recent creations, the Cavalry Bureau.

The Cavalry Bureau was an agency which had been established the previous July to direct the purchase of horses for service in the field, thereafter to collect, train, and care for them, to distribute them to new regiments as well as to veteran outfits which needed remounts, to provide troopers with horse accouterments and arms, and to oversee the inspection of all cavalry units. The War Department had envisioned it as an organization which, by virtue of its specific nature, would satisfy cavalry needs more efficiently than the agencies which had hitherto attended to them, the Quartermaster's and Ordnance departments.

Unfortunately, during its first six months of operation, the Bureau had failed to live up to expectations. In large measure this was the fault of the officers appointed to administer it. Neither of its first two chiefs, Major General George Stoneman nor Brigadier General Kenner Garrard, had been able to cut bureaucratic red tape to expedite operations. In truth, they had been victimized by the same fraudulent practices, perpetrated by unscrupulous contractors, which the Bureau had been created to prevent.

Under the prevailing system, it was often a simple matter for a merchant in horseflesh to deceive the government which sought to purchase his goods. One practice popular with some businessmen was the rebranding of animals to change their designation from cavalry mounts to artillery horses (the latter, usually larger and stronger, commanded higher prices on the market). Another favorite ruse involved dealing in unfit or diseased animals, which merchants could buy cheaply and often sell dearly to the Bureau's purchasing agents, many of whom were susceptible to bribery. Thus, cavalry units continued to be poorly and irregularly supplied, and their men were left with the unhappy feeling that no one in the government seemed willing or able to work in their behalf.

On January 17, 1864 Dana wrote Grant asking if he could spare Wilson for the job of getting the Bureau "into order and honesty." The new general's reputation was that of an intelligent and swift-moving administrator, and Dana felt that "the necessity of him is very great, and I know of no one else who can perform the duty as well as he." If Grant agreed, Wilson could be returned to him as soon as the reorganization had been completed, "say in sixty days."

Grant talked the matter over with Dana's choice and the following day replied: "I will order General Wilson at once. No more efficient or better appointment could be made for that place."

Although he agreed to answer the War Department's call, Wilson had mixed feelings about the assignment. The position, of course, was a vital, prestigious, and highly responsible one. Moreover, it offered him the chance to prove his abilities to the officials of the government by succeeding where others before him had failed. He could hardly resist such a showcase for his talents. But it was a desk job, and by this time he was seriously contemplating an active field command. Then, pondering the matter, he saw he had no choice, in any case. Soon after winning Grant's assurance that whatever the outcome of his stint in Washington he would rejoin the Army for next spring's campaign, Wilson boarded a train and started east.

He arrived in the capital on the twenty-fourth and was greeted by falling temperatures and an almost palpable gloom which had settled over the city during his fifteen-month absence. The gloom had materialized because the Federal war machine in the East, which six months ago had produced the great victory at Gettysburg, had faltered alarmingly. The war had just entered its third winter, with no end to the fighting in sight.

Yet, Wilson exuberantly rode to the War Department for his first interview with the Secretary of War. The meeting surprised both men. Wilson had long thought of Stanton as a ruthless and sometimes petty politician who lacked candor and integrity. Instead he found him forceful and straightforward, and felt he described the situation in the Cavalry Bureau with frankness. At the same time, the secretary was mildly shocked by Wilson's youth, which not even an elegant imperial moustache could hide. Stanton sized up his visitor with some concern, wondering how he might fare in battle against sharp-witted businessmen twice his age.

Yet the secretary laid himself directly on the line when he told Wilson: "I have sent for you because I understand you do not fear responsibility. My life is worried out of me by the constant calls of the generals in the field for more cavalry horses, and by the dishonesty of the contractors who supply us with inferior horses, or who transfer their contracts to sub-contractors who do not fill them at all. They are a set of unmitigated scoundrels, and I want you to reorganize the business, drive the rascals out and put the cavalry service on an effective footing. I don't want you to fail as Stoneman did, nor to say, as Garrard did: 'I cannot hope to surpass the efforts of Stoneman.' Don't tell me you can't swing the job. I give you *carte blanche* and will support you with all the resources of the Department. . . ."

This assurance was all Wilson required. He left the War Department, went directly to the Chain Building, where the Bureau was headquartered, and got to work.

He saw at once that the agency was indeed in chaos, and thus set about to create order. In this he was aided by a West Point classmate, Major James P. Martin, who had served with him on McClellan's staff during the Antietam campaign. With the help of Martin, a clear-thinking officer who could be trusted to fill the important position of Bureau adjutant, Wilson immersed himself in administrative details and studied the records and past practices of the Bureau with particular interest.

In a matter of days, he had developed a plan to reorganize the cavalry examination system by setting up three-man panels of experts, officers and civilians, to oversee inspections at the several cavalry depots administered by the Bureau. Wilson also devised plans to increase the quality of animals purchased by inspectors. From now on, contractors would be excluded from examining yards to prevent them from influencing inspectors' judgments; horses would be placed in the yards twenty-four hours prior to examination, to weed out mounts who would show signs of illness or infirmity over a short period of time; rejected animals were to be permanently branded with the letter "R" to forestall attempts to resubmit them; unfit horses offered in a clear attempt to defraud the government were to be imprinted on their left shoulders rather than on their flanks; and all accepted animals were to be marked with brands carrying the initials of both contractor and inspector.

Such measures were calculated to serve notice that the Bureau would no longer tolerate trickery or dishonesty. Yet they had little effect when first announced, for horse dealers who had the chance to meet Wilson were deceived by his callow appearance into thinking they could easily outwit him and circumvent his reforms.

Several brokers decided to test his vulnerability to influence, by planning dinners in his honor. Some came to his office and personally extended such invitations. They were shocked when Wilson remained calmly at his desk and informed them he had no intention of attending any private affairs. He startled them further by repeating his intention to force them to fulfill any contracts they were awarded in the future. That much said, he showed his visitors the door.

A short time afterward, the Bureau announced its need for several thousand horses—most of them to be sent to Grant's cavalry for the coming campaign—and it prepared to receive bids. Some of the businessmen who had invited Wilson to dinner responded with offers to furnish mounts at the depots in Elmira, New York, Saint Louis, Columbus, Saint Paul, and Indianapolis.

During the period prior to the opening of bids and the awarding of contracts, Wilson grew to suspect that some of the horse brokers were planning to forget their commitments. He therefore called all known bidders into his office for some more plain talk. If any of the dealers intended to break their contracts, he strongly advised them to reconsider. If a winning bidder did not promptly deliver goods he had promised to supply, Wilson vowed to "make it out of his hide." But the businessmen went away without indicating if his words had been effective.

When contracts were let, it became apparent that Wilson could have saved his breath. One of the brokers, who had won a contract to furnish only half the horses he wished to sell, immediately and openly hinted that under the circumstances he did not believe he would fill his quota. Wilson was barely able to control his temper. He suggested that the dealer take heed that the government still owed him for a thousand head of horses previously delivered. Not a cent would be paid until every horse specified under the terms of the new contract was supplied. The next day the merchant returned to Wilson with a different attitude, a smile on his face. Seeing as how the general "had a decided advantage in the matter," he would abide by his rules. And he did.

But the other contractors did not. They either made no attempt to deliver their quota or sublet their contracts illegally. When Wilson sought to learn why, they could not give satisfactory answers.

Wilson allowed the businessmen ample time to deliver their animals. When late in March their contracts expired without proper results, he acted. At once he wrote Stanton that Messrs. Daniel Wormer, Samuel S. Smoot, and John Spicer had "failed in every particular to perform what they have bound themselves for—and have thereby embarrassed the government in its operations. They should be arrested at once and prosecuted under the statute to punish fraud & neglect." A few days later he informed the secretary that Mr. J. M. Moorehead should also be arrested and tried for failing to fulfill his contract at Indianapolis, for transferring his contract to Spicer (himself neglecting a quota), and for deceiving the Bureau as to the selling price of the few horses he did furnish.

To the surprise of everyone involved—including Wilson, no doubt —Stanton fully agreed. Within a few days, a half-dozen businessmen sat in Old Capitol Prison, awaiting trial by court-martial. Military police later rounded up other dealers who in one manner or another had failed to supply the Bureau with goods for which they had contracted. Eventually nine businessmen landed in jail, and six of them were sentenced by a special military commission to spend the rest of the war in the Federal Penitentiary.

Such arbitrary proceedings shocked and astounded a great many entrepreneurs and politicians. Before long, friends of the arrested contractors were pressuring Wilson and Stanton to release the prisoners.

At this time, the Senate was in the process of voting to confirm the promotions of generals recently appointed by Grant and other commanders. Wilson's name was up for consideration, and in a letter to a friend he acknowledged that "animated debate" was raging over his qualifications, apparently because he had no experience in active field command. Now, with political enemies threatening to make trouble for him, the chances of his winning confirmation appeared to have diminished.

After a great deal of thought, he decided to take the problem directly to Stanton. The secretary put his mind fully at rest. When Wilson mentioned a couple of prominent congressmen who had vowed to make Stanton uncomfortable if Wilson were not fired, Stanton cried: "Oh, I know them. They're both damned cowards; neither of them will ever come within five hundred yards of the War Department. I'll take care of them!"

He made good on his promise. He publicly announced his endorsement of the course followed by his new bureau chief, and thus made Wilson unassailable. Political pressure subsided, and eventually—although only after several months had passed—he was confirmed as a brigadier. The contractors worked hard to regain their freedom, and one broker fought his case as far as the Supreme Court, but in the end the new policies were upheld and the businessmen served their full sentences.

Once Wilson's position was secure, he was at his leisure to institute further reforms. He personally made inspection tours to observe progress at all depots and to make on-the-spot recommendations to expedite operations. He hand-picked a staff of special inspectors to attend to such work whenever he could not. He tightened efficiency at the great remount station at Giesboro Point, just outside the capital, and successfully contended with problems which broke out there, including blacksmiths' strikes. He streamlined procedures for transporting mounts and supplies, for distributing matériel to troops in the field, and for awarding promotions to deserving officers and recommending discharges for incompetents.

He also instituted a practice which had far-reaching effects on the size and strength of field units. He decided to supply remounts and new equipment to veteran outfits rather than encourage the organization of new ones. The philosophy behind this was elemental: although state governments seemed to find it much easier to raise regiments than to refurbish those in the field, the latter were more valuable to the war effort by virtue of their experience. With this in view, Wilson also urged the War Department to adopt a policy favoring the placement of re-enlisting veterans in cavalry regiments for which they applied, rather than allow raw recruits or conscripts to fill the ranks. The Union would be better served, he felt, if recruit and conscript joined infantry commands, where highly specialized training was not so crucial a prerequisite.

In sponsoring these reforms, Wilson trod on the delicate toes of state politicians, who regularly distributed commissions in newly organized units among friends and political creditors. However, the chief of the Cavalry Bureau had never felt much love for politicos who hampered the military effort, and he allowed neither governors nor state legislators to sway his judgment.

Perhaps his most intense clash with a politician involved Andrew Johnson, provisional governor of Tennessee and a brigadier general of state volunteers. Early in 1864 Johnson, an old hand at administering patronage, sought War Department authority to recruit twelve regiments of cavalry, to be filled by loyal Tennesseans who would serve for one year. Wilson was firmly opposed to the idea, not only because he found it hard enough to supply regiments in service without trying to outfit new ones, but also because his subordinates in the West reported that the material of Johnson's regiments was poor in the extreme. The Tennessee officers were unlearned and dull-witted, their men undisciplined and lazy. Dutifully Wilson informed Stanton of the situation, called the regiments "worthless," and opined that "it is certainly a ruinous and extravagant policy to place valuable public property in the hands of such irresponsible people."

Because Wilson's influence with the secretary was substantial, and since Andrew Johnson had yet to achieve the prominence which would later propel him into the vice-presidency, the Tennesseans were neither equipped nor authorized to perform duty during Wilson's stint with the Bureau. Eventually, when Wilson left his post, the regiments were permitted to enter national service. Not until then would Wilson learn how bitterly he had alienated Governor Johnson by temporarily frustrating his designs.

Wilson's no-nonsense policies created other difficulties. Because he was incapable of compromise, he often created headaches which he might otherwise have avoided. For example, when his strict regulations regarding the examination of horses achieved wide publicity, several businessmen banded together to circumvent them. When this did not work, the contractors tried another tactic. Soon afterward Wilson had to write Stanton: "The new system of inspections adopted in this Bureau has resulted in working contractors into a fever of excitement and a consequent unwarranted increase of price on their part. They seem to be determined to raise the price of cavalry horses to an exorbitant rate, and therefore I have the honor to request that permission be granted me to authorize the purchase of horses in open market, whenever I may think [it] necessary to protect the public interests." Such permission came through and often he did resort to purchasing animals wherever and from whomever he could, rather than solely from approved bidders. However, this practice proved ineffective for a number of reasons, and, more often then not, the Bureau was forced in the end to pay the extra twenty-five dollars per head which the brokers demanded as compensation for Wilson's stringent policies.

Without doubt, Wilson's most spectacular and most significant reform was his adoption of the Spencer carbine as the primary weapon for mounted troops. This innovative effort more effectively increased the fighting capacity of the cavalry than any other policy instituted by the War Department during the course of the conflict.

Late in 1861 a young New England inventor named Christopher Spencer had patented a breech-loading cavalry rifle holding in its stock, from butt to trigger guard, a tubular magazine. The tube accommodated six shells, with a seventh in the firing chamber; they could be fired as rapidly as the rifleman could eject the spent cartridges. Brigadier General James W. Ripley, then the army's chief of ordnance, had tested the carbine and had formed an adverse opinion of its potential.

The unfavorable report he filed had all but doomed Spencer's chances for contracting to supply the Federal armies with this weapon.

The Ordnance Department's conservative thinking kept rifles such as Spencer's from receiving wide acceptance. During the first year of the fighting, only 8,270 among more than 750,000 rifles contracted for by the government could be loaded through the breech rather than down the muzzle.

In 1863, however, the situation altered. In that year Spencer was able to interest President Lincoln personally in his rifle (which he hoped to mass produce in two models, for both cavalry and infantry service). Lincoln, himself an enthusiastic rifleman, paved the way for its production, in limited quantities, under order to the Federal government. The first samples to be given the cavalry arrived that fall and received some use by Federal horsemen during the Mine Run campaign in December. They were quite favorably received, as indicated by a survey which the Cavalry Bureau had conducted late that year to gather field commanders' opinions as to the effectiveness of the several styles of carbines then in use. Almost to a man the officers whose soldiers had Spencers praised the carbine highly.

Undoubtedly this report influenced Wilson to make a determined effort to equip as many troopers as possible with the weapon. Then, too, he personally experimented with the Spencer and was impressed by its qualities. He saw that its seven-shot capability filled a particular need of horse soldiers; since, compared to infantry, cavalry put fewer men per unit length of front into battle, increased firepower was necessary to maintain its stability against enemy foot soldiers.

At Wilson's recommendation, the government increased its Spencer purchasing quota, and in a few months the carbine was being used with telling effect by thousands of troopers. In the long run, skirmishes and even battles were decided by the added firepower given Federal cavalry by the new weapon, of which Wilson forever maintained, "It was by all odds the most effective firearm of the day."

By this means and through other innovations, Wilson succeeded in transforming the Cavalry Bureau from an inefficient, disorganized agency hampered by bureaucratic fumbling, dishonesty, and outdated thinking into a highly effective, honest, and well-appointed one. He gave unhesitatingly of himself, working at his desk from 8 A.M. to 5 P.M. each day, and spending many of his off hours riding through the capital's defensive lines while discussing ideas for improving cavalry administration with Assistant Secretary Dana (who was lodging at the same rooming house as Wilson). Seeing that his policies won dramatic results, he openly proclaimed his success to others, for the last quality he espoused was false modesty. For example, writing his friend "Baldy" Smith, still in Tennessee with Grant, he observed: "I think I am getting along admirably. . . ."

However, not everyone in Washington considered him the perfect bureau chief. Neither the Quartermaster's nor the Ordnance Department had great praise for some of his policies, just as they had little use for the Bureau as a whole. Their supervisors considered themselves entirely capable of dealing with the needs of the cavalry service, as they had prior to the Bureau's creation. They felt (with some justification) that the new agency often complicated matters rather than simplified them and too often infringed upon responsibilities and privileges they themselves deserved. Wilson often exchanged heated letters with these officers over various disagreements and instances of mutual interference with each other's business.

Some of Wilson's own subordinates also voiced criticism of his administration. Colonel August V. Kautz, whom Wilson had first met in Knoxville and had later made his principal assistant in the Bureau, considered Wilson "an officer of unusual activity of thought and action" but whose program of reform "was not always necessary and perhaps some of it useless. The trait he needed most was fixedness of purpose. He often changed a course of action before he had given it fair trial." Colonel Kautz may well have been correct, for Wilson was so active and so intolerant of practices and personnel that produced no immediate benefits, that he was often inclined to be too hasty, needlessly abrupt, in his judgments.

Wilson did not confine his waking hours to business, although his work schedule was heavy. He would not dine with businessmen with whom the Bureau had dealings, but he did accept other social invitations and soon became a sought-after guest at Washington gatherings. One evening in February he attended a reception given at the White House and had his first opportunity to meet the President and the First Lady. Next day he wrote Baldy Smith: "My Uncle Abe and Aunt Mary are a remarkable pair of birds—particularly Mrs. L. If that be treasonable make the most of it."

On another occasion Mrs. Lincoln invited him to accompany the President and herself for an evening at the theater. This naturally made him feel quite important—an attitude which was rudely shattered when he accepted the invitation, only to learn that the Lincolns had mistaken him by name for the distinguished literary figure, Colonel James Grant Wilson. Once the mistake came to light the First Family seemed rather aloof, and Wilson felt "much bored and disgusted" through the rest of the evening.

Later he also had the chance to attend the theater with General and Mrs. Grant. In late February Grant came to the capital to receive the government's vote of thanks for his victories in the West, and to accept the commission of lieutenant general in command of all the Federal armies.

The promotion came about because late in 1863, when President Lincoln and his military advisors examined the qualities of their field generals, they realized that Grant alone could coordinate the activities of all land forces in the crucial capacity of general-in-chief. Soon after Wilson was installed in the Cavalry Bureau, officials close to the president sought his opinion of how Grant might react to such an offer. Wilson at once seized on the opportunity to increase Grant's standing (and, hopefully, his own as well) by playing politics. He highly recommended Grant for the command, and in a series of letters and then by a personal visit to Grant's headquarters during an inspection tour through the West, he urged the general to accept the commission, provided he received the widest possible authority. To Baldy Smith he later wrote: "General Grant must be *Lieutenant General and commander-in-chief*. . . . He is the only honest and truly brave man the war has thrown up." He also touted his friend Rawlins (now a brigadier) for the position of Grant's chief of staff, and advocated promotions for others on Grant's staff whose talents he valued. Because congressmen and presidential aides recognized Wilson as Grant's close friend, they listened respectfully to his pronouncements on these matters—which fed his ego and increased his pleasure in performing the role of military advisor to the government.

Wilson's urging was one factor in Grant's decision to come east and accept the honor and promotion, as well as to make his field headquarters with the Army of the Potomac, which was waging in Virginia a campaign considered crucial for the Union cause. Grant turned immediate command of the Military Division of the Mississippi to Sherman, while McPherson succeeded Sherman in the Army of the Tennessee; Thomas remained as leader of the Army of the Cumberland.

Grant also decided, after some thought, to retain Major General George Gordon Meade, the victor at Gettysburg, as the Army of the Potomac's commander. Grant would exert his authority as general-in-chief by proposing broad strategy (which Wilson believed to be his forte) and would allow Meade to make the tactical decisions affecting the army's movements. In so deciding, Grant passed over Wilson's objections to Meade's continuance in command. Wilson felt Meade incompetent and believed his well-known temper hampered his relations with his subordinates. Instead Wilson favored the appointment of his friend Baldy Smith, who recently had won his second star in the volunteer ranks. But because of a personality clash between Grant and Smith as well as other factors, the lieutenant general chose, for once, to disregard Wilson's advice.

Soon after Grant came east, he determined to relieve Wilson from the Cavalry Bureau, which had been thoroughly rejuvenated, and assign him to field duty. After some consideration, he offered Wilson a division in the Cavalry Corps of the Army of the Potomac, which was about to undergo reorganization under Major General Philip Sheridan, who had been one of Grant's most efficient field generals in the West.

He foresaw difficulties in assigning Wilson to such a command, since as the Army's junior brigadier Wilson would supersede experienced soldiers more directly in line for the position. But Grant trusted Wilson and knew that the range of his capabilities was vast. He had yet to find an assignment that gave Wilson great trouble.

Wilson eagerly accepted the position. This permitted him to turn down an offer which was made him a short time later—command of the division of cavalry in Major General Benjamin F. Butler's Army of the James, which was also operating in Virginia. Although gratified by Butler's request for his services, he had no great misgivings about passing up that opportunity. Butler's army was much smaller and less prestigious than the Army of the Potomac and was not personally guided by Grant. Through Wilson's efforts Colonel Kautz received a brigadier's star and was given the lesser command.

General Orders No. 154, dated April 7, 1864, relieved Wilson from command of the Cavalry Bureau. At his suggestion, the agency later came under the supervision of General Halleck, who was now Army chief of staff, having been replaced as general-in-chief by Grant. Satisfied that he had brought the Bureau into such a state of efficiency that it would function smoothly under his successor, Wilson said his good-byes to Washington friends, packed his belongings, and boarded a south-bound train.

Hours later, he was in northern Virginia with the Army of the Potomac, reporting to Grant's headquarters for his first service in active field command as a general officer.

★VI★

It's All Right, Wilson; the Army Is Moving Toward Richmond!

Wilson inherited the Third Cavalry Division of the Army of the Potomac, which Brigadier General Judson Kilpatrick had commanded since its formation ten months before. Kilpatrick had left his successor a legacy of problems with which he would have to contend before the unit could retake the field.

A bantam-size Irishman, "Kil-Cavalry" had won a reputation as a hell-for-leather fighter, hard on his men and their mounts. His division had not been quite the same after his ill-advised raid against Richmond in February and March. Although launched in hopes of freeing Federal prisoners in the Confederate capital and perhaps capturing enemy officials, the expedition had fizzled out in the execution, and had resulted only in further casualties to horses and riders. The raid had also cost Kilpatrick his command. During the reorganization under Grant, he was ordered west to Sherman's cavalry, so that Wilson might have the chance to rebuild the division and to restore the confidence it had lost while stumbling toward Richmond.

Wilson was more than slightly eager to surmount the obstacles that lay in his path. This was the first force to be placed under his command for a sustained period and he was intent upon adding its rejuvenation to the list of successes he had engineered to date. Therefore he was determined to leave no stone unturned to secure his reputation as a masterful field commander as well as an efficient desk officer.

His first look at the division came on April 17, when he rode through its winter quarters at Stevensburg. Several things not to his liking at once caught his eye. Kilpatrick had chosen poor locations for his camps and had policed them insufficiently. Some of the troopers appeared to have put on excess weight during the winter, their horses were poorly groomed, and their equipment was in bad order. That night Wilson noted in his diary: "Vigorous measures of reform will be necessary." He both thoroughly understood and wholly approved of the necessity of ruling with a firm hand.

Such measures as immediately came to mind he discussed with Grant, Rawlins, and other headquarters personnel, as well as with his new corps commander, Sheridan. All gave him helpful suggestions and a free hand to carry them out.

"Little Phil" particularly impressed him. When Sheridan had served as an infantry division leader under Grant in Tennessee, Wilson had had little acquaintance with him. But he had had some contact with him in recent weeks, through correspondence between the Cavalry Bureau and cavalry field headquarters. By now he saw Sheridan as a vigorous and pugnacious soldier, a man the Corps truly needed.

His relationship with Sheridan would remain professional rather than personal. In part this was because he considered "Little Phil" a threat to his personal standing with General Grant. The circumstances of Sheridan's appointment to command in Virginia (he was the only field general Grant had brought east with him) indicated that the lieutenant general now considered him one of his most trusted subordinates. Wilson was envious of Sheridan's success in the field, which had brought about this close association, and in fact suspected that Sheridan was using it to oust Wilson himself from his position as Grant's closest advisor and great friend.

Wilson's suspicions in this regard were not confined to his corps chief. Before the war ended, he was destined to break with several friends whom he felt were vying with him for Grant's esteem.

Such one-time allies as Horace Porter, Adam Badeau, and Cyrus Comstock fell into this category. Wilson was personally responsible for securing positions for the first two on Grant's staff, then came to regret having aided them. Porter (who became Grant's aide-de-camp with rank of lieutenant colonel when Grant came east) and Badeau (Grant's military secretary as of March, 1864) were destined to stay by their commander's side during the remainder of the war, while Wilson was fated to spend much of it thousands of miles from Grant's headquarters. Wilson grew deeply jealous of the influence others could exercise upon the man whose friendship and respect he seemed to consider exclusively his own.

Comstock's case was somewhat different. He had replaced Wilson as inspector general of the Military Division of the Mississippi when Wilson went to the Cavalry Bureau, and he too came east with Grant and remained on his staff for the greater part of the war. He incurred Wilson's resentment by complaining to Grant that Wilson had fouled up his inspection reports. Comstock once noted that "Wilson's papers are four months behind hand. I told General Grant that the returns were valueless. . . ." One of Wilson's chief phobias was being made to look incompetent in the eyes of superiors whom he regarded highly; and he regarded Grant most highly of all. Although Wilson had once been close to Comstock, he later described him as "a man of cold and fishlike nature."

Among all of those closely associated with Grant, Rawlins was one of the few to escape Wilson's jealousy. Wilson regarded him as selfless, modest, unassuming and without great personal ambition—therefore no menace to him. Practically all others on intimate terms with Grant—Sheridan among them—remained suspect.

While trying hard to keep from dwelling on such concerns, Wilson went to work to rebuild the Third Division, Cavalry Corps. Despite the sorry state to which it had sunk under Kilpatrick, Wilson saw that it was made of sturdy material. He had not previously known its brigade commanders, Colonels Timothy Bryan and George H. Chapman, but he was acquainted with some of the regimental leaders and from various sources had received favorable reports about their units. The division comprised seven regiments, four in Bryan's First Brigade and three in Chapman's Second. They represented Connecticut, New York, Pennsylvania, Indiana, and Vermont; and a detachment from an Illinois regiment served as Wilson's escort. Many of the 2,000 cavalrymen had performed distinguished service in combat. It was generally believed that two years' time was necessary to fully develop a cavalryman; quite a few of these men had been actively campaigning that long.

Perhaps a greater problem than personnel was Wilson's status as brigadier, which threatened his relationship with other cavalry leaders. As the junior general in the Army of the Potomac he was outranked by several other commanders at the time Grant appointed him to field service in the cavalry. To make way for him, Grant had transferred a pair of senior brigade chiefs, Brigadier Generals George Custer (who had won his star in June, 1863) and Henry E. Davies, to other units. The move naturally upset both men, who considered themselves more rightfully in line for the post which Kilpatrick had vacated. Wilson, who had not attempted to influence Grant's decision (but certainly did not express outrage at Custer's and Davies's treatment), gave the matter less thought than they. Yet he must have suspected that in the future he would encounter hostility from officers he had overslaughed.

Without dwelling on this issue either, he began his reorganization. Calling his first drill, he was shocked to see only 615 troopers turn out. Others, he learned, were scattered over the neighborhood at several outposts, were on detached duty, or were too ill to train. This suggested a laxity on the part of officers responsible for keeping the division in a tight-knit group and in proper field condition. Kilpatrick was at least partially responsible, but some of the colonels seemed also to blame. After investigating conditions, Wilson cashiered one of them and subjected the others to a tongue-lashing few of them would ever forget. From the first, however, he demonstrated a sternness—a determination to exact respect, order, and discipline—which some of his subordinates felt was akin to an obsession. Perhaps they were correct. For Wilson, extremism in pursuit of a goal he considered worthwhile—such as the restoration of an army—was not an ugly thing.

When he finished speaking, he began to act. He rooted through camp hospitals, turning out suspected malingerers; he called in outpost units; he organized long and strenuous drill sessions and closely observed their progress. He instituted a campaign to put equipment and weapons into good condition; he reorganized the division staff from top to bottom; he set blacksmiths and farriers to work providing for the horses. He changed the layout of the camps, overhauling the semipermanent look they had acquired during the winter; and he improved sanitation. By no means least of all, he sent a rush order to his successors in the Cavalry Bureau to provide more than 700 fresh mounts and an even greater number of Spencer repeaters.

Within days, his efforts showed spectacular results. Short hours before he had taken command of his troopers, the assistant inspector general of the Cavalry Corps had turned in a revealing report about the Third Division. The communique abounded with phrases such as "large deficiencies," "considerably disorganized," and "demands much care and attention," and closed with the observation that the division was "not in condition to perform active duty with credit." Less than a week later, Wilson led his reorganized force on parade for the Army brass. Grant and Sheridan were much pleased by the appearance of the Third Division, noting that men and mounts appeared to be in excellent condition. Even the army's chief provost marshal, Brigadier General Marsena Patrick—who found it easy to be critical of his associates—admitted that "it was [a] magnificent review, the best I ever saw. . . ."

Such quick and dramatic results were necessary. The Army of the Potomac would greet the return of spring with a hard-driving movement into the heart of Virginia, and the Third Cavalry Division would be required to play a prominent role.

Grant's plan for the coming campaign was reducible to words which he spoke to General Meade early in the year: "Wherever Lee goes, there you will go also." The Army of Northern Virginia, which time and time again had smashed Federal field armies, would be Meade's primary target. Simultaneously, Butler's Army of the James was to operate in east central Virginia with its two infantry corps (one of them now under Baldy Smith, the other under another of Wilson's old associates, Quincy Gillmore) and Kautz's cavalry division, with the intention of striking Richmond.

In the West, while these campaigns were proceeding, Sherman, with the forces under McPherson, Thomas, and Major General John McAllister Schofield (who had replaced Burnside in the Army of the Ohio), was to strike the Confederate Army of Tennessee, led by Braxton Bragg's successor, General Joseph Johnston, in and around Atlanta. Additionally, General Banks was to move out of Louisiana and against Mobile, Alabama. It was hoped that vigorous spring and summer campaigns would take Johnston's army out of the war, would capture the Gulf's largest seaport, and would blank out half the Confederacy and fatally cripple the Southern war effort.

Throughout April, when not drilling, the Third Cavalry Division —now reinforced by new regiments—performed picket duty along the Rapidan River from Germanna Ford westward to Morton's Ford. Then, as May floated in, the troopers moved from their picket lines and gathered in marching order to take part in Grant's movement over the river, guarding his left flank.

South of the Rapidan was a ten-mile square of second-growth pine and tangled thicket known as the Virginia Wilderness. Grant planned to move by his left from his headquarters at Culpeper Court House, near the cavalry's camp at Stevensburg, into this wealth of undergrowth and reach the open terrain beyond. There he hoped to engage Lee's army, which reportedly was encamped about twenty miles to the south. With 119,000 soldiers, Grant would have a great advantage in numbers when he met Lee's 64,000 men; but unless he fully utilized surprise, Lee might come up to battle him in the Wilderness, where the terrain and dense foliage could neutralize that advantage. In the thick and clotted forest the Army of Northern Virginia might entrap Grant—as it had trapped General Hooker's army at Chancellorsville in May, 1863 —and perhaps rip the invaders to shreds.

Since Wilson held the forward flank (and despite the fact that he lacked field campaign experience), he was called on to lead the Federals' march on May 4. That morning at one o'clock his soldiers broke camp at Stevensburg and began the eight-mile trip to Germanna Ford, screening the advance of the first infantry command to march, Major General Gouverneur K. Warren's V Corps. In early morning darkness Wilson rode at the head of his division, leading his men into their first campaign under Grant. Elsewhere in the vicinity, other infantry corps, protected by other cavalry divisions, were about to cross the river.

This was, quite likely, the most crucial and most suspenseful point in Wilson's career. At twenty-six, he was commanding field troops—the dream of many a West Pointer—for the first time. The next forty-eight hours or so, he realized, might make or break the career for which he had prepared so long and so thoroughly.

The night was black and filled with the distant clatter of mounted troops in motion and with vague noises that indicated the movements of foot soldiers on nearby roads—all of them occasionally softened by the gentle sweep of an early spring breeze. And somewhere not far below the river lay the picket lines which ringed Lee's Army of Northern Virginia, the army which in three years of war had never been defeated on native soil.

THE FIRST UNIT TO FORD THE RAPIDAN was a small force which Colonel Chapman had sent, at Wilson's order, to reconnoiter the far shore. After the force dispersed a small group of Rebel pickets, the balance of Chapman's brigade spent three hours fording the river. Wilson then sent them through the forest down a plank road

Battle Terrain of the Virginia Wilderness

toward a crossroads site, Old Wilderness Tavern, three miles southeast of the ford. When Chapman's men moved off, Bryan's brigade crossed the river.

When he reached the tavern, Colonel Chapman carried out an order General Meade had given the cavalry by sending scouting parties westward and southward along a perpendicular road, the Orange-Fredericksburg Turnpike (often called the Orange Turnpike or Orange Pike). The scouts were to watch for any indications that the Rebels were moving from those directions. As yet Lee's precise whereabouts was a speculative matter, and Wilson had the uncomfortable suspicion that Lee, who made a practice of doing the unexpected, might suddenly come out of nowhere to clash with the Federal troopers in the thick forest.

After Bryan's men forded the river, Warren's infantry crossed on specially constructed pontoon bridges and then followed the cavalrymen to Wilderness Tavern. When the foot soldiers reached the tavern early that afternoon, the reunited Third Division resumed its trek, by angling southwestward toward another forest landmark, Parker's Store. The store was Wilson's ultimate destination on this day. From there he could cover Warren's march and the advance of the infantry in Warren's rear. From there, too, he ought to be able to detect any troops approaching from the suspected location of Lee's headquarters, now due west of the cavalry column.

The Third Division shuddered to a halt at Parker's Store early in the evening, and Wilson then launched another reconnaissance toward the west. He sent one regiment, the veteran Fifth New York Cavalry, along the Orange Plank Road, which ran below and roughly parallel to the Orange Pike. The rest of the cavalry bivouacked near the store.

The Fifth New York moved along the Orange Plank Road about a half-dozen miles before running into a small band of Rebel cavalry. After a short but sharp engagement, the Confederates turned and fled farther westward. Meanwhile, darkness fell and Wilson's main force slept through a peaceful night. At 5 A.M. on May 5 it awoke and, pursuant to orders, pushed eight miles southwestward along a narrow woods road toward a structure known as Craig's Meeting House. There it was to be rejoined by the Fifth New York, which meanwhile remained on scouting duty along the Plank Road between Mine Run and Parker's Store, waiting to be relieved by Warren's infantry.

While these movements were taking place, other Federal cavalry was clearing the way for the bulk of the Army of the Potomac, which was moving without difficulty to the north and east of Wilson's men.

Early on the fifth, all seemed to be going smoothly for Grant's soldiers. Apparently the lieutenant general had succeeded in stealing a march on his usually vigilant opponents.

But danger was in the air. A full corps of Confederate infantry was now only a few miles to the west, coming along the Orange Plank Road directly toward the Fifth New York. And to the north, along the Orange Pike, another corps was driving toward the Federal infantry advance.

In large part, Wilson was to blame for Grant's ignorance of this situation. The scouting forces Chapman had sent along the Orange Pike the day before had not done their proper job; although thousands of enemy infantrymen were approaching in the distance, the Federals saw no one. Possibly their vision was obscured by the glow of the setting sun, which they faced. Even so, Wilson had been ordered to leave scouts along the Pike, but he decided to recall them to the main body late on the fourth without allowing them to make a thorough sighting. He seemed intent on keeping his force as cohesive as possible, but carried his husbandry too far. He feared to weaken his division by detaching units even for a short period of time—a common weakness in an inexperienced commander. He would suffer for that weakness.

Shortly after Wilson moved toward Craig's Meeting House—just as the sun cleared the horizon—the Confederate troops on the Orange Plank Road struck the Fifth New York. Rifle fire was answered by blasts from the cavalry's Spencer repeaters, as the first sustained fighting of the Wilderness Campaign broke out.

The New Yorkers did a splendid job resisting the Rebel advance, although they could throw only 500 troopers against some 20,000 infantrymen. By the rapidity of their carbine fire and because of the dense growth obscuring their position, they made the Rebels believe they had encountered Grant's infantry in force. After a fierce six-hour struggle, the regiment fell back to the safety of Warren's infantry, which was coming up quickly. There it would remain for some time, cut off from the rest of Wilson's division.

Shortly after the fighting began, the main body of the Third Division fought a bitter skirmish near Craig's Meeting House. Brigadier General Thomas Rosser, who when a pompous West Point cadet had irked Wilson and his northern-born friends, came up from the east with a roving brigade of cavalry and struck Wilson's troopers just beyond the meeting house. Sometime after 8 A.M. Rosser drove in the Federal advance echelon, the First Vermont—and then ran hard against Colonel Bryan's brigade. Wilson reported that Bryan's men "after a very sharp fight and several handsome charges, drove it [Rosser's command] rapidly back a distance of 2 miles, taking some prisoners." About noon Wilson called off Bryan's pursuit, for some of the troopers had begun to run low on ammunition.

Wilson now began to fear that the rest of Lee's army was at hand. But he determined to occupy a strong position near the meeting house "and govern myself as circumstances might demand" until told otherwise by General Sheridan. He hoped to receive reinforcements from Warren's infantry, but the truth was that the main body of the army was now eighteen miles to the north and was involved in an expanding battle of its own. Wilson's division was in a tight corner, and was on its own.

Bad news accumulated. At 1 P.M. Colonel Chapman found that the Rebel cavalry in his front had been reinforced by other troopers and was preparing another attack. Before Wilson could make proper dispositions to receive it, however, the Confederates rushed forward on foot. They dashed through the trees in front of Chapman's brigade, making a fearful racket with their rifles and pistols. Chapman's troopers panicked and fled at top speed toward the rear. Mounted and afoot, they sped past a flabbergasted and enraged Wilson, his escort unit, and his two batteries of horse artillery.

Those cannon finally repulsed the Rebels, and enabled Chapman's demoralized men to fall back beyond the meeting house and regroup in rear of Bryan's brigade. Some of them, however, went farther north than necessary, back toward Parker's Store, before halting entirely. Wilson rode through their ranks, cursing their eagerness to retreat, disturbed that they had so completely gone to rout.

He soon had other worries, for as Chapman re-formed, Colonel Bryan brought word that Confederates had gathered in the rear on the road to Parker's Store, blocking the avenue leading north to the main army. Furthermore, said Bryan, all couriers sent to apprise Generals Grant, Meade, and Sheridan of the division's predicament had apparently been captured.

Thus, rather than fulfilling its assigned task of covering the infantry's front and left flank, Wilson's men were cut off not only from Warren's corps but from the rest of the army. Wilson was learning that a vision-dimming and movement-clogging forest was a hideous place in which to fight a first battle.

"Fearing for the safety of my command," he determined to skirt the enemy's flank by following a hidden trail which led to Todd's Tavern, a site fifteen miles to the northeast, near the old battlefield of

Chancellorsville and the reported location of the Federal II Corps. But he had barely begun his movement when he saw Confederates moving in the same direction to cut him off. Realizing that he was heavily outnumbered, he sped up his withdrawal. He pushed Chapman's men ahead of Bryan's and the artillery, and sent them toward the Po River, which they would have to ford to reach the tavern.

Chapman's brigade reached the river near its head and his troopers spurred their horses madly over Corbin's Bridge. Across the river they reached the road to Todd's Tavern shortly before the enemy could gain it. Within minutes, however, a horde of Confederate cavalry appeared atop hills in their rear and then came down to fight.

By hard riding, most of Wilson's division avoided being intercepted. Only the rear guard ran into trouble, and by skillful maneuvering it finally cleared the enemy force, and rejoined Wilson's main force. The next day Wilson sent its commander a bottle of wine for knowing "how to fight *in* and fight *out* of a tight place."

Help was waiting when the Third Division crossed the Po River and neared Todd's Tavern. In the midst of battle, General Meade had taken time to ascertain Wilson's whereabouts and, learning of his predicament, had informed Sheridan. Sheridan had immediately sent Brigadier General David McMurtrie Gregg's Second Cavalry Division (which had held the Federal left flank) to Wilson's aid. Marching cross-country from the east, Gregg had reached the tavern early that morning and had drawn his men up in columns of battle.

Wilson must have sighed with relief. He led his harassed cavalrymen to Gregg's rear and took cover. When the pursuing Confederates reached the tavern, Gregg's fresh troopers charged forward with raised sabers, mixed with them, and drove them back four miles. Wilson's men were safe at last.

Thus, the junior brigadier of the Army had experienced his first battle; his Wilderness fighting had ended. He could claim neither a brilliant victory nor even a moderate success, primarily because he had failed to carry out all of Meade's instructions. He had moved too far south on May 5 to give proper attention to those roads by which the Rebel infantry had swept down upon the Federals, and the scouting parties he had dispatched along the Orange Pike the day before had performed ineptly. Consequently the main army had met Lee's soldiers without timely warning; confused and bloody fighting had resulted, with decisive victory going to neither side.

All in all, Wilson's debut in field command had been ill-starred. He could only hope that better days lay ahead.

IN THE PAST, WHEN IT HAD SUFFERED defeat or had won only stalemate, the army had retreated northward to recuperate and brood over its bad fortune. After the fighting in the Wilderness, it did not. Grant was in command now, and he was determined to use his great fund of manpower to hammer out ultimate victory at any cost. The day after the battle ended, Wilson made his way to Grant's headquarters to determine for himself how well the lieutenant general had thus far withstood the pressures of the campaign. When forty yards away, Grant saw him coming, threw up his hand, and shouted confidently: "It's all right, Wilson; the army is moving toward Richmond!"

Grant's next move would be a push southeastward by the left flank in another attempt to steal a march on Lee. The army would move in the direction of an important road junction near the town of New Spotsylvania Court House, about ten miles from Wilderness Tavern. There he stood a chance of turning Lee's flank and involving him in a battle on open ground in which superior numbers would prove to be the deciding factor.

On the morning of the eighth Wilson was ordered to take his command to Spotsylvania and from there to Snell's Bridge over the Po River, the stream he had crossed to safety three days before. At the same time, General Sheridan intended to march his First and Second divisions to other bridges on the Po and secure them. If Wilson managed to seize and hold the court house town, his associates should be within range to control routes over which Confederate troops would have to advance to contest the Third Cavalry Division.

But matters did not proceed as planned. While Wilson prepared to move off on his errand, General Meade came upon Brigadier Generals Gregg and Wesley Merritt (the latter temporarily commanding the First Cavalry Division) at Todd's Tavern on the evening of May 7, before Sheridan had given them orders, and handed them instructions of his own. He sent Gregg far westward and ordered Merritt to perform various duties, none of which would especially aid Wilson. This was decidedly in opposition to Sheridan's intentions, and the upshot was that Wilson had no supporting troops within range when he entered Spotsylvania.

After a long forced march, the Third Division reached the village about 9 A.M. on the eighth and encountered a mounted brigade of Confederates. Wilson sent a call to Colonel John B. McIntosh, a resourceful officer whom he had recently appointed to head the First Brigade in Colonel Bryan's stead. McIntosh rose to the occasion by charging his cavalrymen through the town and scattering the enemy in several directions.

Wilson then occupied one of the most important pieces of real estate in Virginia. If he could hold it until the infantry arrived, Grant would have a strategic position from which to strike Lee's communications and, if he so chose, from which to march on Richmond.

Wilson's job was not easy, for soon after being driven from the village the Rebel cavalry counterattacked with great force. He was not dismayed, however. He dashed off a report to Sheridan: "Have run the enemy's cavalry a mile from Spotsylvania Court-House; have charged them through the village. Am fighting now with a considerable force. . . . Everything all right."

He should have been more concerned, for everything was not all right. Shortly after he sent his message, part of a hard-marching Confederate advance corps crossed a bridge which had been left unguarded when Meade changed Sheridan's strategy, and came roaring down upon Wilson's men. Aided by the Confederate cavalrymen, the foot soldiers drove forward with such speed as to convince Wilson he had stayed in Spotsylvania long enough. His belief was endorsed when a courier from Cavalry headquarters arrived to tell him to abandon the village and return to the position he had occupied earlier that morning. Realizing that things must have gone awry all along the line, Wilson collected his detachments and led them from the town, permitting the enemy advance troops to reclaim it for the Confederacy.

The Rebels arrived barely in time to stall the approach of the main Federal column. The Confederate infantry repulsed a rather feeble attack by Warren's V Corps and held the town long enough to permit the bulk of the Army of Northern Virginia to come up. When the rest of the Army of the Potomac arrived some hours later, the stage was prepared for another terrible slugging match which would yield thousands of casualties but no appreciable strategic success for either army.

In the meantime, Meade and Sheridan met at Army headquarters and exchanged angry words about the crossed signals. Meade was livid because instead of clearing the infantry's path, some of Sheridan's troopers had clogged the road to Spotsylvania and had kept Warren's corps from reaching the town ahead of the Rebels. Sheridan replied, with just as much heat, that had Meade not given the cavalry orders without his prior knowledge, the trouble would not have occurred and in fact Spotsylvania would now be in Federal hands. The hot-tempered

Irishman also berated his commander for not allowing the cavalry to pursue its proper job—running all of Major General J. E. B. Stuart's Confederate horsemen to earth. If given the chance to cut loose from the rest of the army, said Sheridan, his soldiers would strike Stuart's vaunted legions and smash them to fragments.

Meade relayed Sheridan's reply, which he considered insubordinate, to Grant. Sympathizing with the cavalryman's combative instincts, Grant saw the matter in a different light. Straightaway he sent for Sheridan, talked things over with him, and then granted him authority to move out on his own, head for Richmond around Lee's left and by this means draw the Confederate horsemen into a fight. Once—as Sheridan had confidently predicted—Stuart was whipped, the Federals were to cut railroads in Rebel territory and, if a heavy enemy force gathered in their rear, to move to the James River, south of Richmond. They could draw supplies at the depot of Butler's Army, at Haxall's Landing. That done, they could ride back to the main army.

This was precisely the assignment Sheridan wanted—the first independent maneuver of the rejuvenated cavalry corps. With haste he called Wilson, Merritt, and Gregg to his headquarters for a briefing. He explained the plan, told them that it had been drawn up at his express urging, cursed Stuart, and added: "I know we can beat him, and in view of my recent representations to General Meade I shall expect nothing but success."

At 6 A.M. on May 9 his 10,000 cavalrymen set out. A twelve-mile-long column of riders, followed by horse-drawn artillery and a line of supply wagons, clattered down the old Telegraph Road leading south to Richmond. The route took the horsemen well to the east of the main body of the army, still locked in a bitter struggle with Lee's soldiers near Spotsylvania.

The march began blithely enough. Glad to be free of the maddening Wilderness, Sheridan's troopers rode at a comfortable pace, admiring the fine May morning, the bright, clear skies, and the lovely roadside foliage. General Wilson, in a sensitive mood, found that "the landscape, like that of the entire Piedmont region, was most beautiful, the country fine and rolling, and both fields and streams fringed with growing timber. . . ." The pleasant weather may have taken from his mind the less pleasant thought of the fighting in which he had participated during the past several days. It would do little good to brood over past mistakes.

Almost from the start, a brigade of Confederate riders, and later a full division, followed the Federals at a distance. General Stuart him-

Cavalry Commanders of the Army of the Potomac, 1864—*Photograph courtesy Library of Congress*

From left: Generals Wesley Merritt, David McM. Gregg, Philip H. Sheridan, Henry E. Davies, Wilson, and Alfred T. A. Torbert.

self, with about 2,000 additional troopers, concentrated at a depot along a railroad which crossed Sheridan's route, but arrived after the raiders had passed and had to spur onward to try to cross their path farther ahead.

At first the Federals were blissfully unaware of Stuart's frantic maneuvering, feeling a minimum of pressure from the horsemen to the rear. After a rather uneventful first day out, during which they covered thirty-five miles, they bivouacked near a bridge over the North Anna River.

The next morning, Wilson's regiments fought a sharp skirmish with the Rebels following them, pulling out of formation to cover the other divisions as they crossed the North Anna. The march continued toward the South Anna River and throughout that day progressed smoothly. After daylight on the eleventh, however, bands of Rebels began to appear ahead of the column, falling back upon its approach. It seemed clear that Stuart had pushed some of his troopers across Sheridan's path.

Six miles above Richmond, at the intersection of the Telegraph Road and Mountain Road—an open area fringed by hills near a dilapidated hostelry known as Yellow Tavern—Stuart's legions, dismounted alongside the main road, came into view. Without hesitating, Sheridan drove his leading division, Merritt's, into the enemy. Fighting wildly with sabers and pistols, Merritt's men shoved Stuart's main force several hundred yards east of the intersection and gained access to another route, the Brock Turnpike, which led directly to Richmond.

The fighting seesawed back and forth for quite some time, with the Confederates firing determinedly from behind breastworks and atop nearby hills. But finally Custer's "Michigan Brigade" of the First Division cut down enemy resistance by charging a crucially positioned gun battery and sabering the cannoneers. Wilson's soldiers gave Custer a helpful covering fire, while at the same time General Gregg's division turned about and cracked the Confederate line in the Federals' rear. Soon the raiders had won full control of the road to the enemy capital.

The Federals gained an added dividend. When Custer's "Wolverines" eventually fell back upon Sheridan's main body, one of the Michigan troopers spied a Confederate officer sitting on his horse alongside the battle-filled road. The trooper fired his pistol, and J. E. B. Stuart slumped in his saddle with a mortal wound.

Enemy resistance quickly abated. Badly demoralized by the several Federal attacks, the Confederates scattered in flight. After only a

General J. E. B. Stuart—*Photograph courtesy Library of Congress*

short pursuit, Sheridan allowed them to escape, and for a time afterward he held the field.

Already Little Phil had attained many of his objectives, including besting (although not destroying) the Rebel horsemen and cutting Lee's railroads, a chore which had been carried out by various detachments during the past two days. Now he decided to press farther south toward the Confederate capital, reconnoiter its defenses, then move eastward and link with Butler's army.

The march resumed shortly before midnight. The evening was pitch-black, the roads poor, and the column stopped and started with annoying frequency. The Third Division warily led the way toward the Richmond city limits. From prisoners, Wilson had learned that Confederate veterans and home guards (more than 4,000 of them) had been called out to defend the capital against the Federals.

The raiders' march was also made dangerous by torpedoes which neighboring Confederates had rigged alongside the road. When horses tripped wires attached to these loaded artillery shells, explosions rocked the night; several animals were killed and their riders seriously injured. Wilson watched approvingly as prisoners from the column were then forced to grope alongside the road to locate and disarm the infernal weapons before more deaths could occur. A New Jersey trooper also observed the captives, "their timid groping and shrinking being a curious and rather entertaining sight."

But Wilson found little entertainment in the night march. His men trotted south toward the city and across the line of the Virginia Central Railroad. Beyond the tracks they searched for a road leading eastward to the city of Mechanicsville. Instead they found a junction where several unidentified roads converged. The Third Division halted here just before daybreak, for Wilson did not know which route would lead the column around the city to safety.

As if on cue, a horseman in a blue uniform appeared along the road and told Wilson he was a guide sent by Sheridan. Wilson must have worried that once again he faced a moment of crisis in a situation which meant success or failure to the entire Cavalry Corps. Latching onto the offered hope, he agreed to follow the man's directions, taking a narrow road which he indicated. But he compelled the guide to ride beside Colonel McIntosh, who kept a pistol pointed at his head.

Within minutes the division found itself confronting dark, wide-open areas which looked suspiciously like city outskirts. His tension building, Wilson sent scouts ahead and to the rear. He soon discovered that he had taken a south road and had become separated from the bulk of Sheridan's column, which had marched in the proper direction, eastward. Then a roar of musketry announced that the Third Division had been led into a trap; Wilson was facing an angle in Richmond's outer works, manned by vigilant defenders. In the night, his horsemen recoiled from gunfire which seemed to come from all sides. Horses reared and milled about in confusion, creating chaos all down the column. Fortunately, most of the inexperienced home guards fired above the heads of the cavalrymen, inflicting few casualties.

Wilson tried to rush word of his predicament to Sheridan and at the same time steady his men. Earlier, at the first barrage of rifle fire, Colonel McIntosh had blown out the brains of the spy who had led them astray.

When Sheridan learned of Wilson's plight, he was in the midst of his own skirmish, facing Rebels who were firing from behind timber barricades along the road to Mechanicsville. He ordered a courier: "Go back to General Wilson, and tell him to hold his position. He *can* hold it, and he *must* hold it!"

By the time Sheridan's message arrived, some of Wilson's nervousness had dissipated. His men had taken cover and the Rebels facing them were still conducting their defense poorly. Wilson was outnumbered and outpositioned, but he could afford to remain cool and even flippant. He replied to Sheridan by quoting a well-known humorist of the day: "Our hair is badly entangled in his fingers and our nose firmly inserted in his mouth, and we shall, therefore, hold on here till something breaks!"

While Wilson held his ground, Sheridan decided to ford the Chickahominy River by taking his raiders north across Meadow Bridge, planning later to recross the stream when far from the Richmond defenses. But his advance echelon found that the Confederates had destroyed the floor of that span to prevent their escape. Sheridan therefore dispatched some of Merritt's regiments to repair it with timber from nearby dwellings, while Custer's Wolverines gave them a covering fire.

When the cavalry at last surged over the bridge, they threw back the Confederates, who had gathered on the north bank. In a pelting rain, Merritt's men crossed. In their rear Gregg's division disengaged, and finally Wilson's troopers left their positions to follow. Seeing the Third Division move northward, the Rebels who had faced them sallied forth with blazing rifles. Under the watchful eye of Jefferson Davis, who had come out to witness the fateful struggle from a convenient hilltop, the city defenders at first scattered part of Wilson's division.

But for the second time in a week Gregg's troopers saved the day, by blasting away at the home guards from a wooded ravine, checking their progress. Recovering its composure, Wilson's command rallied, turned around, and broke the Rebel line to bits, pushing its survivors back to their breastworks. Then it followed Gregg's troopers across the re-planked bridge and on the far shore of the Chickahominy took the road which would lead it to Haxall's Landing.

But the Federals were not quite in the clear. Where the road turned southeastward, the remnants of Stuart's command burst from neighboring woodlots. Now guarding the rear, Wilson decided that a strong and swift charge would halt these troopers, who had doubtless followed the Federals from Yellow Tavern. The regiment he chose to deliver the thrust was the Eighteenth Pennsylvania, the unit which had nearly been cut off when crossing the Po River during the second day of the campaigning in the Wilderness.

Wilson entrusted the task to the regiment's commander, Colonel Timothy Bryan, erstwhile leader of the First Brigade. Bryan, an old-line Regular who was inclined to act deliberately, balked at the order. Quite possibly he felt that Wilson had made his decision too quickly, before being able to properly assess the size of the enemy force.

Wilson was enraged. His first instinct in battle was to move decisively and swiftly—sometimes, it was true, too swiftly. But he could not tolerate a subordinate who questioned his orders at such a crucial moment, for he was ever conscious of the necessity of maintaining his authority. With a few terse words he relieved Bryan of his command and ordered the regiment's lieutenant colonel to make the attack, which dispersed the enemy with ease.

Colonel Bryan rode slowly to the rear of his regiment, his active service at a close. He must have been angered and humiliated by the abrupt treatment he had received from his young superior. But he could not deny now that Wilson had guessed correctly about the vulnerability of the enemy, and success was the official measurement of propriety.

Enemy opposition having ended, Sheridan's column rode to safety, recrossing the Chickahominy via Bottom's Bridge and reaching Haxall's Landing on the fourteenth. There it drew needed rations and forage, proceeded farther south, and two days later began its return trip northward, having come 140 miles in 8 days. On its travels it had defeated Stuart's horsemen, killed Stuart himself, cut important rail lines connecting Lee's army with Richmond, threatened the Confederate capital, bested city defenders, suffered some 300 casualties, and,

The Eighteenth Pennsylvania Cavalry Regiment in Winter Quarters—*Photograph courtesy Library of Congress*

incidentally, had acquired a large helping of self-confidence and gained a deep respect for the ability of Philip Sheridan.

For James Harrison Wilson, the raid had been a fitting climax to a fortnight replete with excitement, danger, and hard fighting. He had endured several hours of tangled combat in the Virginia Wilderness. He had fought a series of sharp engagements in and near Spotsylvania. On the expedition he had come under heavy fire at Yellow Tavern, had seen his command nearly cut to pieces through the cunning of a spy, had been assailed in front and rear by citizen-soldiers, and had been challenged at the last by a relentless band of pursuers. Coming through all of it without injury, he had been tempered by battle into an experienced field commander.

⋆VII⋆

Give Parker a Tomahawk, a Supply of Commissary Whiskey, and a Scalping Knife

Moving north by way of White House Landing on the Pamunkey River, Sheridan's horsemen rejoined Grant on May 24 at his new base, Old Chesterfield Court House, about twenty-five miles above Richmond. When Wilson rode to Army headquarters he received a lavish welcome. Grant and Rawlins were as deeply interested in hearing of his exploits on the raid as he was in recounting them.

From them, in turn, Wilson learned that during the cavalry's absence the main army had been quite busy. Moving south after the vicious battle at Spotsylvania, Lee's soldiers had formed a line below the North Anna River, and the Army of the Potomac had followed them and erected a formidable line of its own. Stalemate resulted. Lee's position was partially protected by the South Anna and appeared unassailable by frontal assault. Consequently Grant decided to turn the Rebels' flank by continuing his side-slipping movement. His new objective was one of the Pamunkey River crossings at or near Hanover Town.

To conform to the movement, Grant broke up Sheridan's cavalry and dispatched units in various directions to perform many deeds. On May 26 he sent Wilson's people over the North Anna to demonstrate on the right of the army and threaten Lee's left. Wilson did his job well; Lee received the impression that his opponents were planning to march through that sector rather than toward Hanover Town. Grant then moved as he had intended, and not until the morning of the twenty-seventh did Lee realize he had been deceived. By then, Wilson's division had recrossed the North Anna and had positioned itself to cover the army's right flank as it moved over the Pamunkey.

Wilson's work on the south side of that river, which included scouting and guarding wagon trains, was interrupted on the thirty-first, when his soldiers met Rebel cavalry near Hanover Court House. After a brisk skirmish, the enemy fled at full speed through a shallow creek. Moving on, Wilson received orders from General Meade to wreck four bridges over the South Anna and Little rivers, to impede Lee's countermovements. Late that evening, marching toward its objectives, the Third Division again clashed with enemy troopers, who were roving far afield of Lee's main body. As before, the Federals routed and dispersed their enemy. They then carried out their bridge-burning and also destroyed railroad trackage in the vicinity.

Still more fighting occurred when Major General Wade Hampton, who upon Stuart's death had become commander of Lee's cavalry, came up to battle those of Wilson's troopers who were mangling track. By skillfully meeting Hampton in both front and rear, Wilson managed to hold his opponents off and then withdraw to a safer sector. The next day the Third Division, weary from two days of hard fighting, made a long march till able to connect with the main body of Grant's army.

Early on June 3 General Meade assigned the troopers yet another task. Pursuant to his instructions, the Third Division moved eastward to the town of Haw's Shop, charged through it, and gouged a brigade of dismounted Rebel cavalry from three lines of breastworks.

Pushing farther, Wilson encountered infantry beyond Haw's Shop, protecting the left and rear of Lee's main command. Because the Rebels lay concealed in thick woods shadowed by approaching darkness, he withdrew his men and with a calm precision that clearly indicated his comfortable adjustment to field command, led them back to the Army of the Potomac.

In recent fighting Wilson's division had extended its series of decisive victories, and soon afterward General Meade offered it his heartiest congratulations. Although a clash of temperaments prevented

Wilson from being close to the army leader, he accepted Meade's words with gratitude. But he was sobered by the realization that his command had paid a high price in casualties for its success.

The Third Division had no monopoly on injuries. While its troopers had been attacking, scattering, and pursuing the enemy, the main army had fought an especially brutal battle. At Cold Harbor, five miles south of Haw's Shop, the infantry had been cut down in a series of futile attacks against strong enemy positions. In truth, Wilson had played a role in that fighting, for by engaging the infantry along Lee's left he had also guarded the Federal right flank at Cold Harbor and had conformed to the ordered movements of the nearest infantry corps— led by General Ambrose Burnside, once again serving in the East.

During the next eight days Wilson's men awaited further combat, going forth in patrols to survey the enemy's positions. But they saw no direct action. This was fortunate for, as Wilson reported, the division was "worn and jaded from its exhausting labors" and was on short rations to boot. Furthermore, a number of troopers had begun to complain vociferously about the army's lack of enduring victories. Grant had been in the field for a month, but so far—though he had never retreated—he had won no clear-cut advantage over General Lee.

Sensitive to the mood of his soldiers, Grant knew that the grumbling was not confined to the men of the Third Cavalry Division. Two weeks later, when the army was again moving south, Wilson found the general-in-chief sitting dejectedly in front of his command tent. Regarding him earnestly, Grant asked a simple question which required a complex answer: "Wilson, what is the matter with this army?"

Wilson did not ponder for long, for he possessed all the impatience and self-assurance of youth. The main problem, he replied, was an insufficiency of brains among the subordinate commanders; and almost as vexing was the generals' inability to cooperate effectively with one another. But he added that he had a patent remedy. Grant asked him to reveal it.

Referring to Captain Ely Parker, a full-blooded Seneca Indian who served as Grant's assistant adjutant general, Wilson said: "Give Parker a tomahawk, a supply of commissary whiskey, and a scalping knife and send him out with orders to bring in the scalps of general officers."

Smiling, Grant asked, "Whose?"

Wilson shrugged indifferently. "Oh, the first he comes to, and so on in succession till he gets at least a dozen."

FROM THE SCENE OF THE DISASTER AT Cold Harbor, Grant moved still farther south, toward the line of the James River. He had made up his mind to strike for Petersburg, the rail center which lay twenty-five miles below Richmond and which supplied and supported the Confederate capital. Lee, he realized, would have to move from his unassailable positions around Cold Harbor and race after him.

Five infantry corps drove toward Petersburg, including Baldy Smith's XVIII Corps, borrowed from the Virginia Peninsula, where Confederate generals abler than Benjamin F. Butler had stalled the Army of the James' movement toward Richmond. But Wilson's was the only cavalry division to participate in the race to the strategic city. On June 7 Sheridan took the rest of his corps to the north and west on a diversion toward Charlottesville. He intended to wreak further havoc on railroads above the James and again draw the Rebel cavalry after him and into a fight.

Sheridan's departure forced Wilson to spread his forces quite thin to render adequate protection to both Grant's front and rear. He sent McIntosh's brigade to the right of the army and ordered Chapman's men to its extreme left.

In the hands of a less talented logistician, the Army of the Potomac's movements over the Chickahominy and James rivers might have failed because of the myriad problems that naturally attend such a radical change of base. Under Grant's sure-handed direction, it became one of the finest strategic maneuvers in American military history.

Wilson's duties during the operation included a well-executed feint which he conducted in conjunction with General Warren's infantry on June 12–13. Followed by Warren's V Corps, Wilson led Colonel Chapman's brigade to Long Bridge over the Chickahominy River, a dozen miles below Cold Harbor. The bridge had been destroyed; so he ordered some of his troopers to swim the stream. Securing a footing on the far shore, they helped lay a pontoon bridge, over which their comrades crossed. Then the united cavalry force cleared the way for Warren's men. Afterward troopers and foot soldiers moved westward toward Richmond along roads striking White Oak Swamp, scene of fierce fighting during McClellan's Peninsular Campaign in the summer of 1862.

At dawn on the thirteenth Wilson's soldiers advanced along a wide front between the Chickahominy and the James, alerting Rebel cavalry pickets near Richmond. Word of their coming got to General Lee, who naturally envisioned an attack on the Confederate capital. He sent part of his army to entrench before Wilson and Warren and guard the approaches to the city. He did not know, of course, that Grant's main force was moving across the James, ten miles farther east.

When he learned the truth late that morning, Lee at once sent his own army southward to counter Grant's movements. Some of his soldiers marched in Wilson's direction, and a division of cavalry, commanded by Lee's son "Rooney" (the only Confederate horseman who had not followed Sheridan toward Charlottesville), struck Wilson head-on. The resulting skirmish closed when the Federals pushed their enemy back across White Oak Swamp, retaining a hold on the Chickahominy crossing site.

That evening, with infantry and artillery pressing in, Wilson withdrew a few miles to the south to picket roads toward Richmond, and the next afternoon had a short but vicious fight with the Confederate cavalry at a location known as Saint Mary's Church.

After two more days of demonstrating toward enemy positions, Wilson ended his screening movements. On the sixteenth he took his men south to the James River and in the wake of Warren's corps crossed the magnificent bridge which Grant's engineers had constructed. By 4 A.M. the rear guard of the Army of the Potomac had safely crossed, and Grant's great movement had been successfully performed. Now, for the first time in the war, Grant's soldiers were in position to concentrate on a strategic objective below Richmond—a curious divergence from Federal strategy of previous years, primarily concerned with capturing the Confederate capital.

Soon after crossing the river, Wilson received permission to rest and refurbish his command. In grateful obedience, he marched several miles southward to the Blackwater River, a deep stream which meandered southeast of Petersburg. There he went into camp and for a few days allowed the infantry to prosecute the war.

The infantry did the job rather badly. Once over the James, Grant moved directly on Petersburg, knowing that if he took the city he would control the route to Richmond and thus the movements of Lee's army. The outlook was most promising, for before the Army of Northern Virginia was able to move close to Petersburg, Grant was well within striking distance. Baldy Smith's corps had been transported northeast of the city and had crossed the Appomattox River to strike Petersburg from that direction. And the Army of the Potomac's southward march had provided Smith with handy reinforcements.

But instead of charging onward and taking the "Cockade City" (which was defended by no more than 2,500 soldiers), General Smith halted after capturing some of its outer works, not utilizing his great numerical advantage. Coming up, the Army of the Potomac's advance command was slowed by vague instructions and a variety of other woes, and did little more than Wilson's friend had done. Precious hours slipped past, Smith elected not to launch the assault which would certainly have taken Petersburg and perhaps have won the war, the Confederates in the city feverishly rounded up reinforcements, and by the afternoon of the eighteenth the bulk of Lee's army finally entered Petersburg from the west. With that, Grant's brilliant opportunity faded; a solid army now faced him, as it had at every step he had taken since the Wilderness.

After several unsuccessful attempts to crack the city's defenses, Grant began to consider a Vicksburg-like siege. But such strategy would have to be a final resort, for with lines to Richmond still open both Petersburg and the capital would be sustained in the necessities of life for many months.

There had to be a solution to the dilemma. Thinking long and hard, the commanding general decided to concentrate his attention on the rail lines which ran into Petersburg. Two of them were now in Federal hands, but two others still supplied the city. One, the Petersburg & Weldon Railroad, ran south into North Carolina; the other, the Petersburg & Lynchburg (more familiarly known as the Southside Railroad), led southwestward toward the Tennessee border. At Burkeville Junction, fifty miles west of Petersburg, the Southside crossed the line of a third road operating for benefit of the Confederacy, the Richmond & Danville. Grant at length decided that a properly led raiding force, with the Burkeville depot as its focal point, might rip up enough trackage on all three lines to force the enemy out of Petersburg for want of regular shipments of rations and equipment.

Such a raid was of course the business of the cavalry, the Third Division. Grant talked with Wilson, and Wilson, eager for his first independent assignment, was enthusiastically responsive to the idea. It would provide him with his first great test as a commander in his own right—able to achieve success or suffer failure solely upon the basis of his own merit or lack of same. At this juncture, however, he could not seriously consider the second possibility. Thus he quickly accepted the chance to strike the railroads in concert with the 2,000-trooper division in Butler's army, under General Kautz.

Later—after some inevitable consideration of the less happy possibility involved in the assignment—Wilson began to have second thoughts. He grew concerned that even two divisions of cavalry might find it difficult to ward off defenders south and west of Petersburg. To assuage his fears, General Meade's headquarters assured him that on the day his raid began, the army would extend its left flank across the Weldon Railroad to the depot at Reams's Station, seven miles south of the city. By doing so it would clear enemy troops from country roads, creating an escape route which the raiders might use if necessary. Meade went so far as to predict that in a few days his infantry would be sitting astride the Southside line as well. Although Wilson had never learned to trust Meade entirely, the news somewhat calmed his fears. The evening before he set out he wrote in his diary that his orders, "quite general and comprehensive," were satisfactory.

About 3 A.M. on June 22 his raiders left their camp along the Blackwater. Kautz, who had arrived at Wilson's headquarters two days before, took the advance with his four regiments, followed by the ten regiments Wilson had selected from his division—some 3,300 troopers —two 6-gun batteries of horse artillery, and a long line of ambulances and supply wagons. The weather was warm and muggy, but Wilson rode comfortably at the head of his division, hopeful that Meade would aid him as promised and thus increase the likelihood of his success.

At first the march went perfectly. At 7 A.M. the raiders paused at Reams's Station only long enough to destroy a few hundred feet of Weldon track, thirteen freight cars, and the small depot. Kautz then pushed westward toward the Southside. En route he learned that Rooney Lee's cavalry was in bivouac along the road a few miles ahead. On his own initiative, Kautz skillfully detoured around Lee's flank and without difficulty reached Ford's Station. There, fourteen miles from Petersburg, his troopers wrecked two locomotives and thirty cars, plus four miles of track. Yet Kautz could not prevent observers from fleeing west to circulate the news of his coming.

By the time Wilson's people marched from Reams's Station to the Southside, Rooney Lee was alert. He struck the Federals in the rear, compelling part of Colonel Chapman's brigade to turn around and accept battle. But this interference did not materially worry Wilson; he assumed that Lee's single division would be the only organized force with which he would have to contend, and was confident that it could be held at arm's length.

That evening Wilson ordered Kautz to push on to Burkeville Junction. There, about 3 A.M. on the twenty-third, the cavalry of the Army of the James began to mutilate trackage in four directions. Afterward, Kautz moved south along the Richmond & Danville road, and the following morning the Third Division came up to finish the job at Burkeville and to reunite with Kautz. Meanwhile, Chapman continued

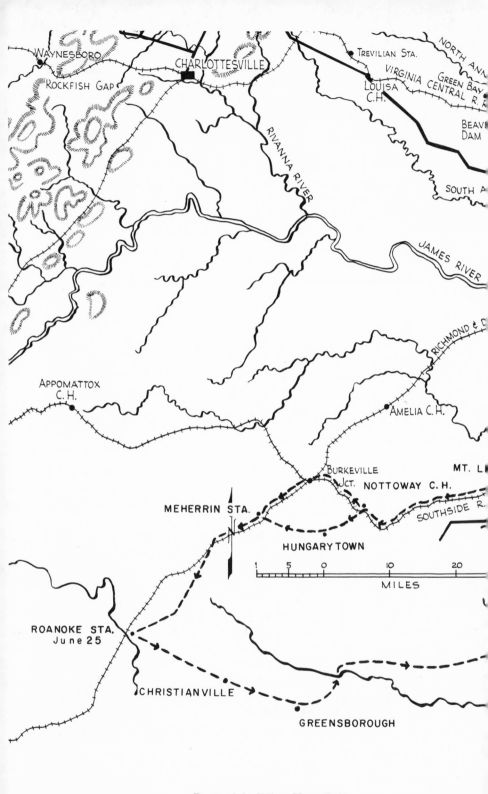

Route of the Wilson-Kautz Raid

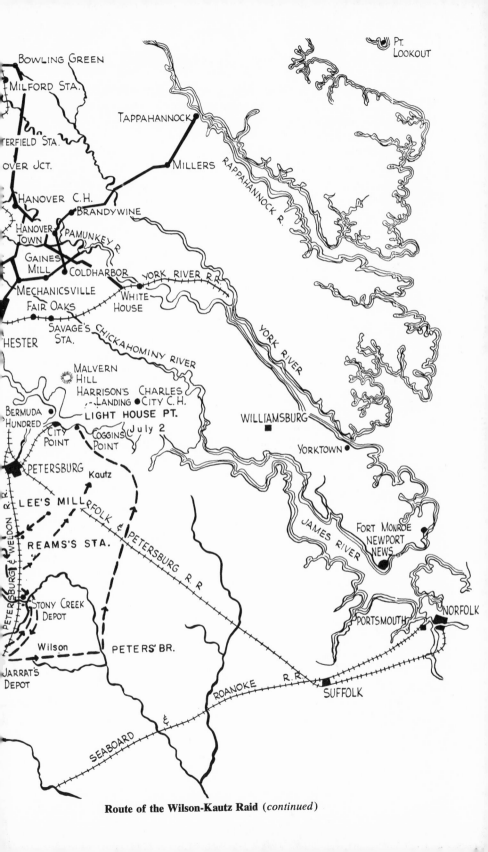

Route of the Wilson-Kautz Raid (*continued*)

to hold the Rebels off. By now Wilson realized that the countryside was beginning to swarm with defenders. But he betrayed no pronounced anxiety when he followed Kautz down the Danville line.

The next two days were spent systematically destroying the R & D. Miles of track, depot buildings, telegraph wire, line shacks, water towers, and various other forms of public and commercial property fell prey to crowbar and torch. The Danville road was a particularly vulnerable target, for its rails were fastened atop wooden "stringers," which rested upon crossties. Wilson's men needed only to pile tree branches or fenceposts near the rails, light a match, and step back. The resulting fire not only consumed stringers and crossties but also warped the strap rails, rendering them useless. The Federals destroyed nearly thirty miles of track in this manner. The R & D had been completed less than two months before; soon it was a line of charred wood, twisted metal, and ashes.

On the afternoon of the twenty-fifth the raiders reached one of their most important objectives, the Staunton River bridge near Roanoke Station. Here Wilson realized he had come as far as possible into the Confederacy. The bridge was defended on both shores by almost 900 Rebels—militia called out from eight counties (initially to watch for the approach of another raiding force led by Wilson's old colleague, General David Hunter), plus civilian sharpshooters and some Confederate veterans on furloughs and sick leaves. Led by Captain B. L. Fairnholt, Fifty-third Virginia Infantry, the force was armed with six cannon, including a battery farther upriver which commanded the approaches to the bridge.

Kautz reconnoitered and then advised Wilson to forego an assault. Wilson agreed that the enemy's position was formidable but insisted that an attack be made. No doubt he considered his image, and the effect which would be produced by his retreating without making an attempt to carry the objective. Thus, Kautz dismounted his troopers and led them through a bottom wheatfield toward the bridge. He was halted short of the span by a massive cannonade and by volleys of rifle fire. Only after launching half a dozen assaults, each of which was aborted, was Kautz able to persuade Wilson to retreat eastward.

Wilson acknowledged that he was, once again, in a precarious situation. Hoping that Grant and Meade had carried out the promise to clear backcountry roads, he turned his column about and that night hurried east through farmland and forest. As he rode, he had to fight Rooney Lee, who continued to pursue and harass him with dogged determination, as well as local defenders, who offered resistance all along his route.

A desperate two-and-a-half-day ride carried his men through several small villages and over numerous streams, until at noon on the twenty-eighth they drew near the Weldon depot at Stony Creek, ten miles south of Reams's Station. From Negroes, many of whom had fallen in with the column in the hope of being led out of bondage, Wilson learned of a sizable enemy force at Stony Creek Station. Hoping to avoid it, he started north along a trail paralleling the railroad and which supposedly ran as far as the point at which the raid had commenced. But he had gone only a short distance before a few Confederates appeared across his path. Soon Rebel infantry and cavalry came crashing out of nearby woods, and the Third Division, now leading the march, had to stop and contest them. The fighting gyrated back and forth, each side seeming to gain the advantage, then to lose it; and while it raged, darkness came on.

It was the most desperate situation Wilson had ever known, and at this point, quite possibly, he wished he had not been so eager to lead his first expedition. He stayed awake throughout that night, as he had for many recent nights, directing his men in battle. The next morning, fatigued to a degree greater than he had ever experienced, he sought to disengage by sending Kautz along another road to Reams's Station. There Kautz ought to find Grant and the Army of the Potomac, and then Wilson's own division would follow him. By now Wilson considered Grant's aid his last hope and put all his faith in the lieutenant general's ability to extricate the Third Division from its predicament.

At full daylight Wilson learned that Kautz had progressed toward the depot without difficulty. Before Wilson marched, however, he left Chapman's regiments in rifle pits to hold back the enemy until the rest of the division could clear Stony Creek Station. The rear guard would be in a perilous spot, for when it came time to withdraw, the Confederates could rush forward and cut it to pieces as it fell back to its horses. Yet Chapman's position at the tag end of the column made his selection inevitable; he accepted the task without comment and never condemned Wilson for the situation.

Fortunately, when McIntosh's brigade made its escape and the enemy came on, Chapman succeeded in extricating most of his command. The rest of the rear guard—including the brigade's greenest regiment, the Twenty-second New York—was captured or forced to the southward, and for a time most of its men were cut off from the main body. Later the survivors rejoined Wilson on the road to Reams's Station. Setting up the suicide squad had been an unpleasant undertaking, but Wilson had betrayed no compunction about it; he was concerned only that his main force evade danger. His single-mindedness was rewarded, for Chapman's tenacity bought the column some time. But the incident reflected a rather cold-blooded professionalism which Wilson never hesitated to adopt whenever he felt it necessary.

The period of grace achieved by Chapman's steadfastness did not last long. At 9 A.M., when he reached Reams's Station, Wilson received the shock of his career. Kautz was there, but General Grant was not; the only others in the vicinity wore gray. Grant had failed to move the Army of the Potomac across the railroad; Confederate Lieutenant General A. P. Hill had thrown back two corps of Federal infantry making such an attempt six days before. Hill had left a full division of Rebels at the depot, later augmented by Hampton's cavalry, which had stopped pursuing Sheridan and had returned to Petersburg for reassignment. Now Wilson had ridden neatly into a trap. He was staggeringly outnumbered, and outmaneuvered as well. As though a nightmare had become reality, he seemed to be facing every veteran in the Confederate Army.

While the lopsided battle raged, some of the men of the Third Division, seeing comrades shot down in droves, began to edge toward panic. Their commander calmed them as best he could, and made necessary dispositions. He dismounted his men and directed them to cover. He set up his artillery, dispatched his wagons and ambulances to the rear, and then sent one of his most trusted aides, Captain E. W. Whitaker, escorted by forty of Kautz's men, toward the headquarters of the Army of the Potomac, which recently had been at City Point, only eight miles to the northeast.

Whitaker miraculously reached headquarters, although more than half his escort were killed or wounded fighting their way through. At noon, when General Meade received the captain's news, the army chief was at first astounded, then deeply alarmed, and then quick to take action. He directed Major General Horatio G. Wright's VI Corps to march to the depot and scatter the Rebels. While the infantry made ready to comply, Meade also collared Sheridan, recently returned from his diversionary operation and a fierce battle against Hampton in which the Federals had come out second best. At first the cavalry commander tried to beg off—his men were worn out, their horses jaded—but finally he agreed to try to rescue Wilson. However, General Wright and he took considerable time readying their soldiers for the trip, and while they did, Wilson was on his own.

At Reams's Station the fighting grew steadily more vicious. Hampton, with two divisions, pushed Wilson and Kautz into a corner in which they were nearly surrounded. Finally it became obvious that the raiders would have to withdraw. Wilson was no longer concerned with saving face; he thought only of retreating with as much haste as possible. About 2 P.M. he had his command remount and head south, abandoning all wagons, guns, and casualties. Aided by the soon-to-be-captured artillery, which slowed the Rebels' pursuit, he and Kautz galloped down roads which they hoped would lead them clear of the depot and thence eastward across the Weldon line.

The resulting march was grueling. Dead-tired and half-starved from days of uninterrupted travel, troopers fell asleep on horseback, despite the presence of Confederates in their rear. General Kautz had a haunting dream while asleep in his saddle and recalled it years afterward: "The most tantalizing vision was that of marching through populous and brilliantly lighted towns; through the windows we could see the tables spread with every good thing and we were not permitted to halt and partake. . . ."

During the march, Kautz's men became separated from the Third Division, for the two forces traveled on divergent trails which were bordered by dense forests. As night came on, Kautz lost touch with Wilson altogether and decided to strike out on a different road to safety. Turning his division east and then north, he cut through groups of pursuing Confederates. One of his men later described the ride as "a wild skedaddle through heavy timber, shells from rebel batteries knocking the branches about our ears. . . ."

Most of the cavalrymen from the Army of the James found their way to safety. Familiar with the countryside from two months' campaign experience, Kautz guided his main force to the Federal lines by 9:30 that night. Then, after giving General Grant, his staff, and Assistant Secretary of War Dana a highly excited account of the raid, and his firm opinion that Wilson's soldiers had been captured, Kautz took his exhausted horsemen back toward General Butler's army, supremely glad to be in friendly territory once again.

Later Wilson would hold Kautz's eagerness to return to Butler—and his unwillingness to retake the field to help rescue the Third Division—against him. Wilson's feelings stemmed also from the fact that Kautz's cavalry fled to safety fairly easily, while Wilson's men were left on their own to suffer additional hardships. The two commanders were never on cordial terms after the raid.

Wilson was not aware of Kautz's retreat until stragglers from the latter's command, who had gotten lost while trying to reach the Federal lines, rejoined the Third Division during its march south. About 2:30 A.M. on the thirtieth, Wilson led his mixed force across the Weldon road, several miles south of Reams's Station, and marched east toward the Blackwater River and ultimate safety. Although many of his soldiers were dropping by the wayside on jaded horses, he ordered his column to speed its march, for Confederates captured along the trail revealed that Hampton was heading toward them on a perpendicular road.

Making a final effort for speed, the cavalrymen pushed on to Blunt's Bridge over the Blackwater, where they halted shortly after midnight on July 1. They found, to their surprise, that the bridge had been burned; the floor was gone, and only the center trestle, in the middle of the deep stream, was still standing.

That trestle saved the Third Division. Without it the troopers would have stood little chance of crossing the river before their pursuers could overtake them. Fortunately Wilson was able to think and act quickly though pressed for time. He located a stable timber and extended it across the trestle. Then he ordered soldiers to cross on the beam and initiate reconstruction from the far shore. Under his supervision, the troopers completed a new span within one hour. In the darkness he moved his entire command across, stacked combustible material on the bridge floor, and turned the structure into a bonfire short minutes before the Confederate advance echelon drew up on the other bank.

Safe at last after a punishing 325-mile expedition, he led his command into camp near Lighthouse Point on the James River, for a long recuperation period. When he rejoined the army, he was greeted as a true prodigal. Until he had sent word of his safety from Lighthouse Point, his commanders had given him up as lost, as a result of Kautz's story.

When they marched into camp, Wilson's men were quite some sight. A correspondent for *Harper's Weekly* found them wearing torn and grimy uniforms, ripped boots, and headgear of almost every description, including many women's hats.

The millinery indicated that considerable looting had occurred during the raid. The wagons abandoned at Reams's Station contained a wide array of valuables ranging from foodstuffs snatched from farms and smokehouses to silver plate, including a communion service which bore the inscription, "St. John's Church, Cumberland Parish, Lunenburg county, Virginia."

Richmond newspapers raised a furor over the stolen goods. In editorials which invoked all manner of earthly torment upon the raiders —and suggested that Wilson's men would have made Attila's Huns seem like merry pranksters—they advocated the hanging of the "mounted thieves" captured during the expedition. The *Examiner* felt that this was the only intelligent way to proceed, for "whenever the game is played on that principle it will be brought to a speedy conclusion."

The to-do did not make an impression solely upon the people of the South. Angry reaction was felt in portions of the Army of the Potomac. Provost Marshal General Patrick was outraged by the reports and wrote that "Wilson's March has been one continuous scene of plunder & burning. . . ." And General Meade called the Third Division's commander to account; he demanded he answer the newspaper allegations.

Wilson sent Meade a reply four days after the raid ended. He denied the charges that he had robbed women and churches, and hoped that Meade would not condemn his command simply because its operations had unleashed the fury of the enemy press. He admitted authorizing his men to forage for things useful to them, but emphasized that he drew the line when it came to pillaging and housebreaking. Then, equivocating a bit, he added: "I can safely say further, no man in my command has ever received any part of his education in lawlessness from me." Kautz later submitted a report similar in tone and content.

Meade accepted Wilson's explanation and dropped his investigation. But Wilson, who believed that personal animus had prompted Meade's inquiry, continued to regard his commander with rancor. He was angered not only by Meade's investigation but also by Meade's failure to rush reinforcements to Reams's Station more quickly than he had (Sheridan's cavalry and the VI Corps had reached the depot long after Wilson and Kautz had retreated). Wilson mentioned his feelings to Grant, which (as Wilson knew it would) helped spur the lieutenant general's occasional thinking about ousting Meade from command of the Army of the Potomac. The incident demonstrated that Wilson felt the best way to vent his anger at any superior he disliked was to complain to his mentor; Grant usually lent a sympathetic ear, and Wilson could always hope he would cashier the offender.

If Meade was seeking to attach personal blame to Wilson for his men's activities during the raid, his efforts were futile. Indications are that Wilson was conscientious in attempting to prohibit looting. As Kautz later wrote: "Wilson succeeded in exciting a very hard feeling against himself among the men. I saw him during the march on several occasions cursing and berating men for straggling and pillaging, which he should have left to his staff and provost marshalls. . . ." At the same time, this report helps explain why Wilson remained an unpopular commander to many of his troopers. When displeased by men under him as well as by those who ranked him, he was inclined to shout out his anger. He seemed not to understand that citizens in uniform do not like to be yelled at very often.

At first glance, the results of Wilson's raid seemed impressive. In destroying some sixty miles of track on three important railroads, he had dealt the enemy a powerful blow. On the other hand, he had lost all of his artillery and wagons, and had suffered 1,300 casualties (although a majority of these, initially listed as missing in action, later straggled back to their units). Furthermore, his achievements were later nullified when the Confederates ran wagon trains around the broken track to haul supplies to Petersburg, while working furiously to repair the damage.

It became quite clear, once all the facts were in, that the expedition had fallen far short of its goals and that only by a combination of good fortune and the stout fighting of those same men whom he had berated for straggling, had Wilson's command escaped capture en masse. In the final analysis, it appears that most of the troubles which the cavalry suffered can be attributed to Wilson's excessive confidence in finding ready aid at Reams's Station. Quite simply, he had put too much faith in the army's ability to secure the railroads immediately south of Petersburg—a feat not to be accomplished until the following winter. Lacking contingency planning, Wilson barely was able to act quickly enough to pull out of Reams's Station with his command intact.

Personal verdicts came in quickly. Meade wrote his wife that the raid was "quite a serious disaster," and had yielded only two discernible results: "Our cavalry is no longer superior in numbers to the enemy & what is worse has lost its prestige. . . ." Artillery Colonel Charles S. Wainwright called the raiders "terribly careless," for they had been "caught by the enemy completely with their breeches down." George Custer wrote his wife, Libby, that "the upstart and imbecile" Wilson had met defeat through "his total ignorance and inexperience of cavalry." And even General Grant, who had authorized the raid, echoed a harsh term in describing Wilson's initial independent mission: "I regret the disaster. . . ."

DURING HIS RECUPERATION PERIOD, WILSON learned that Grant and Lee were still at an impasse. Petersburg had been solidly fortified and fully occupied by the Confederates, and the Army of the Potomac had moved as close to its works as it seemed likely to venture for some time. Barring a dramatic breakthrough, the stalemate would drag on for months.

At about this time, activity was intensifying in another theater. The Federal forces in Virginia's Shenandoah Valley, under General Hunter, had beat a retreat, enabling the Rebel army in that sector to move almost at will. One of the principal Confederates in the Valley was Major General Jubal A. Early, a feisty, quick-witted soldier who commanded some 14,000 men, of all arms.

In early July, while Wilson remained in camp near the James River, he was surprised to hear that "Old Jube" was marching down the Valley toward the Federal capital. After throwing the countryside into a panic, Early then came up to the outskirts of Washington, skirmished with its garrison troops, and only when reinforcements arrived from the Army of the Potomac did he turn away and head back to the Valley.

The politicians and garrison soldiers breathed more easily upon Early's withdrawal. But in later weeks, Early became more and more of a wide-ranging menace, to the alarm of the government officials. To take the Confederate forces in the Shenandoah out of the war for good, and to lay waste to the "Breadbasket of the Confederacy," Grant organized the Middle Military Division. The department encompassed wide areas of Maryland and upper Virginia and was defended by a newly organized force, the Army of the Shenandoah, consisting of the VI, VIII, and XIX infantry corps and three divisions of cavalry. To head the force Grant chose the energetic Sheridan and sent him into the Valley on August 1, with orders to destroy Early.

Two of the cavalry divisions assigned to Sheridan were from the Army of the Potomac—Wilson's, and Brigadier General Alfred Torbert's; in the Valley they would join a third unit under Brigadier General William W. Averell. Torbert was subsequently given charge of all three divisions, while command of his own unit devolved upon Wesley Merritt, who had led it previously on an intermittent basis.

On the fourth of August Wilson moved his command from Grant's left flank to City Point, where it embarked upon transports for the trip up the James River and eventually to Washington. By now the reinforced division contained eleven regiments, still divided between two brigades, plus three artillery batteries—an aggregate of almost 5,000 officers and troopers. During months of campaigning under Wilson the unit had been fashioned into one of the most reliable cavalry forces in all the Federal armies, its bad fortune on the railroad raid notwithstanding. Still, the mishaps which had occurred south and west of Petersburg nagged the troopers. They vowed to recoup their lost prestige once in the Valley.

In Washington they went through a thorough refit at Giesboro Point, the great cavalry depot which four months ago Wilson had administered as head of the Cavalry Bureau. The division received fresh horses and new equipment, plus enough Spencer carbines to arm every man. Then the troopers rode through the streets of the capital, heading for the Potomac River and the great valley which lay southwestward. Years later Wilson fondly recalled that march: "It was a beautiful day, the division was in better condition than ever before, many had new uniforms, the guidons were unfurled, the brigade bands playing and the column of platoons, with clanking sabers and clattering hoofs, made its impressive way by Pennsylvania Avenue and Georgetown to the Potomac bridge and country beyond. . . ."

His men reached Leesburg, Virginia, just east of the Valley, on the evening of the twelfth, and the next day they marched in the direction of Berryville, the strategic village to which Sheridan had recently advanced. Two days earlier, Sheridan had sallied forth from Harpers Ferry, West Virginia, at the top of the Shenandoah, toward Berryville, to contest the Confederates. General Early had promptly fallen back farther south to await reinforcements promised him by General Lee. When the new troops, infantry and cavalry, arrived, they gave Early a total force of 23,000 effectives with which to confront the approximately 40,000 which Sheridan then had on hand.

After Early received his additions, Sheridan decided to return to Harpers Ferry, destroying military resources as he went. One of Wilson's first tasks in the Valley was to cover the rear of the withdrawing army. On the sixteenth he protected Sheridan's wagon train following a skirmish with part of Early's army at Cedarville.

On the twenty-fifth, Sheridan learned that his adversary had divided his force, only a portion of which was following the Federals. Possibly Early was about to launch another invasion of Federal territory with the bulk of his army. That day Sheridan dispatched General Torbert, commanding Wilson's and Merritt's divisions, to reconnoiter northward toward the Potomac River and ascertain Early's intentions.

Wilson was glad to be given an opportunity for action, for he had been kept idle for almost two months: "I was anxious that my division, newly armed and equipped, should show what it could do." It could do quite a bit, as it proved when it crossed the line of the Baltimore & Ohio Railroad above the town of Kearneysville and then struck cavalry screening the movements of a Confederate infantry corps, which it pushed back a half-mile or more. Sixty-some prisoners yielded information that the large force was indeed heading north, as Sheridan had feared. Wilson relayed the news to Torbert and received orders to fall back to a safer area. The instructions came a few minutes too late, for a Rebel counterattack forced the Third Division to withdraw with great haste and in poor order.

At the outset of the general withdrawal there occurred an event which Wilson forever believed was caused by Wesley Merritt's jealousy. Perhaps as a result of a guilty conscience, he felt that Merritt had never forgiven him for moving directly from a desk job in Washington to a field command, over Merritt's head. Therefore Wilson was entirely willing to believe a rumor that Merritt had suggested to his friend and superior, Torbert, that Wilson's command bring up the rear of the column on this day, with orders to delay the Rebels till the First Division could get out of the way.

Whatever the circumstances behind the order, Wilson was indeed commanded to cover Merritt's rear. But he extricated his division by falling back slowly in open order, his rear units firing constantly from the saddle. Their accuracy, of course, was ragged, but the steady barrage of shots kept their pursuers at a comfortable distance until the main force could outrace them and join Sheridan in camp near Harpers Ferry.

That same evening, orders came for Wilson to move toward the Potomac River crossings near Sharpsburg, to guard against any Rebel attempt to ford the river and menace the North. The Third Division marched through the night, across Blue Ridge Mountain valleys near which its commander's ancestors had lived. The next morning it moved over terrain Wilson vividly recalled from his Antietam campaign experience.

Aided by Custer's brigade of Merritt's division, Wilson's men later held mountain gaps near Boonsboro, Maryland, to prevent Early from moving in that direction. But after a few hours of uneventful vigil, Wilson realized that the enemy had given up its invasion scheme, apparently lacking sufficient strength to implement it. Recrossing the Potomac on August 28, he made a quick march through the lovely country beyond to rejoin the main army at Berryville.

He remained in camp there from the thirtieth until September 13, resting and again refitting his command. Only portions of the division remained active, for their sole opponents in this area were partisan rangers under Lieutenant Colonel John S. Mosby, who often called on Wilson's men in early morning hours with blazing pistols, and rode off before pursuit could commence. General Early had withdrawn deeper into the Shenandoah Valley and then, after a skirmish with detachments of Sheridan's infantry, marched to Winchester, beyond Opequon Creek and several miles southwest of Sheridan's headquarters.

On the thirteenth part of Wilson's division took to the roads and delivered a telling blow at the enemy forces nearest it. McIntosh's brigade, sent to develop Early's positions at Winchester, dashed upon a Rebel camp in front of the village. The horsemen galloped through the astonished troops, capturing 16 officers and 145 enlisted men—a coup which was primarily the work of a single regiment, the Third New Jersey. The size of the captured force made the operation one of the most successful in the history of American cavalry warfare. Wilson rejoiced; at last his division was garnering favorable publicity.

Four days afterward, Ulysses Grant came to the Valley to personally initiate a decisive campaign against Early. To date, Sheridan had been unwilling to come to grips with the Confederates, and thus had little to show for his six weeks in the Shenandoah. His failure to crumple Early's understrength army had deepened the gloom with which Grant's inability to take Petersburg had infected the Union. Wilson greeted the general-in-chief at Sheridan's headquarters and, foreseeing a chance for his division to win further glory, heartily endorsed Grant's opinion that the Army of the Shenandoah should "go in" after their opponents.

In the small hours of September 19, after Grant had departed, Sheridan moved out for the showdown. He planned to strike Early in front of Winchester and break his army into human flotsam.

Wilson's division led the Federal advance, clearing a path for the infantry. His orders called for him to move up the pike which ran to Winchester, wrest control of the Opequon Creek crossings from the enemy, and move a short distance toward the town through a ravine which lay between Winchester and the creek. Since only infantry could

negotiate the ravine where it narrowed close to the town, it was impera-
tive that the cavalry capture the Confederate outposts at its mouth,
enabling the foot soldiers to reach the maneuverable terrain farther on.
While the Third Division did its work, Sheridan's other mounted units
would ford the Opequon above Wilson's crossing and threaten the
Rebels' right flank.

Wilson did his job admirably. At dawn General McIntosh's men
rushed over the Opequon, charged through the ravine, fought mounted
and on foot against Rebel cavalry, and succeeded in capturing the
earthworks which covered the western entrance of the defile. Many
Confederates became casualties and captives, although McIntosh's
brigade also suffered heavily.

The infantry now had a clear path toward the town. However, it
could not use it right away. Supply wagons, mistakenly directed along
the army's route of march, slowed the advance of the VI Corps to a
shuffle. Hours passed before the Corps could sort itself out and move
through the ravine, followed by the XIX Corps. Part of the VIII Corps
was at first held south of the creek to block Early's retreat, should the
Confederates be routed. The first foot soldiers to enter the gorge found
Wilson's men still at their posts, their guidons staked atop the captured
earthworks.

In due course Wilson's troopers were ordered to form on the left
flank of the VI Corps. From that sector they watched Sheridan's attack
at last go forward just before noontime. As the infantry drove toward
the Confederates, the Third Cavalry Division swept around the Rebel
right and late in the afternoon opened fire with its Spencers. The enemy
was stunned by the flanking movement, and began to waver. Deceived
by the volume of carbine fire into believing that all of Sheridan's horsemen had massed in that area, Early dispatched his own cavalry in
force, to stop Wilson. Later, as the battle raged all along the line, the
Confederate commander also grew concerned about his other flank,
which Merritt's cavalry and some infantry units had begun to roll up.
Soon Early saw that retreat was inevitable.

Early's horsemen, led by Major General Stephen D. Ramseur, yet
another of Wilson's Academy classmates, were able to neutralize the
Federal threat by fighting long and desperately. In the thick of the
action, both of Wilson's brigade commanders were wounded, Chapman
by a spent bullet and McIntosh by a slug which smashed his leg below
the knee and caused its amputation. Reinforcements were sent to Wilson, but gathering darkness made fighting in that area indecisive and
valueless. As night came on, Early massed his army along a pike lead-

ing south, which Ramseur managed to keep free of Federals. Time and again Wilson tried to cut across Early's retreat route, but his frustration was not relieved; he simply could not overcome the frantic, last-ditch efforts of his opponents. Despite his rage, he was held a mile and a half from the important avenue of withdrawal.

Finally, Wilson recalled his units for the night. The next day the Third Division, with the rest of Sheridan's army, resumed the pursuit. Again Wilson led the way, but because rough terrain slowed his progress and since the Rebel rear guard—infantry and cavalry—put up fierce resistance, he was unable to bring the enemy to bay.

Even so, the Federals' victory had been overwhelming, and the Third Division had done a particularly effective job. As Wilson later remarked, Winchester was the first large action of the war in which foot soldiers and cavalrymen were employed in proper conjunction. Sheridan had been ordered to defeat Early and he had done so precisely and soundly.

But the little Irishman could not be content with anything short of his enemy's destruction. His pursuit continued. On the twenty-first he sent Wilson south to attack Early's rear guard at Front Royal. The Third Division encountered the Rebels in a dense fog which compelled its leader to issue orders exclusively by bugle. After some 250 buglers called the regiments into line and signaled the charge, the troopers shattered the Confederate force and sent its pieces scurrying southward up the Luray Valley in the direction of New Market.

That same day, joined by two-thirds of Merritt's division, Wilson went up Luray to get behind Early's army near New Market and cut off his retreat. At the same time, Sheridan moved to strike Early's main force near Strasburg, several miles farther north; he hoped to crush the battered enemy between his main army and his cavalry.

During the trip up the valley, Torbert was in overall command of Sheridan's horsemen. Unfortunately, he lacked the aggressiveness of Little Phil and Wilson, and consequently made an unpardonable blunder which permitted Early to escape. At daylight on the twenty-second he reached the town of Milford and found two brigades of Rebel horsemen under Brigadier General Williams C. Wickham blocking the pass. The Confederates held what seemed to Torbert very strong positions, their left flank skirting the Shenandoah River and their right resting on a knob of the Blue Ridge Mountains. Unaware that Sheridan had pried Early's main army out of Strasburg earlier that afternoon, and unwilling to commit himself to a costly attack on Wickham without that knowledge, Torbert decided to withdraw without a fight. Because he turned his cavalry about and went back down the valley, he permitted the Rebels to escape southward, where they were again reinforced by General Lee.

Afterward Torbert moved his troopers across the lower end of the Shenandoah Valley, where they destroyed railroad track, captured enemy-held towns, and once again started after the Rebels. After a strenuous march, during which they far outdistanced Sheridan's infantry, the Federal horsemen came upon Early's rear guard near Waynesboro late on the twenty-ninth. Here Early suddenly turned front and gave battle, realizing that the Federal cavalry had outstripped their supporting units. Torbert once again lost his nerve and ordered a quick withdrawal from the scene.

Wilson again secured the cavalry's rear until Merritt's horsemen could clear the field. When the withdrawal began, the nearest Rebel troops—infantrymen—came forth from behind roadside barricades, "their rifles flashing in the gathering gloom," as Wilson remembered, "like an innumerable swarm of fireflies."

Wilson dismounted and personally exchanged shots with the Confederates, to impress upon his men the importance of holding their ground. By now he had become expert at inspiring his men by his example. The Rebel movement halted.

After full darkness came on, Wilson remounted to make a last reconnaissance to determine if his rear echelon had managed to disengage. Riding forward alone—his staff officers having ridden off on errands—he suddenly became a common target for several enemy sharpshooters. He swung his horse around and galloped back to his retreating division, aware now that he himself was the last to withdraw.

He could see nothing in the darkness but the bursts from the Rebels' guns, and only the enemy was audible; it seemed as though his division had vanished from the land. Then he took a wrong road and landed in a deep ravine, where he was sprayed with rifle fire from two sides. Fortunately, the sunken road caused the shells to fly over his head. "I had already drawn my revolver," he later wrote, "and as I caught the flash of the nearest rifle I fired in return, aiming low and hoping to kill. My speed was fast, and yet I had time before getting clear of the enemy to empty both pistols, and this I did with as much deliberation as I could bring to the task."

Even after he had safely passed through the ravine, his ordeal was not over, for he heard horsemen approaching in the darkness. Supposing them to be Rebels, he hastily reloaded his revolvers. Then he heard a shouted challenge: "Halt! Who comes there?"

Immensely relieved, he recognized the voice of one of his colonels, who had returned with a party of men to locate him. At once he identified himself, fell in with the detachment, and rode back to the rest of the division.

Years later, looking back upon his predicament in the ravine, he described it, simply, as "the narrowest escape of my life."

WILSON'S CAMPAIGNING IN VIRGINIA was at an end. In October Sheridan would again smash Early, turning apparent Federal defeat into decisive victory at Cedar Creek. But Wilson would not be there to witness it, for on September 30 Sheridan (quite possibly at Grant's urging) relieved him from command of the Third Cavalry Division and ordered him to take control of General Sherman's cavalry in Alabama, Georgia, and Tennessee.

Wilson was ambivalent about the transfer. He had led the Third Division for more than five months and felt quite close to it. On the other hand, the new assignment meant an increase in rank (he would be assigned to duty by brevet as major general of volunteers) and it gave him command of an entire corps of horsemen. It certainly appeared to be an upward step.

He never learned precisely why Sheridan might have chosen him for the position. Although in some respects the cavalry chief thought highly of him, they never had attained an intimate association either in personal affairs or in matters of command. The tone of their relationship probably was a contributing factor. Wilson's transfer would allow Custer, Sheridan's close friend, to move up to division command.

Wilson did not know it at the time, but as he closed out his affairs in Virginia and prepared to travel west, he stood on the threshold of glory. The coming months would find him at the apex of his career, during which he would win a singular reputation as a dynamic and successful field commander.

Wilson was not particularly introspective, and did not have the ability to accurately weigh his own strengths and weaknesses. He boldly emphasized his talents as a soldier and rarely acknowledged those flaws which limited his military effectiveness. In truth, he possessed more than his share of both strong points and failings, and might have done well to assess them, to determine how he might multiply the former and diminish the latter and thus increase his chances of winning renown under Sherman.

His flaws and dubiously distinctive traits would have greatly hindered many another soldier. His most enduring characteristic was his vast personal ambition, which he had displayed time and again both in his private relationships and in his unending quest to secure position and rank, which he craved—no matter where the best interests of his country might be said to lie.

In Wilson's eyes, however, his own best interests *were* those of his country; he felt the nation was best served when it recognized, rewarded, and fully utilized the talents of its ablest defenders—including James Harrison Wilson. Thus, he thought nothing of using influence and favoritism to achieve desired goals or of manipulating those under him and (whenever possible) those who ranked him, for his own ends. He had been born and bred on the success ethic, and success was all that truly mattered to him. The Army system, which stressed the desirability of succeeding or at least covering up failure as much as possible, merely solidified his desire to advance his career by all means practicable.

Often he had to convince himself that if perceptible error was attributable to a project in which he was involved, his associates were guilty of the error, not he. Therefore, his troubles during his railroad raid were caused by Grant's inability to keep his promise (which he expressed through Meade) to secure Reams's Station, as well as by Meade's, Sheridan's, and Kautz's unwillingness to hurry reinforcements there. Neither were his troubles in the Wilderness his own fault; he had been placed in jeopardy because the main army had allowed the enemy to interpose between it and the Third Division, blocking Wilson's retreat route.

Wilson's preoccupation with success was inevitably linked to his obsessive fear of being blamed for mistakes. He was concerned not only with absolving himself of guilt when directly associated with a military performance of doubtful value. He had to divest himself of culpability in *any* situation, even when (as regards the expedition following the fall of Fort Pulaski) his being held responsible might appear highly unlikely to most observers. One can imagine Wilson worrying about such guilt to the extent of losing sleep over it. Perhaps, in the last analysis, the obsession was rooted in his personal life and family background. He came from a long line of unusually successful and enterprising men—men who had conquered an untamed land, who had been stalwarts in war as well as in civil life and seemingly capable of handling any responsibility which devolved upon them. Even Wilson's younger brothers had become war heroes and officers of great talent. He simply could not permit himself to become the first notable failure in his family. The credo he had noted when beginning his studies at West Point would remain with him throughout his life. He had to succeed, or be dishonored—"and this I could not bear."

His ability to dispose of all evidences of failure—at least to his own satisfaction—made Wilson less than modest. Being a dynamic, energetic young man who impressed others by his confidence and his impatience with ineptitude, he was generally regarded as gifted. Such regard was a large factor in building his self-esteem even further, for praise invariably swelled his ego. Like many earnest young men, he quickly won friends; and such friends, including Generals Grant and Rawlins, bolstered his faith in his own abilities by continually praising him or, at any rate, speaking words which he could usually interpret as praise.

Wilson was drawn particularly close to men such as Grant and Rawlins because he perceived them to be honest and unassuming, not forever grasping after the main chance. Yet, like many highly individualistic people, Wilson was often intolerant of individualism in others, and felt threatened by the ambitions of such singular men as Sheridan and Custer. He regarded them as out to best him in a personal contest —a race toward fame and universal esteem—and thus could not afford to be friendly with them.

He felt threatened not only by those trying to grasp rank or position which he himself coveted, but also by those whom he narrowly conceived to be trespassing upon his exclusive bailiwick. His close association with the Union's most famous general made him childishly jealous of men such as Horace Porter and Adam Badeau, who he felt were seeking to steal into his old place at Grant's right hand. Wilson considered himself Grant's ablest advisor and thus regarded others as faulty or lacking in energy—if only in comparison to himself. He could rationalize his jealousy by proclaiming that his successors were either a bad influence on the general or were so avidly self-seeking as to wish to maliciously discredit Wilson's own achievements as staff officer. The latter was a crime of which he considered Cyrus Comstock particularly guilty.

Wilson displayed a curious double standard in his attitude towards authority and rank. Since a youth (and perhaps because he had become the head of his family while in adolescence and was forced to exert authority on a par with his elders), he had displayed no awe towards those whom society regarded as his superiors. As a soldier in his mid-twenties, he still would not cowtow to rank simply on the basis of rank itself; in fact, he seemed to feel an urge to openly proclaim his lack of fear vis-à-vis established authority in uniform. His close association with General Grant ideally suited this inclination. Wilson could permit himself to be abrupt and critical towards Watson Smith during the Yazoo Pass expedition and Ambrose Burnside in Knoxville, in the belief that Grant's power would keep him safe from all possible consequences.

On the other hand—as Colonel Bryan had learned at the close of the Richmond raid—Wilson would not tolerate anyone who questioned his authority or suggested that his orders were, just possibly, ill-considered. This intolerance of criticism when exercising authority stemmed as much from his iron-handed attitude towards command as from his boundless self-esteem. He believed that a leader of mettle, who knew his ideas to be viable and appropriate, was duty-bound to make his men obey them at all times. To permit a subordinate's hesitation, to leave room for someone to second-guess him, could lead only to slackness of discipline—to disaster. And if a commander had to shout and gesticulate to his men to maintain his authority and firm control, so be it. In truth, Wilson rarely hesitated to shout when he deemed it necessary. He would berate his men in appropriate terms whenever they beat a disgraceful retreat or looted the homes of civilians.

With such character traits, Wilson drew the enmity of many who came into sustained contact with him—associates of equal rank as well as those under his command. He seemed almost to cherish his enemies and to work as hard to keep them as he did to maintain friendships with other men. Perhaps this was inevitable, for he found it supremely difficult to forgive any wrong, tangible or imaginary. He was able to assume a neutral or casual relationship with few persons; he regarded most as either strong allies or bitter foes.

Wilson's flaws were easy to find because he displayed them so dramatically and so often. But he also possessed many remarkable—perhaps less readily evident—virtues, which ably suited him for command and which would ultimately bring him a degree of glory not achieved by any other soldier as young as he.

Perhaps his strongest point was an energetic, get-things-done style, which usually produced dramatic results. His great virtue, as also his vexing limitation, was his firm belief that he could do things better than almost anyone else; and, for the most part, he may well have been correct. Certainly he was inclined to act more swiftly and more decisively than many of his military associates; the flaws which seemed to cripple other commanders most seriously—irresolution and sluggishness of action—never hampered him.

Wilson always stood ready to do what was asked of him. He could be counted on to carry out instructions, discharging all responsibilities as best he could; and he was not afraid to commit his troops to battle or to lead them into a dangerous corner if he thought such would aid the design of the general plan. Moreover, he was an able student of tactics and strategy; his wide reading in such subjects and the wealth of training he had received at West Point more fully fitted him for command than many civilian-soldiers, such as General McClernand, and older but less dynamic West Pointers such as McClellan and Burnside.

Wilson was intensely patriotic. He loved and revered his country with a fervor which had grown out of his youthful interest in American history and the principles of Constitutional law. Perhaps better than most of his associates, he understood the concepts of national union which he was fighting to maintain and the urgent necessity of doing his utmost to preserve the united democratic system.

Although a stern disciplinarian, he exercised discipline to keep his soldiers a cohesive, tight-knit force, which would assure their collective proficiency and therefore their common safety. Moreover, he was concerned about lending encouragement to his men and bolstering their morale. In the midst of battle he could be counted on to exercise a stabilizing influence by exemplifying coolness and clear thinking.

In addition to displaying solid talents in field command, Wilson had proven himself a gifted administrator, by substantially increasing the efficiency of the Cavalry Bureau and by raising the Third Division to a level of order and proficiency it rarely if ever had attained under its previous leader. Such talents would come in handy when he headed west and took charge of Sherman's sprawling, disorganized command.

Aided by such strengths, Wilson was steadily learning the skills of command, if only by trial and error. By now he had made his share of mistakes—obvious, glaring mistakes, many of them stemming from simple inexperience—and he would make even greater mistakes in future months. But he had also demonstrated intelligence, bravery, and steadfastness in command, and they too would be displayed in the campaigning that lay ahead.

His formative adventures in field command were now behind him. He had fumbled during his first campaign, in the Wilderness, through failure to make certain his men carried out all assigned orders. He had done much better at Spotsylvania, taking and for a time holding the town, unlocking a door which the Army had been unable to open wide.

He had fought vigorously at Yellow Tavern and had given a creditable account of himself in other fighting during Sheridan's raid on Richmond. He had maneuvered expertly during Grant's crossing of the Pamunkey, the Chickahominy, and the James. On his raid below Petersburg he had fumbled again—and barely avoided a disaster greater than had befallen any cavalry command—but had survived, winning the opportunity to make amends. He had done his penance in the Shenandoah Valley, achieving particular success and winning favorable publicity at Winchester.

To be sure, his record was spotty. But as an indication of the interplay of all his strengths and weaknesses—his solid talents and his unenviable shortcomings—it did not augur ill for his future. The most significant fact to be drawn from all of it—the fact of greatest importance to General Sherman and his cavalrymen—was that Wilson's career seemed definitely in its ascendant stage.

#

I Regard It as the Highest Honor Ever Paid Me

H ad William T. Sherman not lacked confidence in
cavalry power, Brevet Major General Wilson
might never have had the opportunity to display his talents in Tennessee
and later in Alabama and Georgia.

In general, Sherman was a discerning man with a sharp eye for
military talent. But he had a blind spot which prevented him from
measuring the value of his mounted troops. He felt that on occasion
they did well enough at raiding, skirmishing, and gathering intelligence.
But they could not compare with infantry in fighting potential.

It was true that Sherman's foot soldiers had won the majority of
the glory during the recently concluded campaign to chase the Confederate Army of Tennessee, now under General John Bell Hood, from
Georgia. But at present Sherman was forced to concentrate on cavalry
matters; hence Wilson's coming.

Sherman was no longer preoccupied with overwhelming his 40,000 Confederate opponents, now based in Alabama. He had already decided to turn his back on Hood and march eastward, burning out the state of Georgia and then sweeping up the Atlantic coast to link with Grant in Virginia. But he could afford to do this with only a portion of his force, for troops would have to remain behind to deal with Hood, once Hood was again ready to fight. General George Thomas could handle that job from his headquarters in Tennessee, but Thomas required the services of a capable cavalry commander, which the western armies seemed to lack.

Searching for such a commander, Sherman had immediately asked Grant for help. He would welcome the transfer of any general who had proven his ability in Virginia—including Wilson, of whom Sherman had heard fine things. Grant straightaway conferred with Meade and Sheridan, and from the meeting of their minds came the order sending Wilson west, dated October 1.

Flattering endorsements accompanied Wilson's departure from Virginia. Apparently they were calculated both to assure Sherman that a proper choice had been made in his behalf and to assuage the disappointment Wilson naturally felt at having to leave the Third Division. One of these paid Wilson what he considered the greatest compliment of his life. Grant wired Sherman on the fourth: "I believe Wilson will add fifty per cent. to the effectiveness of your cavalry." The words had the desired effect, for soon afterward, Wilson wrote Baldy Smith about his new assignment: "I regard it as the highest honor ever paid me."

From Harrisonburg, Virginia, Wilson traveled to Washington City, Baltimore, Wilmington, and Philadelphia, visiting friends and acquaintances at every stopover. His most important call was paid on the Andrews family. Despite the important assignment drawing him westward, he was sorry to have to leave Wilmington; no telling how much time would pass before he could see Ella again.

Several days later, he reached Nashville, where General Thomas had made his headquarters as "the most central point of operations" against Hood. But the greater part of Thomas's old Army of the Cumberland was with Sherman in Alabama and temporarily under the immediate command of Major General David S. Stanley.

On the twenty-third Wilson at last found Sherman, just across the Tennessee border in Gaylesville, Alabama. The commanding general was most happy to see him, and they chatted informally for some time before getting down to the case at hand. At this point, Sherman obliquely revealed his distrust of cavalry's effectiveness. He briefly mentioned Grant's recent suggestion that Wilson make the march to the sea with his new command while the rest of the army remained in position to deal with Hood. But Sherman was captivated by his desire to "make Georgia howl," and felt that cavalry alone would not be able to accomplish on the march everything he hoped to achieve with his infantry. Then, too, he believed that the thousands of soldiers he would send to Nashville before starting on the march would be entirely sufficient to cope with the Army of Tennessee.

Since horseflesh was in such short supply that little more than a division of cavalry could immediately be mounted, Sherman wished to take only that many horsemen with him through Georgia. He wanted Kilpatrick, who had been sent him when Wilson received the Third Division, to lead them: "I know Kilpatrick is a hell of a damned fool, but I want just that sort of man to command my cavalry on this expedition."

This more than faintly hinted of Sherman's prejudice against mounted soldiers. But he added that he wished the rest of the cavalry in his sphere of authority to be mounted and organized under Wilson for service in Tennessee. Magnanimously, he spoke of Wilson's new command: "Do the best you can with it, and if you make any reputation out of it I shall not undertake to divide it with you." His cavalry chief was properly grateful.

The day after their conference, Wilson was duly announced as commander of cavalry for all of Sherman's forces. The order thus detached his unit from the authority of all subordinate army commanders and also designated it the Cavalry Corps of the Military Division of the Mississippi.

Leaving Sherman's headquarters, Wilson spent several days at Marietta, Georgia, outfitting Kilpatrick's 5,000 troopers for the march. The task was made difficult by "Kil-cavalry" 's continuing recklessness with the health of his animals. Wilson grew discouraged when he found that Kilpatrick would require many more fresh mounts than expected, depriving Wilson's men of a like number. Wilson would start his reorganization at a great disadvantage.

While Kilpatrick's division was remounting, Wilson traveled to the camps near Sherman's headquarters for a look at those horsemen he would retain under his command. He saw at once that the task lying before him was considerable. His new force was roughly seven times as large as his old Third Division (and his reorganizational problems in Virginia had been formidable enough). The Cavalry Corps, M.D.M., was said to consist of seventy-two regiments—by far a greater number than any other general of comparable rank, Federal or Confederate, had ever commanded.

As if this unwieldy total was not bad enough, the units lay scattered between eastern Tennessee and southwestern Missouri. Furthermore, convalescent and dismounted troopers—the great majority of the corps—were consigned to hospitals and remount depots in several large cities such as Louisville and Saint Louis. Finally, the majority of the horsemen lacked serviceable equipment and weapons.

Another man might have thrown up his hands in defeat from the outset. Even Wilson must have considered the idea. Late in October he wrote Rawlins that his effective force should have totaled more than 20,000 but "what are the facts now? We cannot raise 6,000, and because horses, arms, and equipments have not been furnished." Soon he was pleading with his former associates in the Cavalry Bureau to rush delivery of remounts, all manner of supplies, and thousands of precious Spencer carbines.

His job did have some compensations. Like the Third Cavalry Division, his new corps was disorganized and poorly supplied, but was composed of excellent material. He could see its potential even if Sherman could not; in fighting caliber, in the potential of its men, and not in size alone, this western command might prove to be the greatest body of cavalry ever assembled in America.

Then, too, Grant had promised him the help of veteran officers from the Army of the Potomac, the selections to be Wilson's. After careful deliberation, he sought the services of men such as Custer, Ranald Mackenzie, and Emory Upton, each a West Point colleague who had shown promise in command in Virginia. He was unsuccessful, for a number of reasons, in securing the transfer of the first two, but perhaps the most talented of the candidates—Upton—replied that he would be delighted to join Wilson as soon as he recovered from battle wounds. The wounds had come at Winchester, where the youngish, neatly bearded general had led his VI Corps infantry brigade through the ravine after Wilson's troopers had secured it. Even with shrapnel pieces in his thigh, Upton had directed his soldiers onward, by barking orders from his stretcher. Talented in all arms of the service, he would be of great help, in many ways, to Wilson.

While reorganizing and remounting his corps, Wilson swept the old house clean. He transferred a number of fusty or lax subordinates including such venerable cavalrymen as Major General George Stoneman and Brigadier General Benjamin Grierson, the Vicksburg raider In their stead he placed energetic young officers whose talents were

General Emory Upton—*Photograph courtesy Library of Congress*

widely known in the Army. In so doing he caused a great deal of grumbling, most of which, of course, came from the displaced generals. But Wilson held no awe of age or rank and cared little for reputations he did not consider deserved; besides, Sherman had given him carte blanche, and therefore repercussions from such radical alterations did not trouble him.

After shuffling his personnel, Wilson called out those troopers who had mounts, inspected them with a critical eye and then, on October 26, led them on an expedition southward toward Blue Mountain, Alabama, "during which I got acquainted with . . . the bearing, behavior, equipment, and mounts of the men and gathered information about that part of the country." He did not encounter any large enemy force, but did find evidence to confirm one of General Grant's suspicions, a possibility which Sherman had discounted: Hood's army had left its base at Florence and, having been reorganized, was moving north toward the Tennessee River, undoubtedly with the intention of invading Tennessee.

When Sherman received this intelligence on the twenty-ninth, he hurriedly concentrated the 60,000 infantrymen he would take with him to the sea. Until this time he had toyed with the notion of taking Wilson and as many troopers as could be mounted, with him. Now Sherman made up his mind: the brevet major general would indeed join Thomas in Nashville.

The next day, Wilson began his trip north. Some of his cavalrymen rode with him; others, including thousands of dismounted troopers, awaited him in the Tennessee capital. Still others under his authority were stationed in dozens of nooks and crannies throughout the West.

He did not shrink from the thought of the work waiting for him in Tennessee. But he could not look forward to it cheerfully. Later he wondered: "Perhaps if I had known what was expected of me when I left camp at Harrisonburg for my new field of duty and responsibility on that bright morning of October 2, 1864, I should not have gone with a heart so buoyant."

Given the circumstances, this seems quite likely.

WHEN HE RETURNED TO THOMAS'S HEADQUARTERS on November 6, he had a long interview with his new superior. Thomas, as Sherman, gave him a free hand to reorganize the cavalry. Unlike Sherman, Thomas did so not only of necessity but also because of a genuine concern for the well-being of his mounted troops. Years before, Thomas had been a field officer in a distinguished regiment, the Second United States Dragoons, whose lieutenant colonel had been a soldier named Robert E. Lee. His experience had given Thomas an enduring interest in cavalry operations.

Wilson and he shared many views as to how horse soldiers ought to be employed. Both decried the relegation of cavalry to a defensive role; they desired to give it a full share in the waging of battle. They agreed that the horse was merely the means of transporting the soldier to the battlefield, on which he should dismount to fight with saber, pistol, and repeating carbine. They also advocated the utilization of massed cavalry to attack and hold objectives in conjunction with—not merely in preparation for—infantry power.

When their conversation focused on particulars, Thomas revealed his concern about the course which Sherman had elected to pursue. He had tried in vain to convince Sherman to permit the cavalry to prove itself by making the march through Georgia on its own. He fervently hoped that Sherman had left him troops sufficient to deal with Hood, who was generally regarded as a daring, hard-fighting commander. Yet Thomas would not have enough soldiers to face his opponents on an equal footing until all of the 40,000 infantry Sherman had promised him arrived on the scene—including Major General Andrew Jackson Smith's XVI Corps, which was based in far-off Saint Louis.

After the conference ended, Wilson mulled over Thomas's concern. Wilson did not entirely trust Sherman's judgment (for one thing, he was aware of Sherman's prejudice against cavalrymen) and was still a firm believer in Grant, who shared Thomas's worry about the menace posed by the Army of Tennessee. But Wilson must have finally decided that his only course was to serve Thomas as best he could with the materials at his command, regardless of the military situation. Soon he had immersed himself in the details of dispensing the equipment on hand, drilling those cavalrymen who had reported to Nashville, and scouring the countryside for additional horses.

His troopers reacted to his methods of reorganization in various ways. One cavalryman felt that he "set a noble example to his troops by remaining at the front and sharing the hardships and dangers with his men." Others saw him as a sobersides and a martinet, a man hard to admire. Among other things, he seemed far more concerned about horses than about their riders: "He swore that the *horses* had to be well taken care of, if the men starved," one observer wrote disgustedly, adding that such a philosophy "made the whole army despise him."

Most antagonizing was Wilson's apparent holier-than-thou manner, which had particular reference to his stand against liquor. On one occasion at about this time he found that some of his staff members had procured a demijohn of whiskey, which they had been sampling avidly. When he discovered the source of their pleasure, Wilson ordered the owner of the jug to dash it to the ground. His officers regarded him silently as the demijohn was thrown down and shattered, and for several days thereafter, as Wilson reported, they "scarcely spoke to me." Yet this did not concern him as much as the upholding of his authority.

One can see that this aspect of Wilson's personality won him few friends. Since youth he had hated drinking with a passion and was convinced that under no circumstances—certainly none concerning an army in the field—did it serve a useful purpose. In general, he was undoubtedly correct. But he never allowed room for others' opinions. Too often he remained unaware that he was forcing his own moral philosophy on the men under him, using his established authority to make it stick.

Despite making enemies along the way, Wilson succeeded in creating a system out of near-chaos. His command took on particular shape and substance on November 9, when he announced orders regarding the formation of divisions. Eight such units were originally projected, but through lack of serviceable horses only seven were eventually organized, six of which were under his immediate authority (Kilpatrick's was nominally under his command but, being with Sherman, was of course beyond Wilson's reach). The division commanders were Brigadier Generals Edward M. McCook, Eli Long, Upton, Edward Hatch, Richard W. Johnson, and Joseph F. Knipe. All were men of energy and ability, and only the last two were older than Wilson by more than ten years; he found it easier to work with men approximately his own age—men whose ambitions he could better understand and whose abilities he could more accurately gauge.

Seeing that his efforts at reorganization were bearing fruit, he informed Thomas blithely that his program would be completed by November 12. But when that day arrived, only 4,300 mounted cavalrymen were in the field; and they had been there for some time. These were Hatch's Fifth Division, some 2,500 troopers, and two brigades—one from the First Division, about 1,000 strong, under Brigadier General John T. Croxton, and the other from the Sixth Division, led by Colonel Horace Capron and consisting of 800 riders.

All of these, under the overall supervision of General Hatch, had recently moved from the western part of the state to the vicinity of Pulaski, a town about 75 miles south of Nashville and not far from the Alabama border. They were keeping watch on the northward-marching Rebels (who by now had crossed the Tennessee River) and were working in close cooperation with the bulk of the infantry sent to Tennessee by General Sherman. The 23,000 foot soldiers confronting Hood included part of Major General John McAllister Schofield's XXIII Corps and all of General Stanley's IV Corps, with Schofield holding the top command.

Schofield's soldiers did their best to observe the enemy's approach. Although Thomas had ordered them to avoid a battle, they were also directed to slow the Rebel invasion by any means practicable, so that Smith's corps could reach Nashville and insure its safety. The major portion of the reconnaissance chores fell inevitably to the cavalry; General Hatch did a fine job of gathering and evaluating all necessary intelligence.

However, Hatch's men were vastly outnumbered by their more than 10,000 opponents in the Confederate cavalry, and during a series of skirmishes below and then above Pulaski the Federals were forced into a retreat. Hatch's difficulties stemmed from the talents of his opposite number in gray, Major General Nathan Bedford Forrest, the "Wizard of the Saddle." A hulking, heavily bearded former slave dealer from Tennessee, Forrest had never read a military textbook, yet was the most consistently successful commander of mounted troops produced by the war.

On November 21 Wilson left Nashville, where many of his cavalrymen remained dismounted and idle, to assume command of those horse soldiers facing Forrest. He must have felt quite uneasy. He was on the verge of seeing his first action in the West as a corps leader. But more than half of his force was not available for service and those few with horses and equipment were pitted against a corps of veteran Confederates led by a renowned fighter.

He arrived on the scene of action, several miles north of Pulaski, on the twenty-third, and at once superseded Hatch. Carefully observing the approach of his enemy, he continued Hatch's retrograde movement, conforming to the withdrawal of Schofield's infantry. The next day both troopers and foot soldiers retired to the town of Columbia, thirty miles north of Pulaski and just below a bend in the Duck River. Forming on the north bank of the stream while Schofield at first remained on the shore below, Wilson was somewhat cheered by the arrival of several regiments fresh from the remount camp at Louisville, Kentucky. Any reinforcements were welcome.

But he was still outnumbered by a wide margin, and his present task was formidable. The safety of Schofield's force and the defense of Nashville depended, to a great extent, on the vigilance of his troopers. He was particularly concerned for the safety of his friend and commander, Thomas, and wished to perform creditably before his eyes—as he had once wished to favorably impress General Grant. Therefore he positioned his troopers with a view toward observing the Duck River fords east of Columbia, as far in that direction as Huey's Mill. In that sector Hood was likely to advance along a route which Wilson believed would carry him to Nashville and perhaps to the Federal-held territory beyond. Wilson also realized that if the Confederates could move into upper Tennessee, cross the Ohio River, and invade Kentucky as well, the Federal war effort would face a crisis of epic proportions.

For all of his precautions, Wilson quickly found himself in trouble. Forrest's cavalry, in advance of Hood's main army, came up to the lower shore of the river, influencing Schofield to move to the other bank and to emplace his men west of Wilson's headquarters. But Wilson did not expect the Rebel cavalry to force a crossing of the river so soon afterward. Citizens of the area reported the stream too swollen to be forded; Wilson believed them. No doubt he also believed that his picket force was sufficiently strong and vigilant to delay any such attempt long enough to permit the infantry to come up.

Therefore he was shocked when, shortly before noon on the twenty-eighth, he received a report that Rebel horsemen were already splashing through the river near Huey's Mill, five miles east of Columbia. On the basis of previous intelligence, he could only tell Schofield: "I can scarcely credit this, though will find out at once."

Riding to the sector in question, he found that the report had been painfully accurate. A firefight had broken out there between troops under General Croxton and a much stronger contingent of Confederates. Forrest had succeeded in crossing near Huey's, overwhelming pickets under Colonel Capron, who had been posted below the stream, and isolating other Federal units along the line of the so-called Lewisburg and Franklin Turnpike, which ran northward from the river. In fact, at four divergent points east of Columbia Rebel horsemen were forcing their way across the Duck River, threatening to crumple the Federal left flank. By all indications, it was going to be a rough day for the Cavalry Corps, M.D.M.

Cursing the scarcity of horseflesh which had made him such an underdog, Wilson pulled his men to safer positions. He did this so hastily that some units, who were slow to get the word, found themselves cut off at the river and encircled by the enemy.

In his eagerness to withdraw, Wilson made the most serious tactical error of his military career. Instead of falling back via routes which would enable him to fulfill his primary job—to serve as the eyes and ears of the army—he led his troopers up the Lewisburg Pike, in a direction that carried them far from Schofield's main force above Columbia. In placing himself in a position from which he could not readily inform Schofield about the enemy's movements, he compounded his errors in misjudging Forrest's capabilities and those of his own pickets at the river.

He frantically tried to regroup his cavalry along the pike, but Forrest's swift pursuit at least temporarily prevented this. Farther and farther north raced the Federal horsemen, while along Duck River some of their isolated comrades hung on desperately, temporarily preventing a portion of Forrest's command from crossing in their front.

On his retreat, Wilson did send a courier to Schofield with the news of Forrest's crossing, and he added some very significant information: Forrest was moving north along a path which would enable him to turn in Schofield's rear near Spring Hill. The last-named was a hamlet eleven miles above Columbia; the towns were connected by a broad road, important to Schofield as a line of retreat. Wilson stressed Spring Hill's importance by telling Schofield—quite rightly—to "look out for that place."

Wilson repeated the warning later that afternoon, by which time he had succeeded in regrouping his cavalry at Hurt's Crossroads, along the pike. He reported, first, that Forrest's men, still in hot pursuit, had clashed with his rear guard all along the pike. But he hoped to hang onto his new position and keep the Rebels from driving farther northward. Then—at I A.M. on the twenty-ninth—he informed Schofield that Hood's infantry was reported ready to cross the river, too: "I think it very clear that they are aiming for Franklin, and that you ought to get to Spring Hill by 10 A.M." Wilson assumed this would be sufficient to convince Schofield to pull back to the hamlet. While Schofield did so, Wilson would hold the pike and thus protect the army's flank.

Because of slow couriers, General Schofield did not receive Wilson's latest dispatch until sunrise on the twenty-ninth. By that time he was more concerned with ascertaining the whereabouts of Hood's forces than with securing Spring Hill. Hood's dispositions remained a mystery to Schofield, for his cavalry scouts had been driven apart from him. Fearing for the situation in his front, Schofield did not take time to ponder the perilous situation in his rear.

Hood's infantry had crossed Duck River east of Columbia, but Schofield did not know this. Therefore, when he received Wilson's urgent dispatch, instead of withdrawing his main army, he sent out scouting patrols to bring word of Hood's crossing. Finally, in partial response to Wilson's message, he sent a small force—two divisions of the IV Corps, under General Stanley—to Spring Hill. He ordered Stanley to entrench at the little village and guard the army's wagon train, which soon would be sent there too.

One of the main reasons for Schofield's decision to remain at the river with most of his army was a telegram he had received the evening before from General Thomas in Nashville: "If you are confident you can hold your present position, I wish you to do so until I can get General Smith here." Not sharing Wilson's great concern for Spring Hill, Schofield thought he could delay Hood's movement across the river until nightfall, thus aiding Thomas. Even after he had received confirmation of Hood's crossing, Schofield felt he could prevent most of Hood's men from getting over and keep those Rebels already across from moving very far north.

Meanwhile, Wilson's situation was worsening. By the morning of the twenty-ninth, he had assembled most of his men at Hurt's Cross-roads—including many of the once-isolated troopers, who the night before had cut their way free from the enemy at the river. But not even a united Federal command could withstand Forrest's pressure. Some time after dawn the Confederates again struck Wilson's rear guard, dismounting to exchange carbine fire with the Federals. Wilson had already retreated much too far, but he saw that he would have to withdraw even farther. He drew his men into columns and led them five miles north to Mount Carmel.

At Mount Carmel, too, the Confederates struck the rear echelon. By now Wilson must have felt enraged as well as harassed; would Forrest never let up? The answer came sooner than he expected. The fierce skirmish that broke out lasted but a short time, and then, abruptly and mysteriously, ended. Suddenly the wooded area south of Wilson's position was very quiet.

Had the Confederates retreated? Wilson rode forward with scouts and searched about, but was greeted only by light carbine fire. Most of Forrest's soldiers had indeed drawn off—somewhere. Perhaps they were moving to get in the Federals' rear. But Wilson quickly discounted that possibility, and then had a fearful thought: Forrest might have skirted his flank entirely and galloped northward to attack General Thomas and thinly defended Nashville.

The prospect must have pained Wilson acutely. What would Thomas say if Wilson had allowed his opponents to sneak around him and menace the very city which the army was most concerned in protecting?

Feverishly Wilson remounted his command and pushed toward Franklin and Nashville. Not all of his subordinates approved of the decision; some felt Forrest might have turned westward toward Spring Hill. But Wilson could only concern himself with the possibility that he had put General Thomas's safety in jeopardy. Furthermore, Spring Hill no longer worried him; he assumed that Schofield had followed his advice and by now had all or most of the infantry there.

Still out of touch with the main army, Wilson raced toward Franklin at top speed. En route, passing directly east of Spring Hill, he heard firing coming from that direction. Perhaps a portion of Forrest's command had gone there, after all. But he kept riding, fearing that most of the Confederate cavalry had stolen a march on him, making him look inept—a stigma he could not bear.

He reached the town of Franklin late in the day, but did not find any Rebels in the vicinity or, for that matter, farther north. When his scouts turned up no evidence that any enemy riders had passed that way at any time during the day, Wilson was entirely mystified. He had the vague but unpleasant notion that he had been cozened, though he could not have said how.

The truth was that Forrest never intended to ride northward to challenge General Thomas on his own. Late that morning he had withdrawn from Wilson's rear to move directly to Spring Hill, leaving behind only a token force to hold Wilson in place. His plan had worked better than he knew. Not only had he chased the Federal cavalry away from Duck River and interposed between them and their main army, but he had sneaked into Schofield's rear without being molested by Wilson. By holding Spring Hill long enough for the rest of Hood's soldiers to come up, Forrest could destroy Schofield's army. Sooner or later, Schofield would have to move northward to rejoin General Thomas. Blocking his only retreat route, the Confederates could crush him to death.

Thus, the initial phase of the Confederates' plan had worked well. It continued to progress smoothly when Hood left one infantry corps at Columbia to occupy Schofield's attention, then sent two others along

Forrest's route toward Spring Hill. Schofield was fooled; he remained unaware of the threat to his rear.

Just as it reached the crucial stage, however, the Rebels' plan faltered. They did not expect to find even a small force at Spring Hill, and thus General Stanley's well-entrenched soldiers beat back Forrest's attack early that afternoon (the noise of which Wilson heard while riding toward Franklin). When the bulk of Hood's infantry came up at 4 P.M., it too was stopped abruptly. Stymied by conflicting and incoherent battle orders, the foot soldiers—who ought to have overwhelmed Stanley with ease—could not capture the hamlet, pry the Federals out of it, or even move across the Spring Hill road to separate Stanley from Schofield. The short winter day drew to a close before Hood could remedy the situation.

Finally, Schofield perceived the danger at his back. He started his men northward at 5 P.M., which should have been too late, but was not.

The Federals moved through the night, although they could spy the glow of the enemy's campfires a few miles east of the road. Those few miles had spared them; by hard marching they evaded Hood's trap and moved northward to safety.

Schofield and Stanley went as far as Franklin, which they reached at dawn on the thirtieth. Soon afterward the Confederates awoke and found them missing. Enraged and frustrated, Hood ordered a speedy pursuit.

When Schofield reached Franklin, Wilson was there. His trip north from Mount Carmel, in fancied pursuit of Forrest, had accomplished nothing except to place him in the proper spot to reunite with the Federal infantry. In his eagerness to save his command by any possible route, and because of his obsession to protect Nashville, Wilson had left the foot soldiers sightless and vulnerable; only a military miracle had saved him from being largely responsible for a disaster.

However, Wilson was eager to make amends for his sins of omission and commission during the past two days. He sent his troopers along the north bank of the Harpeth River, which flowed above Franklin, to guard Schofield's flanks, rear, and wagon trains. Croxton's single brigade was positioned below the stream. Most of the cavalry, however, were deployed on the left flank of the army, the body of which remained below the Harpeth in and near the village.

Schofield took cold comfort from Wilson's dispositions. Angered by the cavalry's ineptitude, he wired General Thomas on the morning of the thirtieth: "I do not know where Forrest is. He may have gone

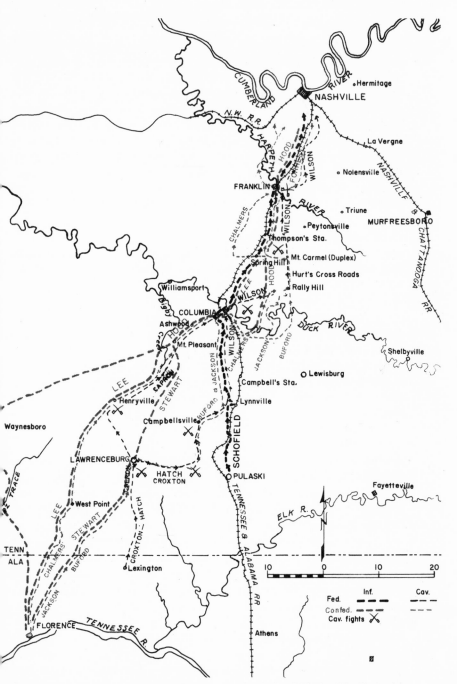

Routes of the Union and Confederate Forces in the Spring Hill-Franklin Campaign

east, but, no doubt, will strike our flank and rear again soon. Wilson is entirely unable to cope with him." This dispatch must have set Wilson's teeth on edge, for he had worked so hard to avoid receiving a bad report, which would inevitably cross Thomas's desk.

Wilson's determination to better his record was mighty. When the Confederates came up to the Harpeth that morning, Forrest's cavalry initiated the fighting. Two of his divisions struck Croxton's men, who were stationed along the Lewisburg Pike. However, General Hood had decided to send the rest of the cavalry to face the extreme Federal right, where they ultimately saw little action. Thus, for the first time, Wilson fought Forrest on approximately equal terms.

At first the Federals were again hard-pressed. Croxton's brigade resisted the attack until 2 P.M. and then, on Wilson's orders, withdrew north of the river. There it joined Hatch's cavalry and some other units which this very day had joined Wilson from the remount camps. The combined force then prepared to meet Forrest's advance.

Fighting furiously, the Confederate commander forced his way across the Harpeth, aiming to strike Schofield's rear and cut off his retreat route toward Nashville. For a time he placed Wilson's position in jeopardy. But today he could not exploit his initial advantage. The battle raged for most of the afternoon, but shortly after five o'clock, the dismounted Federals were able to throw the Rebels back across the river and to keep them there. For the first time in his career, Nathan Bedford Forrest had been forced into a withdrawal after a battle against approximately equal odds.

While the cavalry fought, the opposing infantry forces grappled with each other with particular savagery. Hood's opening attack was successful, but finally was stalled by Federal reinforcements. Their entrenched infantry and the strategically placed artillery tore the Rebels to shreds, and no fewer than six Confederate generals were killed or mortally wounded.

Early that evening the Federals found the opportunity to cross the Harpeth and march toward Nashville. A night of travel would carry them to safety behind Thomas's fortifications. There—even if General Smith's corps had not yet arrived—they ought to be able to contest a further advance by Hood.

At the start of the withdrawal, Wilson reached Schofield's headquarters and found the army commander in an enthusiastic mood. He greeted Wilson warmly—as well he might, for Wilson's tenacity had kept the all-important retreat route open. In fact, Schofield acted as though he had had no reservations whatsoever about his cavalry's effectiveness and had never doubted Wilson's command abilities in a telegram to General Thomas. He told Wilson: "Your success is most important; it insures the safety of this army. . . ."

And so, once again, success had removed the mark of failure and culpability which for a time had stained Wilson. But Wilson alone knew just how close he had come to being branded indelibly, and the realization sobered him. Above all else, he wished no repeat performance.

★IX★

Dang It to Hell, Wilson,
Didn't I Tell You
We Could Lick 'Em?

T he march from Franklin to Nashville was not without incident. During Wilson's withdrawal— his men held their positions till most of Schofield's foot soldiers could disengage and then fell in to protect their rear and flanks—Forrest came up with some of his troopers and struck the end of the column, hoping to gain a measure of revenge. He failed miserably. Wilson's men immediately changed front, soundly thrashed the Rebels, and chased them off— demonstrating that they had acquired an amount of self-confidence which made them hard to defeat, even by the Wizard of the Saddle.

The march continued along various roads and country lanes to within a few miles of Nashville, where the Federals rested, in relative comfort and safety, for the night. About daylight on December 1 they entered the city and took up positions behind its extensive works.

Wilson's men did not remain in the city proper. That evening they trotted across the bridge over the Cumberland River and went into camp near the suburb of Edgefield. There they could rest, refit, and absorb those recently remounted troopers who had reported to Thomas during his main army's absence.

After encamping his troopers, Wilson reported to Thomas and from him received heartiest congratulations for his role in the great victory at Franklin. The general said nothing of Schofield's uncomplimentary dispatch of the day before. He too could afford to be gracious, for the main army had delayed Hood long enough to permit Andrew Jackson Smith's corps to approach within supporting distance of the city. Thomas had few worries now. If Hood could be decisively defeated by 23,000 soldiers, as at Franklin, he ought to be no match for the almost 40,000 Federals now in or near Nashville.

Because of such confidence, Thomas could allow General Hood to make the next move. And in the interim, he could give his attention to administrative matters. He was especially interested in reorganizing the cavalry, for he projected a large role for his horse soldiers in any future campaigning. Therefore, on the very day that Wilson reached Edgefield, Thomas wired Grant in Virginia that he would not consider confronting the Army of Tennessee, which was already moving north from Franklin, until all the cavalry could be remounted and re-equipped.

Grant relayed the message to President Lincoln, General Halleck, Secretary Stanton, and other high government officials. Their reaction was sharp. Stanton quickly replied to the lieutenant general: "The President feels solicitous about the disposition of General Thomas to lay in fortifications for an indefinite period 'until Wilson gets equipments.' This looks like the McClellan and Rosecrans strategy of do nothing and let the rebels raid the country. The President wishes you to consider the matter."

Grant did consider the matter, and came to agree with his superiors. He had never been on the most cordial terms with General Thomas, and felt he possessed some critical failings. Primarily, he thought Thomas prone to move slowly when speed was an urgent necessity. At present he worried that Thomas might remain in Nashville so long that the Confederates would slip around his flank, cross the Cumberland River, and penetrate Federal defenses in Kentucky.

Accordingly, on December 2, he dashed off a wire to Thomas, in which he alluded to Hood's possible intentions: "Should he attack you it is all well, but if he does not you should attack him before he fortifies." That same day he wrote again, stressing the need for quick action: "You will now suffer incalculable injury . . . if Hood is not speedily disposed of. . . ."

Thomas was not alarmed. He knew that Hood had been much weakened at Franklin and now stood little chance of moving his entire army over the river before troops from Nashville could contest them—if he had such a maneuver in mind at all, which Thomas doubted. In Thomas's mind, Grant and the Washington officials were inordinately and unnecessarily concerned.

This difference of opinion between Thomas and Grant left Wilson in a difficult situation; never before had his loyalties been placed in such conflict. He had long been a Grant partisan and the lieutenant general remained his great friend as well as his mentor. But by this time he had been serving directly under Thomas for two months—had known him personally for a year—and felt quite close to him, too. For a number of reasons, he may now have felt closer to him than to Grant. His natural inclination was to take the part of his immediate commander, the general who exercised the greatest power over his military career. Moreover, he had long admired Thomas's soldierly ways (Thomas even looked the part of the warrior; Grant did not), and his sympathy was particularly drawn by Thomas's interest in cavalry warfare. By this time, too, Wilson's once idol-like worship of Grant may have diminished. Grant had made what Wilson considered unforgivable strategic errors which had injured Wilson's career and personally wounded his feelings. Foremost of these, in Wilson's mind, was Grant's inability to make good on the Army's promise to secure Reams's Station, which had caused the Third Division much embarrassment as well as danger during the Petersburg railroads raid.

Whatever the extent of his friendship with Thomas, Wilson endorsed his plan of wait-and-see, especially since it would provide him with much-needed time to refurbish the cavalry. He, too, felt that Grant and the Washington authorities were obsessed with the thought of speed. Better to proceed cautiously and prudently and thereby make certain that in the coming compaign they would neutralize Hood's threat.

During the first week and a half in December Wilson organized his new arrivals into brigades, and "clothes were drawn for the men, the horses were rested, reshod and well fed, extra shoes were fitted, new arms were issued, old ones were repaired, and equipments of every kind were put in order." He kept in daily touch with his commander, informing him of the steps taken to improve the condition of the corps and what work remained to be done.

His program was complicated by several problems, one of them posed by Governor Johnson of Tennessee, who recently had been elected vice-president of the United States and would be sworn into office, under Lincoln, in March. He and Wilson clashed over the latter's ideas about regimental efficiency.

Wilson believed that the regiments under his authority were of fine quality—with the exception of twelve. These were the state units which Johnson had succeeded in pressing into one-year service following Wilson's departure from the Cavalry Bureau. Passing time had not improved the caliber of the regiments, for the Tennesseans were still fond of deserting; upon his arrival in Nashville, Wilson found less than half of them on hand for duty.

He thought it best to cashier the Tennessee commanders and replace them with more capable officers with whom he had become familiar. That done, he would incorporate all the regiments into his field divisions rather than allow them to continue serving as a glorified bodyguard to the vice president-elect.

Before Wilson carried out his plans, however, Thomas suggested he talk things over with Johnson himself. Accordingly, Wilson visited the Tennessee Executive Mansion and politely sought Johnson's opinions on the subject. Their conference soon degenerated into a confrontation in which the gentlemen hurled invective at one another. Johnson felt that Wilson wished to malign the reputation of the Tennessee soldiers. Wilson replied that the soldiers themselves had done that job, and well. The interview closed with no appreciable result other than the fact that a long-standing personal feud had been revived. Afterward, Wilson went out and reorganized the Tennesseans exactly as he had intended.

Another of Wilson's pressing difficulties was the scarcity of serviceable horses. During the Spring Hill/Franklin campaign, hundreds of mounts had broken down. Within a week after returning to Nashville, on the other hand, the number of Federal troopers had increased to about 10,000—without a comparable increase in fresh animals. With the officials in Washington clamoring for an early campaign, Wilson realized that only so much time remained in which he might secure mounts; and he dismissed the thought of again taking the field with only a fraction of the soldiers in his command.

To some degree, he had brought these troubles upon himself. The stringent standards he had imposed upon horses contracted for by the Cavalry Bureau had resulted in a shortage of qualified animals and a consequent insufficiency of horses available to field troops.

Fortunately, General Grant came to the rescue. He persuaded Secretary Stanton to give Wilson authority to impress all available

horses in Tennessee and Kentucky, as well as "every species of property necessary to put your command in an efficient condition." Greatly
relieved, Wilson at once drafted the formal orders, and between December 5 and 9, several of his regiments hunted down all privately
owned mounts, including every hack, omnibus, and carriage horse in
Nashville and Louisville. Representatives of the Quartermaster's Department handed their owners vouchers promising future compensation
by the government.

The cavalrymen blockaded cities where seizure orders were in
effect, to prevent riders from escaping with serviceable animals. Then
the troopers went to work. One soldier, who entered Louisville, later
recalled: "Horses were taken out of stables, street cars, wagons and
buses, and in the afternoon they were found in cellars, parlors, garrets,
and all sorts of out-of-the-way places, where their owners had hidden
them."

Wilson's activities angered a number of departmental commanders, including Brigadier General Stephen Burbridge, who headed the
District of Kentucky. Burbridge was preparing to repel what he saw as
an impending Confederate invasion of his bailiwick, and thus was concerned about gathering enough horses to mount his own troops.
Rumors later indicated that he went so far as to steal several hundred
of the horses seized by Wilson's men and corralled in Lexington, Kentucky prior to shipment to Nashville. No doubt Burbridge protested to
his superiors about the impressment of other animals in his area, but
his shouts must have fallen on deaf ears. For one thing, General Grant
had a low opinion of Burbridge's abilities and only one half-hour after
securing War Department permission for the impressment, he asked
Stanton if Burbridge ought not to be relieved of his post. In the end,
Burbridge stayed on, but had no power to stop Wilson's men from
spiriting away Kentucky horses.

Few animals indeed escaped seizure. A traveling circus playing
Nashville lost its trick riding horses. Even the spirited bays who pulled
the carriage of Andrew Johnson were commandeered, much to their
owner's chagrin. Johnson felt—perhaps with justification—that Wilson
had ordered their seizure as a means of further antagonizing him. Later
he complained vociferously to General Thomas, but without recovering
his horses. Soon afterward associates heard Johnson refer bitterly to
Wilson as a "bumptious puppy."

The practice may have been drastic, but it yielded desired results
—some 7,000 horses. Within a few days Wilson was able to mount two
full divisions and to remount all of Hatch's troopers, for an aggregate

saddled force of 12,000. But at that juncture two-thirds of McCook's division was called to southwestern Kentucky to chase guerrilla raiders, leaving only one of its brigades, Croxton's, within Wilson's reach. Even so, the cavalry corps had been noticeably strengthened; it was now at its most efficient level. On December 9 Wilson told Thomas that in two days he would be able to resume offensive operations.

By then, Hood's army had moved into siege positions a few miles below Nashville. Realizing that the city was now too strongly held to take by assault, the Confederate commander waited to receive a Federal advance and indicated no intention of moving over the Cumberland River into Kentucky.

Hood seemed to feel that he was obliged to meet Thomas in battle on Thomas's own terms—as though he were in a position from which he could completely destroy the Federals. His logic was hard for his opponents to fathom; by all indications the outnumbered Rebels were in anything but a secure spot. But, thankful for such favors as this, General Thomas fully accepted Hood's challenge and made plans to strike him as soon as Wilson's people were ready.

Then the unavoidable occurred. On December 9 a winter storm, gusting snow and sleet over the countryside, swept down upon both armies, temporarily ending thoughts of combat. The ground froze and snow drifted into great piles, and the Federals scurried into warm corners of their lines while their enemy huddled miserably inside field tents.

The weather struck the cavalry severely; many horses froze to death, and those not affected by the chill could not easily negotiate the frost-covered earth. In consequence, Wilson could not carry out Thomas's order to break camp outside Edgefield, recross the Cumberland, and take position with the infantry at Nashville.

Word of this further delay in operations quickly reached Washington, intensifying the fears of the government. If Thomas did not move out at once and initiate battle, the officials believed, Hood would slip away through the storm and create havoc farther north. Their worries were reflected in Northern newspaper reports which predicted a Confederate invasion of hitherto inviolate Federal soil.

On a national scale, in fact, the Union was in a state of concern. The war in Virginia was dragging on without Federal triumph imminent; Sherman was driving through Georgia without thus far having achieved any dramatic success; and the price of gold was rising—a signal that the country seemed to be losing faith in the value of the Yankee wartime dollar.

Displaying symptoms of the prevalent mood, Grant buffeted Thomas with a storm of telegrams, each more agitated than the preceding, urging him to attack Hood. When Grant sent an especially anxious wire, Thomas decided to call a conference of his corps commanders. On the evening of the tenth, the generals assembled at his headquarters in the St. Cloud Hotel, where he read Grant's positive order to attack. After stating his desire to obey only after the bad weather had fully subsided, he asked for his subordinates' opinions. Wilson felt that although Thomas would be relieved to have them endorse his view, he did seem genuinely interested in hearing them speak their minds.

Since Wilson was the junior corps commander, he was given the honor of speaking first. All eyes turned toward his place at the foot of Thomas's command table. Everyone knew of Wilson's close association with Grant; they did not fully know the extent of his regard for his new commander. They were silent, waiting for him to speak.

Wilson may well have done some deep thinking during that silent interval. But finally, in a clear voice, he endorsed Thomas's opinion. He added a graphic argument to support his stand: if troops tried to charge across the ice-covered battlefield, their first volley would send them slipping and sliding in every direction.

One by one, the other generals had their say. Each granted that Wilson had made a strong point, and they joined him in concurring wholeheartedly with Thomas's view of the situation.

Relieved that the decision had been made, the generals donned their overcoats and gloves and went back through the snow to rejoin their commands. All of them, that is, but Wilson, whom Thomas asked to remain for a few minutes.

Thomas was most grateful for Wilson's support; his may well have been the most welcome of all, precisely because of his relationship with the general-in-chief. Now, when they were alone, Thomas released his pent-up feelings about the high command in the capital: "Wilson," he lamented, "the Washington authorities treat me as if I were a boy. They seem to think me incapable of planning a campaign or of fighting a battle, but if they will just let me alone till thawing weather begins and the ground is in condition for us to move at all I will show them what we can do." In a particularly determined voice, he added: "I am sure my plan of operations is correct, and that we shall lick the enemy, if he only stays to receive our attack."

Again Wilson assured him that he wholly believed in the wisdom of withholding the attack. Their conversation then grew more chatty and lasted for some hours, before Wilson at last left headquarters and recrossed the river to Edgefield.

Thomas's concern about the fears of his superiors was justified. The day before the conference—unknown to him—Grant and Stanton had worked out a plan to relieve him of his command and compel his successor to move at once against the enemy. But, soon after drafting the necessary orders, Grant received word from Thomas that he would march out of Nashville as soon as humanly possible, perhaps the next day, and he decided to withhold the orders at the last minute.

But Thomas could not advance on the tenth, for ice still coated the ground, hindering the movements of soldiers, horses, artillery, and wagons. The day afterward, however, the weather began to moderate, the earth to thaw. On the morning of the twelfth, Wilson was able to recross the river with his cavalry and take up positions outside Nashville.

All of Thomas's soldiers were ready to move by the morning of the fifteenth. By then the battle plan was smooth and polished. Four infantry units would head southeastward toward the enemy—the corps of Smith, Schofield, and Major General Thomas J. Wood (who had relieved Stanley, wounded at Spring Hill, in command of the IV Corps), and two divisions under Major General James B. Steedman. Steedman held the Federal left, and Wilson's cavalry the far right.

As at Franklin, Wilson's task was made easier by the Confederate battle plan. General Hood had directed 60 percent of his cavalry, under Forrest, to make a two-day march in what would prove a futile attempt to capture the Federal garrison at Murfreesboro. A single division of horsemen, led by Brigadier General James Ronald Chalmers, remained to contest Wilson.

Though unaware of Forrest's absence, Wilson was confident that his men would succeed in their endeavors. He had taken several steps to assure this. First, he had personally oriented his division and brigade commanders to the ground they would cover this day. Then, he had assembled the subordinates at his headquarters, where he verbally discussed the dispositions. To further insure a flawless operation, he had given each commander a copy of the orders. Finally, a staff officer had been instructed to lead each division into a position in which it could conform to the general plan.

In spite of so many precautions, things began badly for the troops along the Federal right when ordered to move out at seven o'clock on the morning of December 15. A thick fog had settled upon the ground, delaying the advance of both cavalry and infantry for an hour and a half. Then, when the mist dissipated, a division from Smith's corps marched across Wilson's front just as the 12,000 cavalrymen prepared to push forward. The mistake postponed the army's advance until almost ten o'clock and sent Wilson into a towering rage. Once again he saw himself as an orderly, methodical soldier surrounded by the sloppiness and incompetence of others.

When the confusion finally abated, the advance got under way with a fair degree of precision. Hatch's Fifth Division trotted alongside Smith's corps, Knipe's Seventh Division remained to their rear along the so-called Harding Pike, and thousands of other troopers—including a brigade which still lacked horses—moved down the pikes farther to the west.

The fighting on the right began when Hatch's division crossed a deep creek and encountered Rebel infantry farther to the east. Hatch's first brigade, under Colonel Robert R. Stewart, rammed into the enemy and with rapid carbine fire caused them to fall back swiftly. A charge led by the Twelfth Tennessee—one of the regiments Wilson had withdrawn from Andrew Johnson's authority and had reorganized under capable officers—also cleared some of Chalmers's Rebel cavalrymen from Hatch's path, enabling the Fifth Division to sweep farther eastward.

The cavalrymen soon encountered a detached Rebel redoubt guarding Hood's left flank. The four-gun battery it enclosed would have been a formidable obstacle for soldiers used to fighting afoot; most cavalrymen would have regarded it as unassailable. But Wilson had Hatch dismount his second brigade, Colonel Datus Coon's, and with help from the Federal infantry, send it against the enemy guns. Thanks to the XVI Corps and also to a covering fire from Hatch's horse artillery, Coon's men broke through the Confederate position and by 1 P.M. had captured all four guns. Some of the troopers then turned the cannon against Confederates posted on a nearby hill; others vied with General Smith's infantrymen in rushing a second redoubt, 400 yards to the right of the first. Cutting loose with their Spencers, Coon's brigade took four more guns and over 200 prisoners.

Flushed with success and still filled with energy, Wilson's soldiers charged a third gun emplacement, this time without infantry support, took four more guns, and chased nearby Rebel infantry into a valley. Only after this third assault and with evening coming on, did the horse soldiers cease their advance. By now they had pushed as far as the Hillsboro Pike, which ran southwest from Nashville. Knipe's soldiers, supporting Hatch's right, had gone even farther eastward, snaking around the Confederate flank and striking the Granny White Pike, directly in Hood's rear.

By Wilson's efforts, the Confederate left flank had been thrown back about four miles. Elsewhere along the battle line, Thomas's infantry had battered the Rebel army in a series of vicious attacks. The Confederates' position had become precarious, nearly untenable. Had their opponents been able to recoup the three hours they had lost to fog and mismanagement that morning, they might have driven Hood from the field.

While Hatch's soldiers, covered by Knipe's division, had been smashing their way to success, other of Wilson's units had gained headway against the Army of Tennessee. After skirmishing with Rebel infantry near the Cumberland, Johnson's Sixth Division and Croxton's brigade had chased their foe into the distance and had then moved close to the rest of Wilson's force, to extend and in turn receive support.

That evening, after deploying his troops, Wilson rode north to Thomas's headquarters, a mile below Nashville, to receive orders for the next day's operations. Thomas—who that afternoon had witnessed a rare event, dismounted cavalry fighting side by side with infantry to carry strong enemy emplacements—greeted him warmly. He bestowed upon his cavalry leader compliments which Wilson felt "might well have made an older and better soldier blush." He then instructed Wilson to press Hood's flank and rear at daylight with as much force as he could muster.

But when rainy dawn came on the sixteenth, the enemy struck the first blow. The Confederates pushed back Knipe's pickets and temporarily regained the Granny White Pike—a crucial highway, one of only two leading south which Hood could use as a retreat route. In a furious counterassault, Knipe's men again took possession of the pike, and beside them Hatch came up to smite the Rebels' flank and rear. The fighting raged back and forth across an area of rocky, tree-covered slopes known as the Brentwood Hills. By noon 4,000 of Wilson's cavalrymen had worked their way to the top of the steep hills and had taken position directly in the rear of Hood's line. Some of the troopers, facing northeastward, were now firing in the direction of their infantry comrades facing the other side of the line.

By this time Hood's position was extremely tenuous. Wilson's troopers intercepted a message in which Hood begged General Chalmers "for God's sake to drive the Yankee cavalry from our left and rear or all is lost."

Wilson saw that if Thomas's foot soldiers could exploit the gains his troopers had achieved in the Confederates' rear, the enemy line would collapse. He sent word to Schofield (whose men had been held in reserve the day before and today had interposed between Wilson's and Smith's corps) to at once strike the Rebels in front of him. Receiving no immediate response, Wilson galloped off to Thomas's headquarters, detouring around the enemy. As he rode off, his men pressed against the backs of Hood's soldiers, their carbines flaming.

At headquarters, he found both Thomas and Schofield, calmly surveying the field. Since it was nearing four o'clock in the afternoon and a drizzling rain was dimming the light, Wilson wasted little time in suggesting an assault. But neither of his listeners reacted quickly, which made him wonder if perhaps Grant might not be correct in supposing that Thomas acted too deliberately. Never in his life had Wilson been so concerned with quick action. After some thought, however, the commanding general finally ordered Schofield to make an attack as the cavalry leader had suggested. Only then could Wilson ride back to his men.

When he rejoined them, he saw that his errand had been unnecessary. In his absence some of Smith's infantrymen had punched a hole through the Rebel flank near the point at which it angled west and then south; and General Hatch had driven his dismounted division against a fortified hill which formed a salient on Hood's extreme left. Hatch had carried the Rebel entrenchments before Smith's infantry could reach them from the opposite direction. It was raining heavily by now, and in a frantic effort to escape the Confederates began to splash across the muddy field, heading southward and eastward. "Our line, thus pierced, gave way," General Hood recollected years later. "Soon thereafter it broke at all points, and I beheld for the first and only time a Confederate Army abandon the field in confusion."

The Rebels' headlong flight caught Wilson by surprise. Because he had kept his horses to the rear, and because the rear had gotten farther and farther behind his hard-driving troopers, he had to bring up the animals from a considerable distance, to make an all-important effort at pursuit. Thomas wished the cavalry to head south and cut the remaining avenue of retreat, the Franklin Pike, the road which both Federals and Confederates had followed north to Nashville two weeks before. But with the exception of Croxton's brigade, which had been held in reserve beside its horses on the sixteenth, the cavalry could not follow with anything approaching the required speed. While Croxton pounded off through the sodden darkness to try to prevent Hood's escape, the rest of Wilson's troopers ran to the rear to find the cavalry jumpers which short days before had pulled buses and wagons.

When finally mounted, the Federals started off with great enthusiasm, but rode only a mile before being halted. General Chalmers, having foreseen Hood's collapse, had taken up a line to the south beside the Granny White Pike, along which most of Wilson's men were moving. His astuteness was rewarded when the Federals came up to fence-rail and fallen-log barricades which had been placed across the pike, and could not pass. A firefight broke out which Wilson later described as "one of the fiercest conflicts" of the war. A brigade under Colonel Edmund Rucker, composed largely of Tennesseans, did most of Chalmers's fighting; their opponents included some of the Tennessee regiments in Wilson's command. In the hand-to-hand melée, the colonel of a Loyalist unit found himself dodging saber blows from Colonel Rucker himself, who at one point reached out, grabbed the reins of his antagonist's horse, and shouted, "Well, you are my prisoner!" The Federal called out, "Not by a damned sight!" and battled until comrades came to help him. Another Federal officer challenged Rucker, somehow managed to exchange swords with him, and was forced to duck swipes from his own saber. The strange battle ceased when a stray pistol shot broke Rucker's sword arm, compelling him to surrender. That night, behind Federal lines, surgeons amputated Rucker's arm, and he convalesced in bed at Wilson's headquarters, although neither he nor his host got more than an hour's sleep.

By the time the outnumbered Confederates fled from the muddy road, it was midnight. Influenced by the late hour and an erroneous report from Rucker that Bedford Forrest had arrived on the scene with his main force "and will give you hell tonight," Wilson decided to recall his units and place them in bivouac. Pursuit would resume at dawn.

That night was achingly cold as well as damp, but Wilson seemed not to mind the weather. The sharp activity of battle and the warm glow of victory kept him alert and vibrant. An indication of his alertness had come shortly after he had begun his pursuit from Nashville. Standing beside his horse along the Granny White Pike, he whirled quickly when he heard the heavy thud of hooves coming toward him in the darkness. In the rain he could barely perceive the outline of a horse and rider. Then General Thomas's voice boomed: "Is that you, Wilson?"

Wilson replied quickly, aware that the general's voice was high with excitement. Which was understandable, for Thomas had just won a complete and precise victory. He had won in spite of criticism and doubt from his superiors. In fact, although Thomas would not learn the truth for some time, Grant's impatience had prompted him to dispatch another general to take command in Tennessee two days before the battle. At the last minute, Grant had even made preparations to go west and himself relieve Thomas. But those steps had been proven unnecessary, and Thomas's deliberation and prudence—as well as Wilson's— had been vindicated once and for all.

Now, savoring his personal triumph, the usually reserved commander threw back his head and shouted into the night:

"Dang it to hell, Wilson, didn't I *tell* you we could lick 'em?"

NEXT MORNING, THE PURSUIT RESUMED feverishly. Although by this time the remnants of Hood's army had a large head start, Wilson felt certain that his swift riders could overtake them. They could then brush aside the Rebels' rear guard and run wild through their ranks, creating so much pandemonium that the Federal infantry could come up and completely destroy the Army of Tennessee.

During the seventeenth the troopers again met Chalmers in battle, and Chalmers did his dogged best to slow them. This he did, but he could not hope to win more than a temporary advantage. Soon he was retreating, following Hood's dejected infantrymen as they moved toward Franklin.

After the fighting ended at 7 P.M. the previous day, Wilson had sent General Johnson's division down the Hillsboro Pike, west of the main pursuit column, to cross the Harpeth River and reach Franklin before the Rebels could make a stand there. Now Johnson did his utmost to obey, swinging his troopers in a wide arc south of the stream. But he was so slowed by the continuing rain and the rough, muddy ground that when his troopers reached the heights above Franklin they saw the Confederates sweeping through it.

When Wilson's main force came up to the river, it pushed across at and above Franklin. With Johnson on the Federal right, Croxton on the left, and Hatch and Knipe between, the troopers raced furiously after Hood's men, hoping to catch them, sweep around their flanks, and halt their withdrawal for good. But Hood was obsessed with pushing south as quickly as possible, and since his men raced along a smooth road while the Federals on their flanks galloped over difficult terrain, the Confederates kept well ahead of their pursuers.

Late that evening, exhausted by their break-neck pace, the Rebels shuddered to a halt about one mile above the West Harpeth River. In open fields north of the stream they set up artillery to sweep Wilson's line of march. Hatch's division came up and braved cannon fire until it reached the enemy cavalry and infantry along the road. Ordering a charge, Wilson sent other units into the fight as reinforcements, including his escort, a company of the Fourth United States Cavalry. With drawn sabers the Regulars charged the guns, sliced at the artillerymen, and forced the cannons to be drawn back to safety. Finally the Rebels fled into the night, and Wilson's troopers rushed forward, yelling at the top of their lungs.

The pursuit continued intermittently through much of the evening, although there was no sustained contact between the forces. That night was wet and harsh, made particularly miserable by hunger pains, for the armies had moved far afield of their supply wagons. Wilson was forced to order his men to stretch their already depleted five days' rations to last seven days.

The eighteenth was spent in hit-and-run fighting. Wilson's men struck the Rebels' rear time and again and skirmished fiercely but without decisive results. That day, however, the Confederates were able to push across Rutherford's Creek and then Duck River, both of them swollen by rain, and destroy the bridges, forcing their pursuers to attempt a fording operation.

But fording was not possible; the waters had risen too high. Taking precious time, Hatch's men stripped local houses and barns to rebuild the span over Rutherford's Creek. This required two full days, primarily because the army's pontoon-bridge train had been misdirected while on its way to the head of the column. Then Wilson lost three more days in making his way over Duck River and in awaiting the arrival of necessary rations and forage.

During that time, Hood put miles of rough ground between them; and Forrest, who had been recalled from Murfreesboro, rejoined the main army and organized a mighty rear echelon with troops of all arms.

The delay also enabled the advance of the Federal infantry, Wood's IV Corps, to come up in the rear of the cavalry, stalled on the bank of the stream. The foot soldiers waved their caps and cheered, saluting the horsemen's efforts at pursuit. The tribute was of the sort that Wilson had long craved and considered overdue.

On December 24 the pursuit finally resumed. Redoubling their efforts, the troopers spurred their horses as hard as they could, short of risking their collapse. They rode through freezing rain, capturing dozens of stragglers who trickled back from Hood's column.

That evening, after a furious march, they again closed in on Hood's rear guard, close to Pulaski. In that area, two sharp shirmishes broke out. During the first, Croxton's men routed one of Forrest's divisions and wounded one of his brigadiers. A short distance farther on, the Rebels halted at the mouth of a ravine through which the road passed. Without warning, the plucky Confederates rushed forward, split the line which General Johnson's division had hastily formed, and captured a Federal artillery piece—their only trophy of the retreat. When the balance of Wilson's command deployed for a full-size fight, the enemy drew off, dragging their prize with them.

As the chase went on still farther, the Confederates neared the ultimate safety of the Tennessee. Once they crossed that broad river on their long pontoon bridge, their pursuers would be foiled. The thought pained Wilson, as did the realization that the weariness of his men, the poor condition of their mounts, and the extremely harsh lay of the land was slowing his pursuit.

But when he wrote General Thomas on the twenty-fourth about his concern over his decelerating pace, Thomas assured him that "your progress is not considered slow, under the circumstances, but, on the contrary, is quite satisfactory to the major-general commanding. . . ."

To prove his earnestness, Thomas wired General Halleck the next day and, as a Christmas present of sorts, recommended Wilson for the full rank of major general of volunteers "for the excellent management of his corps during the present campaign."

On Christmas Day, General Forrest, now deep in the Tennessee Valley, set a trap for the Federals, into which they neatly fell. Concealing his rear guard, he sprang from ambush upon his pursuers, routed Wilson's advance, and caused it to fall back upon the vanguard of the column. But Wilson recovered his composure and sent General Hatch forward. Coolly braving enemy fire, the Fifth Division chased the Rebels from neighboring slopes, captured fifty of them, and hurried after the rest.

The long and exhausting race through middle Tennessee at last drew to a close on the twenty-seventh. Aware that Hood's soldiers were almost to the river, Wilson sent a flying battalion of 500 hand-picked riders, on the best horses, to make a last-ditch effort to reach the Tennessee first. Through that day and night the 500 charged ahead furiously, but succeeded in rounding up only a few stragglers. Reaching the river the next morning, they found that Hood and his soldiers had crossed during the previous evening, had taken up their pontoon bridge, and had wrecked all other spans. The Army of Tennessee was gone, having rushed out of its namesake state with as much speed and determination as it had displayed when invading it five weeks before.

Wilson could do nothing but draw in his detachments and allow his men an extensive rest. A number of unavoidable circumstances—and a few lamentably unfortunate, such as the errant pontoon train—had prevented him from catching Hood's soldiers.

Nevertheless, he was comforted by the results of his efforts. By anyone's standards, the pursuit recently concluded was one of the most devastating in American history. Having come 175 miles since the afternoon of December 16, his command had suffered several hundred casualties and a great number of disabled horses, and had lost one cannon. But in that period they had captured, in a series of skirmishes and engagements, 32 guns, 11 caissons, 12 stands of colors, and no fewer than 3,200 prisoners. Moreover, they had viciously harassed the remnants of a beaten but still dangerous army—not enemy cavalry alone, but foot soldiers and artillerymen as well. It was a record of which Wilson's soldiers could be deeply and justifiably proud.

HOOD'S RETREAT CARRIED HIM AS FAR as Tupelo, Mississippi, where his army lay down to die. As a fighting force, the Army of Tennessee was finished; from almost 40,000 soldiers at the start of the late campaign, it had been reduced to fewer than 20,000 effectives.

Hood asked to be relieved of his command, and the Confederate government promptly granted his wish. His soldiers then disbanded, many of them returning to their homes, about 4,000 others drifting south to Mobile, Alabama to join an army there, another 5,000 trekking to North Carolina, where General Joseph Johnston was recruiting a force to oppose Sherman, who, after sweeping to the coast, was about to turn northward. Only Hood's cavalry remained intact. Forrest's command had been decimated during the campaign, but its commander did not consider himself defeated. He longed for the chance to repay Wilson for forcing him into so humiliating a withdrawal.

Forrest realized that such an opportunity would come in the not-distant future, and so did his subordinates. Only one week after crossing the Tennessee to safety, he received some observations from General Chalmers. The Federal cavalry had done well at Nashville, wrote Chalmers, because Wilson had rested and recruited it so carefully that when "the time for action came . . . he moved it out fresh and vigorous with telling effect." The Confederate horsemen needed a similar respite if coming campaigns were to be waged successfully. And Chalmers closed his letter by indicating the nature of those campaigns: "Every man in your command is anxious that you should have a fair trial of strength with Major-General Wilson. . . ."

The Plain Truth
Is They Were
Invincible

F ollowing Hood's escape, Wilson's cavalry stood in dire need of its third extensive refit in six weeks. Nine hundred of its men had become casualties during the Nashville campaign, 6,000 horses had broken down, and countless weapons were missing or unserviceable. To remedy the situation, Wilson withdrew his corps to Huntsville, Alabama, fifty miles above the Tennessee.

From Huntsville, on New Year's Day, the battle-weary cavalry marched westward to better campsites between Waterloo and Gravelly Springs, where they went into winter quarters. The troopers built cantonments (log cabins and lean-to stables), discarded useless firearms, and obtained fresh animals in any manner possible.

When the new reorganization commenced, Wilson began to plan for the future. He envisioned a revitalized corps larger than any force he had previously commanded in the field—in fact, larger than any

mounted command ever assembled on the continent. He wrote from
Alabama to a friend: "With twenty-five thousand men properly organized, armed and mounted, I hazard nothing in saying, more may be
done by the army in the next campaign, than ever before. The rebels
can be thrown entirely on the defensive. Their cavalry can be broken
up or driven behind their Infantry for shelter, their rail-roads and other
lines of communication can be cut, and finally their Infantry itself can
be attacked and harassed beyond endurance. . . ."

The men who would enable him to attain many of these goals
began to arrive in force, soon after the winter camp had been established—the First Division, from southwestern Kentucky; the Second,
from the remount camp at Louisville; and the Fourth, from its point of
assembly at Saint Louis. For the first time since coming west, Wilson
had on hand each of the six divisions under his direct and immediate
authority.

With these long-absent troopers came the officers who would lead
them: McCook, returned from his 17-day, 400-mile pursuit of the
Rebel guerrillas; Long, who commanded the largest as well as perhaps
the most efficient unit in the corps; and Upton, at last recovered from
his battle wounds. Wilson greeted each warmly and gave him a thorough opportunity to rest and strengthen his troopers to ready them for
the resumption of field operations. In their behalf, he placed another
order with the Cavalry Bureau—this time for 10,000 animals, plus as
many Spencer repeaters as were available.

Throughout January and February the cavalrymen remained in
their camp, drilled whenever weather permitted, and familiarized themselves with all facets of mounted service. The methods Wilson used to
train and discipline his troopers antagonized the usual small percentage, but others felt, as one soldier later remarked, that Wilson "succeeded in establishing throughout the entire command an *espirit du
corps* hitherto unknown among them. . . ."

Drill was one of Wilson's obsessions, and sometimes the single-
mindedness with which he advocated it brought him into conflict with
his colleagues. He was determined that his men would become so profi-
cient that they would reward him with a magnificently successful campaign, come spring; and this sometimes prevented him from considering
the best interests of the Army as a whole. On one occasion, General
Smith sought to borrow some of Wilson's cavalrymen for outpost duty
around his nearby infantry camp. Wilson flew into a rage and told
Smith, with unnecessary vehemence: "You can't have *a man:* if you
are going to move against the enemy or need me I'll go with my whole

force. If you simply want me to do picket duty for you—I shall not do it for I was sent here to rest, recuperate and prepare my command for active service—and I intend to do it. This habit of calling upon Cavalry to protect Infantry must be broken up or we shall have no Cavalry!" Smith, who ranked Wilson, must have been surprised by this little lecture, and may well have felt that Wilson, in his quest for achievement and fame, was being perversely uncooperative. But his only reply was, "Very well."

During the winter, the government ordered Thomas's army to be fragmented, and the decision had far-reaching effects upon the cavalry. First Schofield's and then Wood's corps were ordered eastward, and Smith's command was sent south, that they might serve in areas where large-scale campaigning was still in progress. Soon afterward the authorities determined that a cavalry division ought also to go southward, to cooperate with Major General E. R. S. Canby, who was launching an expedition to capture Mobile, one of the last bastions in the Deep South. With angry reluctance, Wilson chose Knipe's troopers for the assignment, then had to strip horses from other units so that the Seventh Division could make the journey.

In addition, Johnson's division was detached from the corps and returned to middle Tennessee, where it would operate, dismounted, against Confederate irregulars who harassed Loyalist citizens. The order came directly from General Thomas, and again Wilson had to comply as graciously as possible—which he did not find easy.

Another matter which vexed him was the continual insufficiency of horseflesh. Despite new attempts at impressing mounts in Alabama and Mississippi, the approach of spring found the corps so critically short of animals that Wilson was forced to make a painful decision. Because most of Hatch's 6,000 men had given their horses to Knipe, Wilson resolved to leave the Fifth Division in camp when time came for the corps to retake the field. General Hatch accepted his commander's decision with good grace. He even volunteered to donate hundreds of his soldiers' Spencer carbines to the men of Croxton's brigade, since Croxton, who would campaign actively in the spring, had few reliable weapons.

To aid General Canby in his movement against Mobile, Grant and the War Department proposed a number of diversionary operations, and in so doing initiated Wilson's spring campaign. While other Federal horsemen swept eastward, the Cavalry Corps, M.D.M. would move south into Alabama, to demonstrate against the Confederate-held cities of Selma and Tuscaloosa, thus distracting the enemy's attention.

The plan was a great disappointment to Wilson. Although it did offer his men the chance to operate in the field against Forrest's cavalry, it did not authorize his longed-for drive into the depths of the South, where, working independently, he could crush the last working parts of the Confederate war machine. More significantly, he could perceive little if any opportunity to win personal glory by undertaking a mere supporting assignment with only 5,000 of his troopers, as General Grant wished.

Nevertheless, on February 23 Wilson dutifully assembled his command at Gravelly Springs prior to making the journey Grant had proposed, and General Thomas came down from Nashville to inspect it. Almost 17,000 officers and troopers paraded in review. The men were rugged and looked eager for campaigning; their sabers were polished, their carbines and pistols clean and ready for use. Such horses as they had—only 10,000—were in good condition. Also at Gravelly Springs were 250 supply wagons, 56 pontoon-train wagons, and 3 batteries of horse artillery. The men had been issued 5 days' rations and 100 rounds of ammunition, plus forage stock and fitted horseshoes, and the supply wagons held ample quantities of supplemental supplies. Whatever their fortunes during the 300-mile trip to Selma, they would at least ride, eat, and defend themselves in fine style.

Perhaps the sight of so many well-appointed horsemen made Thomas realize the staggering blow such a force, if given the chance, could strike the Deep South. After the review, he met with Wilson in private, and they discussed how the cavalry might be utilized to maximum effect. At length, Thomas made a decision which materially affected the future of the corps. He gave Wilson authority to mount an independent campaign against not only Selma and Tuscaloosa but also Montgomery, Columbus, Georgia, and other important manufacturing centers in the interior of the Confederacy. Wilson was also instructed to whip Forrest and, if possible, join Canby near Mobile and assist him in his expedition.

This was all Wilson could have desired. Renown might come to him yet. Thanking Thomas profusely, he set about revamping his plans and briefing his subordinates about the change in orders. A new enthusiasm took hold of him, and he wrote excitedly to his friend Adam Badeau: "If we get Montgomery—and separate all of the forces they have west of the Atlantic the game is all in our own hands."

To accomplish his goals, however, he would definitely have to do as Thomas wished—whip Forrest and whip him for good—something no other Federal commander had been able to achieve. In mid-Febru-

General Nathan Bedford Forrest—*Photograph courtesy Library of Congress*

ary, preparing for his trip into central Alabama, he had sent scouts all along the projected route and with their help had arrived at a fairly accurate idea of Forrest's plans, strength, and position. Three days after the review at Gravelly Springs, in an effort to gain further information, he sent one of his staff officers, Captain Lewis Hosea, to negotiate an exchange of prisoners with the Confederate cavalry leader at his headquarters at West Point, Mississippi. But Hosea's main purpose, as Wilson noted, was "to interview that wily commander, to study his frame of mind. . . ."

Hosea, a young, observant West Pointer, was surprised to find Forrest "of aristocratic mien." In a letter to his family, the captain remembered that "I had the honor to present the compliments of my general, our cavalry Murat—Wilson—to him, in the hope of meeting him upon some future occasion. He at once accepted this as a challenge, which the friendly message might be construed to convey, and with a curl of his lip he said: 'Jist tell General Wilson that . . . whenever he is ready, I will fight him with any number from one to ten thousand cavalry, and abide the issue. Gin'ral Wilson may pick his men, and I'll pick mine. He may take his sabers and I'll take my six-shooters. I don't want nary a saber in my command—haven't got one'."

The captain replied to this obvious exaggeration by mentioning that Wilson was a West Point man and a skilled tactician who put great faith in the value of the saber. "Wal, I never rubbed my back up agin a college," Forrest replied quickly, "but I'd give more for fifteen minutes of the 'bulge' on you than for three days of tactics!"

HEAVY RAINS, PROBLEMS WITH WAGONS, AND the scarcity of forage delayed Wilson's expedition for more than three weeks. The situation bothered him not only because it gave the Rebels time to strengthen their defenses but also because Grant, who had formally approved Wilson's new project, wished him to move as quickly as possible, to be of service to General Canby.

On March 7 Wilson wrote Adam Badeau, now serving as Grant's personal secretary, and urged him to explain the delay to the general-in-chief: "Tell him I shall not lose a moment I can possibly avoid in getting away." But two weeks later he was still in camp in northern Alabama, awaiting forage stock. He wrote Badeau again, stating that he was "greatly provoked at our delay—but am powerless to help it. . . . I hope we shall be off in time to do good service. My command is certainly in a magnificent condition, well armed, splendidly mounted, perfectly clad and equipped, and will turn out a heavier fighting force than ever before started on a cavalry expedition in this country. . . ."

The long-awaited operation finally got under way on March 22, nearly three months after the cavalry had gone into winter quarters. The extended period of training had yielded a powerful return. The 14,000 cavalrymen who headed south that morning—12,500 of them mounted, the rest afoot, serving as train guards—were confident that it would be they who got the "bulge" on their opponents.

As the troopers rode through northern Alabama, Federal armies on many fronts were moving against their enemy. In Virginia, Grant had begun his campaign to chase the Confederates out of Petersburg and toward final defeat; in North Carolina, Sherman was moving northward with implacable progress; in Alabama, Canby was driving toward the Gulf Coast; and in Florida, Tennessee, and sundry other theaters of combat, other operations against the faltering Confederacy were proceeding apace.

At the start of his expedition, Wilson and his men passed over a wide expanse of barren land, fringed only by longleaf pine, sedge grass, and dwarf palmetto. Farther on they encountered swamps and savannahs and forests of willow trees, live oak, and overhanging moss. Wilson himself described the terrain encountered in the early going: "It was throughout a hilly, gravelly and barren region . . . broken here and there by the small clearings of poor white folks. The valleys are deep and narrow and the roads which threaded them much of the way were often almost impassable for lack of bridges and from the presence of quicksand and quagmires." The people of this area, one of Wilson's soldiers observed, were "very ignorant and poor, but of Union proclivities."

In this region the enemy might have placed Wilson's corps in a precarious position, for the hills and streams prevented quick movements to facilitate mutual support. The problem was heightened because the three divisions moved along individual and divergent routes, which Wilson correctly foresaw would help disguise his destination. But had Confederates been able to gather among the columns, they might have stopped the Federal advance before it was fairly under way.

They could not stop it because they lacked a concentrated, fast-moving force. The only available defenders, beyond the local militia, were Forrest's cavalrymen; and Forrest had scattered his command—less than half as many men as Wilson boasted—across a wide area that stretched from eastern Mississippi to central Alabama.

Now a lieutenant general assigned to defend parts of three states, the wily Forrest commanded two divisions of veterans led by Brigadier Generals Chalmers and William H. Jackson, and a pair of brigades under Brigadier General Philip D. Roddey and Colonel Edward Crossland. But when he heard about Wilson's approach, approximately March 26, Forrest realized he had to collect these units before he could thrust them at the raiders. As Wilson's columns came on, Forrest tried to cover Selma and also cut across the Federals' trail. Later he decided to unite with Chalmers several miles above Selma, hoping that Jackson could strike Wilson's men in the rear and delay them to permit the juncture.

During their first five days on the march, the Federals covered 100 miles. But their march was not free of difficulties. Long's division, impeded by the pontoon train which traveled with it, and occasionally moving over wrong roads, suffered a substantial delay in reaching its first port of call, Russellville. And when Upton's troopers crossed bridgeless waterways swollen by recent rains, horses foundered in the raging current, wagons were swept away, and some cavalrymen drowned. Once the Federals forded both forks of the Black Warrior River, however, they passed a turning point. On the other side the roads were better and the land less rugged. If they could only contain Forrest, they should be able to reach Selma with ease.

On the twenty-ninth the raiders reached Elyton, about twenty miles below the Black Warrior. The next day, while in this insignificant town which was destined to become the great iron and steel city of Birmingham, Wilson detached General Croxton's brigade and sent it on a diversionary maneuver. To lead Chalmers's men astray, Croxton was to turn westward toward Tuscaloosa and there destroy the Alabama Military College, as well as public property, bridges, and railroad track, then rejoin the main body of the command near Selma. Wilson's decision to slice 1,800 troopers from his force indicated that he had become such a deep believer in the power of his soldiers as to be confident he could handle any opposition.

After Croxton's departure, the main force pushed on from Elyton and headed for the Cahaba River. Upon reaching the stream the next morning, they received word that part of Chalmers's division was about fifty miles below them, moving eastward toward Selma. Realizing that all of Forrest's people would soon be after him, Wilson stripped his command to its lightest marching order, emptied and abandoned his wagons, then pushed over the Cahaba.

Early on the afternoon of the thirty-first, the main force reached the town of Montevallo, southeast of the Cahaba bridge. Arriving there in advance of the other divisions, General Upton found enemy cavalrymen waiting for him just beyond the village. The crucial moment—the first confrontation of the campaign between Wilson and Bedford Forrest—had come.

The Rebels advanced toward the Fourth Division through fields which bordered the road leading to Selma, planning to strike from three directions. At first Upton's skirmishers withdrew slowly before them, falling back upon the main force in the village. When they had retired to within a few hundred yards of Montevallo, Wilson, who was beside Upton, surveyed the scene through field glasses. Forrest's force on hand appeared quite small; a swift charge ought to scatter it. Coolly he turned to his division leader and said, "Upton, I think you have let them come far enough; move out!"

Minutes later, Upton's men trotted down the Selma road in columns of fours, ready for the showdown. Then the Fifth Iowa, leading the advance, spurred into a charge, sabers swinging and pistols cracking. Its men rammed into the nearest body of Rebels, including part of General Roddey's brigade, and steadily forced them back. Forty Confederates became captives; the rest fled south, Forrest with them. After a five-mile retreat, they attempted to make a stand alongside a creek. But Upton's artillery and the men of his first brigade, led by the charging Third Iowa, caused the Rebels again to flee.

That night, after permitting the enemy to move toward the town of Randolph, far to the south, Upton's soldiers bivouacked fourteen miles below Montevallo, still congratulating each other on their first victory of the campaign. Wilson's confidence was strong, his spirits high; already he could smell success—and glory.

The next morning he had Upton push on to Randolph, in the hope of striking other roads which would lead them to Selma. Wilson looked ahead to his first significant objective, the capture of that vital manufacturing center on the Alabama River. But he felt he could take Selma without great loss, if his men gave their maximum effort, and were aided by a little luck.

Good luck came his way with dramatic speed. Shortly before dawn, some of Upton's outriders captured a Rebel courier riding from General Jackson to Bedford Forrest. The papers he carried revealed the location of each of Forrest's units and his plans for the campaign. Wilson learned that the Confederate leader, with a small portion of his command, aimed to join Chalmers and with him strike the Federals' front, and that Jackson's division was riding eastward from Tuscaloosa toward Centerville to attack Wilson from the rear. The dispatches also revealed that a small enemy band held the Cahaba River bridge at Centerville, over which both Jackson and Chalmers would have to pass to join their chief.

Shortly after this remarkable fund of intelligence fell into his hands, Wilson received a pertinent dispatch from Croxton's wide-riding detachment. Croxton reported having struck the rear guard of Jackson's division north of Tuscaloosa the night before. Instead of moving directly on that city, as ordered, Croxton would follow Jackson and compel him to fight, to keep him from menacing Wilson's main column.

Wilson quickly formulated a plan to aid Croxton and also prevent Jackson and Chalmers from causing trouble. Late that morning he detached the rest of McCook's First Division and sent it to the Centerville bridge, about a dozen miles westward. McCook was to look for Croxton and bring him back to the rest of the command; if possible, meet and best Jackson; and destroy the span, to trap the two Confederate divisions on the far side of the river. He was then to take the handiest read to Selma.

Although Wilson would not learn the facts for quite some time, McCook would accomplish only a part—but the crucial part—of his mission. He would take Centerville, would move beyond it in a futile attempt to locate either Croxton or Jackson, and would retreat over the bridge and fire it. Consequently, Forrest would find himself unable to receive aid from the balance of his command, and Wilson would no longer have to fear for the safety of his rear or right flank.

Late on the afternoon of April 1, Forrest again attempted to halt Wilson, but, as at Montevallo, with only a few thousand troopers. Near Ebenezer Church, twenty miles north of Selma, he placed himself across the raiders' path. When General Long, now leading the Federal advance, came up to the town, he found the Rebels posted behind fence-rail barricades along a roadside creek. Once again Wilson grew supremely confident after examining the strength of the enemy. How did Forrest expect to make headway against them with so few soldiers?

Calmly Wilson told Long to dismount one of his most experienced regiments, the Seventy-second Indiana Mounted Infantry of the old "Lightning Brigade" (a sobriquet derived from the blazing power of its Spencer repeaters). With inexorable power the regiment drove in the enemy's skirmishers. Simultaneously, another Hoosier unit, the Seventeenth Cavalry, charged the Rebels' artillery on horseback and with drawn sabers.

As fighting swirled along the creek, Upton's division tipped the

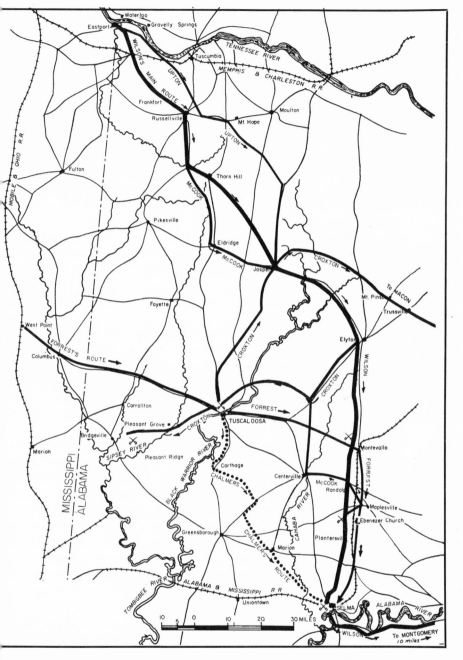

Routes of the Union and Confederate Forces During Wilson's Selma Raid—*Map adapted from Plates LXXVI, (1), CXLIX, and CXLIX of the Atlas to Accompany the Official Records.*

balance in the Federals' favor by coming up quickly, dismounting and then charging beside Long's men, breaking the enemy line by force of numbers. Led by a bloody, saber-slashed Forrest, the Confederates drew off toward Selma, abandoning 200 of their wounded and 3 of their cannon. After a hectic, 25-mile pursuit, the Federals allowed their opponents to enter the fortified city, then bivouacked several miles above it at sundown.

The next morning, finding the roads clear, Wilson moved off on the last leg of his march to Selma. Good fortune again rode with him; that afternoon Upton's soldiers encountered an English civil engineer who had helped construct the Selma fortifications. Now disenchanted with the Confederate cause, the man willingly sketched a detailed plan of the city's outer and inner works. Wilson digested the information as he rode on. It did not make for pleasant reading, however, and probably gave him his greatest worry of the campaign.

When in midafternoon the raiders reached Selma, 300 miles from the starting point of their expedition, Wilson found that the Englishman's information was complete and accurate. The city, defended by about 6,000 soldiers under Forrest and a half-dozen other generals, was protected supremely well. Situated on the north shore of the Alabama, it was covered by a 400-yard front of timber abatis—sharpened logs standing 7 feet high—behind which was a cleared space of about 200 yards, thickly strewn with cross-wire baskets and mined with torpedoes. Behind these barriers was a nine-foot-tall palisade with a ditch in front, protected by logs and interwoven wire. Inside the palisade was a platform two feet above the ground, upon which sharpshooters had been positioned, and in rear of the palisade were other manned ditches, earthworks, star-shaped gun forts at angles in the line, and field and siege gun emplacements boasting an array of artillery ranging from light 6-pounders to a "monster" 64-pounder cannon.

Selma looked impregnable. But Wilson had had time to theorize about weak points, and at his back were 9,000 skillful and confident troopers experienced in fighting on foot against difficult objectives as well as campaigning on horseback. In particular, he felt the residual effects of the smashing success those men had achieved in battle against Forrest.

After deep and careful thought, he formulated plans for a full-scale attack, to be conducted under cover of darkness. Long's division was moved from the path it had taken into the city and placed on a road farther to the right, while Upton's men remained on the direct Selma road. Long was ordered to strike the city from his new position with a dismounted force of 1,500 troopers, reinforced by other units from his division. Upton, keeping his main force concealed in neighboring woods, would penetrate a thick swamp with 300 men and assault the enemy works at what was probably their weakest point, the extreme left flank. A blast from one of the Federal batteries would trigger both movements.

Wilson had the satisfaction of seeing the various units move into their assigned positions before darkness fell, and with a minimum of difficulty. Again he began to sense impending victory—the sweetest sensation he had ever experienced. However, at 5 P.M., before the signal gun fired, the assault was precipitated. The sudden arrival of Chalmers's long-delayed cavalry, making a futile attempt to fight its way into Selma, threw the rear of Long's division into confusion and forced the advance units to move out against the city.

Although begun prematurely, Wilson's attack did not falter. As the Second Division charged forward, bands of freed slaves who had joined the Federals during their march rushed ahead of the soldiers with axes and, ignoring the hail of enemy bullets, chopped holes through the palisade to allow the dismounted cavalrymen to pour through. Long's troopers threaded their way across the obstructed 600-yard approach, reached the wall, went through it and, in some places, climbed over it, leaped across the ditches farther forward, scaled the steep parapet, and at last closed with the defenders in hand-to-hand fighting. An observer saw the cavalrymen gain entrance to the inner works by scaling the wall "as boys play leap-frog, the more active 'boosting' their comrades," and he heard them cheer wildly as they swarmed inside the fortified line. By this time rifle and cannon fire had ripped jagged gaps in the Federal lines, but the survivors came on.

Three hundred of Long's men became casualties after entering the fortifications. Long himself was shot in the head and partially paralyzed; both of his brigade commanders, Colonels Abram O. Miller and Robert H. G. Minty, were also wounded, and several regimental leaders were killed or severely wounded. But the Federals continued to pour through the embrasures and over the parapet, their carbines ablaze. Before them, the defenders began to fall back, then flee.

When Long's attack reached its apogee, Upton's men came charging through the gathering darkness against the left flank, scaling the works and flooding into the city. By then the field was covered for a mile and a half, as Wilson said, "with a whirlwind of battle."

Soon after Upton's men went forward, Wilson himself—caught up in the frenzy of the attack—entered the fight. Believing that his conspicuous presence would lend encouragement to his soldiers, he mounted his dapple gray gelding, Sheridan, and galloped to the left of Long's division, followed by his escort from the Fourth Regulars.

His presence did bolster his men, but it also drew the fire of the enemy. As he closed in on the outer works, he could hear Confederates shouting to comrades to fire at him. Moments later, Sheridan went down with a bullet wound, hurtling Wilson through the air. He was slammed onto the ground with a terrific impact, which left him slightly dazed but did not inflict serious injury. Finding that his horse was able to regain its feet, he slowly remounted and rallied his escort, then led it again toward the works.

In all quarters, his attack was proceeding smoothly. Upton was entering the defensive line in his sector, putting his opponents to flight. The Federal horse artillery was shattering the inner works, raining shrapnel and canister on the defenders. And Long's men were still throwing themselves over the parapet and into the city.

The battle inside the works continued for several minutes, the Confederates steadily weakening. Finally their line crumbled and broke apart, and they began to throw down their guns and cry, "We surrender!" Others tried to run for the rear, stumbling and falling as the Federals swept toward them, still firing. "For God's sake, Yanks," the cry went up, "don't butcher us all!"

Final victory came before full darkness settled over the city. Wilson entered the works and found that some of his soldiers had collected scores of prisoners, while others were chasing those who had fled eastward. The brevet major general was in lofty spirits, which could not be lowered even by the news that Forrest and many of his troopers had escaped. He went among the units which had seen the heaviest action, offering congratulations. To the men of the Lightning Brigade, who had made an especially vigorous charge, he doffed the ornate forage cap which he always wore, and said: "Men, I now see how it is you have gotten such a hell of a name!" The troopers responded with a cheer.

Wilson's speech-making was short-lived, for he had to turn to more pressing matters. After they had broken the Rebel line, some of the Federals, plus many of the freed slaves, took the first opportunity to plunder the city. In a short time flames were raging through Selma. At once Wilson formed a fire brigade and took steps to halt the looting. The firemen had indifferent success, but the campaign against plundering yielded quick results, for Wilson decreed capital punishment for all house-breakers.

Since a prime purpose of the expedition was the destruction of

Selma's industrial resources, Wilson later added to the flames. But on the night of the attack he did his best to save property not earmarked for ruin. Despite his efforts, small fires raged throughout the night, giving an eerie illumination to the thousands of cavalrymen, captives, and citizens scurrying out of their path.

As a metaphor of the Confederacy's ruin, the flames were particularly apt. Unknown to Wilson, a city almost 700 miles from Selma was also ablaze. That same afternoon Federal troops had marched into a fire-gutted Richmond, a week after taking Petersburg by storm. The end of the war was at hand.

FOR EIGHT DAYS THE TROOPERS REMAINED in Selma. They rounded up Confederate stragglers, pursued Forrest's escapees, and guarded municipal property and the approaches to the city. Headquartered in a city hotel, Wilson enforced the protection of citizens, tended to the casualties of both armies, refitted his command, drew up plans for the rest of the campaign, and then sent his subordinates to dispose of the property with military value.

The process of destruction was systematic and thorough. Machinery and products which would not burn were dismantled, mangled, or thrown into the Alabama River. Then, on a night when heavy rains insured that fires would not rage for long, they put to the torch select buildings, under the immediate direction of one of Upton's brigade leaders, Colonel Edward F. Winslow. The most significant target was the great Selma Arsenal, which consisted of two dozen buildings. A cavalryman watched as it was fired: "The scene was hideous and unearthly beyond anything we had ever imagined. The explosions continued for three hours, much louder than any we had ever heard, and of sufficient violence to shake the earth for miles around, making the city a perfect pandemonium. . . ."

Other structures razed included the C.S.A. naval foundry, the Selma iron works, the powder mill and magazine, the nitre works, a large machine shop, and scores of outbuildings, plus fifty acres' worth of factories and warehouses of lesser size. In addition, Wilson's troopers had already seized 2,700 prisoners, more than 2,000 horses—invaluable as remounts—32 cannon, 66,000 rounds of artillery ammunition, and 14,000 pounds of gunpowder.

On April 7 Wilson left Selma in the hands of his generals and rode a few miles to the southwest to meet General Forrest for a conference which had been set up days before. In a stately mansion in the town of Cahaba the two commanders came together face to face for the first time, prepared to negotiate another exchange of prisoners. Forrest was nursing wounds received at Ebenezer Church; withal, he seemed in good physical condition. Yet Wilson found him "neither so large, dignified nor striking as I expected."

The two opponents regarded each other warily at first; it was a delicate and rather tense moment. Wilson—once the underdog but now the man with the edge—could afford to be gracious, however, and soon an almost friendly atmosphere prevailed. Their conference followed a sumptuous dinner which the master of the house had prepared for his visitors. During the meal the opponents chatted informally. Reciprocating Wilson's cordiality, Forrest admitted at one point: "Well general you have beaten me badly—and for the first time I'm compelled to make such an acknowledgment." Wilson accepted the compliment, but remarked that his victory had not been without cost. Forrest candidly replied: "If I had captured your entire force twice over it would not compensate us for the blow you've inflicted upon us."

The conversation also gave Wilson some valuable information concerning the whereabouts and fortunes of Croxton's roving brigade. Apropos to the prisoner topic, Forrest mentioned that he had captured very few of Croxton's men, that his brigade had moved far to the southwest after striking Tuscaloosa, and that it was—to Wilson's relief —still at large.

After Forrest promised to refer the exchange question to his superiors, Wilson rode back to Selma to make preparations to leave it for good.

Convinced that General Canby could capture Mobile without direct assistance from him, Wilson sent messengers to bring him word of Selma's fall and then prepared to push farther to the east rather than to the Gulf city. Cut off from communications with the other armies and thus ignorant of the momentous news being made elsewhere in the beleaguered Confederacy, he marched his men out of Selma on April 10 and led them toward Montgomery, first capital of Jefferson Davis's government. To resume the expedition the troopers crossed an 870-foot-long floating bridge which Wilson's engineers had thrown over the Alabama, despite a rich variety of difficulties, including a treacherous current.

In contrast, the capture of Montgomery posed no great problems. The troopers reached it at 7 A.M. on the twelfth, and its mayor surrendered the city to the advance guard, McCook's division (which after the battle on the second had rejoined the main column in Selma). A trooper observed that the townspeople received the cavalry "if without manifestations of joy, at least without any evidences of dislike." On their part, the troopers behaved flawlessly, riding through the city with precision and composure. "Not a man left the ranks," Wilson proudly recollected, "not a loud word was uttered, and not an incident happened to hurt the feelings of the misguided people. It was an example of discipline, order, and power lasting nearly all day. . . . Many witnessed it from the windows, doorsteps, and sidewalks with silent respect, which showed clearly that the great Rebellion was at an end. . . ."

While in the city Wilson heard an unsubstantiated report that both Petersburg and Richmond had fallen and that Jefferson Davis had fled into the Deep South. But because he could not secure details or official confirmation, Wilson decided to push on to Columbus and points east. After a single night in Montgomery, the Federal cavalrymen returned to the road, spent the next three days marching through the country, and on April 16 arrived at the Chattahoochee River and the twin Georgia cities of Girard and Columbus.

Upton's men, supported by Long's division (now commanded by Colonel Minty) captured Girard in the early afternoon and without much difficulty. Wilson then concentrated on the more important objective. Columbus (population 12,000) was one of the last manufacturing citadels in the Confederacy. It produced a massive quantity of matériel for the Rebel armies, including cannon, rifles, sabers, pistols, boots, uniforms, drums, and ammunition. Despite its great value, only militia, some of Forrest's veterans (minus their leader, who had remained in Alabama with his main force), and local defense brigades defended the city. In overall command was Major General Howell Cobb, one of the state's most famous spokesmen for secession. However, the major portion of the field troops were led by Colonel Leon Von Zinken, a German-born militiaman. Convinced that his lines of defense would repel any attackers, Von Zinken had gone on record with the prediction: "If tem tam Yankees come, I make vun hell of a tam fuss!"

At Columbus, three bridges crossed the Chattahoochee—a foot bridge at the lower end of the city and a foot and a railroad bridge three-quarters of a mile upriver. Cannon, rifle pits manned by marksmen, and other works defended them. Before the close of the afternoon, Upton's division tried to capture the lower span but was repulsed by heavy rifle fire, after which the Confederates burned the bridge. Reporting his failure, Upton told Wilson that if darkness was not coming on he would like to strike the upper works of the city with dismounted men, pass others through gaps in the defensive lines, and have them secure one or both of the other bridges. Wilson, who usually saw merit in a bold, decisive idea, liked the plan and ordered it carried out. Upton was skeptical that a night attack would succeed. But once his commander reminded him of its effectiveness at Selma, he exclaimed: "By jingo, I'll do it; and I'll sweep everything before me!"

He did—with help from the enemy. At 8:30 P.M. his dismounted men carried the rifle pits around the upper works and allowed their mounted comrades to ride through the defenses, beyond which they unexpectedly encountered a second strongly held line. They might have been stopped but for the confusion of the defenders, who, hearing horsemen approaching in the darkness, believed that other Confederates were riding up. Before discovering their error, they permitted many of Upton's soldiers to pass over the foot bridge and enter the city. By then the Rebels had other troubles, for some of the dismounted Federals had moved up to the second defense line, while others were charging redoubts to their right and left. Both Federal forces received aid from the mounted troopers, who recrossed the bridge to battle the enemy sharpshooters. One of Wilson's staff officers observed that the fight was "all dark except when the scene was illuminated by flashes of the guns and glaring brilliancy of volleys from forts and rifle pits. . . ."

Moving into Columbus, the cavalry spread out and attacked the flank of those troops guarding the upper railroad span as well as those still encamped near the burned bridge. By 11 P.M. the city had fallen with 52 guns and 1,200 prisoners; General Cobb had escaped toward Macon, and Colonel Von Zinken had paid for his overconfidence. Overflowing with enthusiasm, Wilson rode into the city and once again extended hearty congratulations to his troopers. Nothing at all seemed capable of stopping them.

His enthusiasm was doubly justified. That same afternoon, while Upton directed preliminary maneuvers against Columbus, McCook's division—again detached from the main column—attacked Fort Tyler, some thirty-five miles north of Columbus, and captured it after a bitter struggle. The First Division—which heavily outnumbered the 200-odd defenders—charged against three sides of the square earthwork, killing its commander and namesake, Brigadier General Robert C. Tyler, and eighteen of his men, wounding twenty-eight others, and occupying the adjacent city of West Point, Georgia. A Wisconsin trooper later commented: "No slaughter-house could have been bloodier than was the inside of Fort Tyler, where the dead and dying were piled knee deep."

On April 17, two columns of Wilson's cavalry crossed the Chattahoochee at Columbus and West Point, and took roads which converged in the direction of Macon. En route, the advance guard of Minty's division achieved an important feat by capturing the Double Bridges over the Flint River, about fifty-five miles east of Columbus. The success was owing to furious charges by Minty's own regiment, the Fourth Michigan, and by the Third Ohio, whose men chased off the Confederate bridge guards.

Early on the evening of the twentieth, twenty miles west of Macon, Wilson's cavalry entered its last large skirmish of the war. Some 200 Rebels who had assembled at the crossing of Tobesofkee Creek set fire to the bridge as the Federals approached, and peppered away at the troopers from the far shore. But the Confederates did not expect the raiders' advance guard to charge over the bridge through the flames, secure the far bank, and chase them out of their entrenchments —all of them occurred in rapid succession. Flabbergasted, the defenders threw down their arms and fled in confusion.

The officer who had led the charge, Lieutenant Colonel Frank White, continued toward Macon with his regiment, the Seventeenth Indiana, riding at the point of the column. A few miles farther on, he met Confederate Brigadier General Felix Robertson, who carried a flag of truce and a communication from General Cobb, now in command at Macon. The message was addressed to "The Commanding General, United States forces."

The letter went down the column to brigade and division leaders before it reached Wilson. Eventually the brevet major general found that it contained a telegram appraising Cobb that Generals Sherman and Johnston had entered into a truce pending the surrender of Johnston's army in North Carolina. It seemed apparent that Cobb expected Wilson, in view of this, to suspend all operations and to refrain from entering Macon.

Wilson had no intention of doing so, but his course was actually decided by Colonel White, whose advance unit charged on Macon, scattering Robertson's truce party. White's speed prevented other Rebels from burning bridges which commanded the approaches to the city. Shortly after sundown that night, the cavalry marched into Macon without opposition.

By the time Wilson rode in, his soldiers had taken full possession. He soon encountered an angry Howell Cobb, who accused him of violating explicit orders to obey a general armistice. Cobb demanded the cavalry be informed of the truce and be quickly withdrawn from the city.

Wilson replied that he had received no verification of the truce news, nor orders in that regard from any superior. But he was anxious for further information. If an armistice was truly in effect, did it mean that not only Johnston but also Lee had surrendered? General Cobb declined to reply, but one of his subordinates did, affirmatively. No longer doubting that the war had ended, Wilson agreed to maintain strict order and peace in the city, adopting the attitude that "any man killed on either side is a man murdered." But he refused to withdraw a single trooper until specifically ordered to do so by his commanders. He dashed off inquiries to Sherman via Rebel communication lines, but not until the next evening did he receive orders "to desist from further acts of war and devastation."

And so the fighting was officially over. Although this meant that he would not continue toward Virginia to join Grant—a course he had decided on before pushing through the Deep South—Wilson was relieved that the long years of conflict had ended.

Even after receiving Sherman's message, he kept his troopers in and near the city which he had captured complete with almost 2,000 troopers and men and 60 guns. He established his headquarters in the Lanier House, Macon's principal hotel, and deployed his men to be ready for whatever might be required of them in the future. The troopers maintained order and discipline and, except for firing a 200-gun salute to celebrate the war's close, created few disturbances.

During the next few days, Wilson received other important news. President Jefferson Davis was believed to be fleeing through Georgia to escape Federal authorities; Sherman and the War Department were bitterly at odds over the lenient terms he had extended to General Johnston; and (as Wilson learned during the last week in April) Abraham Lincoln had been assassinated in Washington. The president's murder sobered him and plunged his entire command into mourning. To his friend Badeau he wrote that he was "painfully agitated" by the intelligence and found it hard to believe that "so atrocious a crime could have been committed on the eve of peace." Though he had met Mr. Lincoln only a few times, he had come to regard him as a gifted military commander, an adroit politician, and, at bottom, a sensitive and compassionate man. Wilson's gloom was deepened by the realization that his old enemy, Andrew Johnson, was now president and commander in chief of the Army.

On the twenty-ninth Wilson greeted the arrival of General Croxton's brigade, almost a month after its detachment from the main force, near Elyton, Alabama. Croxton amazed his commander with the story of his activities during that period. Marching and countermarching along a roundabout route to accomplish its assigned duties and to elude larger enemy forces, the brigade had covered 653 miles over rugged country. Its men had captured several cities including Tuscaloosa, had ripped up a great many miles of railroad track, and had taken 300 prisoners. Most important, Croxton had engaged Jackson's cavalry division, giving General McCook time to destroy the Centerville bridge—one of the events upon which the success of the expedition had hinged.

Croxton's accomplishments added bulk to the already weighty results of Wilson's campaign, the largest and most successful cavalry operation in American history. In 28 days, Wilson's troopers had marched an average of 525 miles and had captured 5 fortified cities and towns, 23 stands of colors, 288 pieces of artillery, 6,820 prisoners, and 100,000 stands of small arms; they had destroyed 7 iron works, 7 foundries, 2 rolling mills, 7 collieries, 13 large factories, 2 nitre works, a military college, 3 C.S.A. arsenals, a powder magazine, a naval armory, 5 steamboats, 2 gunboats, 35 locomotives and 565 cars, several railroad depots and bridges, 235,000 bales of cotton, and immense quantities of quartermaster's, ordnance, and commissary stores; and, once peace was established, they had paroled 59,878 captives, including 6,134 officers. In the process, they had lost 13 officers and 86 men killed, 39 officers and 559 men wounded, and 7 officers and 21 men missing. Finally, they had rewritten the books which specified the manner in which mounted troops were to be utilized in the field. Moving in mass against stationary objectives, including well-fortified cities, they had demonstrated the unconquerable power of a hard-driving, highly mobile force.

There was, however, a tragic aspect to the expedition—an aspect which qualified its value. In the final analysis, it did not achieve any material strategic success. The Confederacy was in its last throes before the raid began, and it died several weeks before the raid ended; therefore, the losses sustained by Alabama and Georgia at Wilson's hands did not contribute to Federal victory and in fact constituted a vast and needless waste of human lives and resources.

Of course, Wilson had received no information about the war's close until weeks after the fact and had thus been obliged to continue his destruction until he received further orders. Yet, even in later years, he could never bear to acknowledge that his great expedition—the principal achievement of his career—had been of no strategic help to the cause of the Union, although men such as Grant and Sherman were not so hesitant to speak the truth.

Of course, too, this overview of the campaign's effectiveness could not be derived until long after the expedition ended. From Macon Wilson could see only that his men had achieved the most spectacular feat of arms in American cavalry warfare. And he gave those soldiers full credit for making him, at twenty-seven, the country's most successful cavalry commander. Writing Badeau from Macon, he expressed the conviction that his campaign would convince everyone that "my corps of cavalry was the best in the world—that my division and brigade commanders were the truest men of the day and my sixteen thousand sabres the brightest and most heroic of all in modern times." And he attributed their fantastic success to a fact which he stated without fear of being accused of exaggeration:

"The plain truth is they were invincible."

★XI★

*It Is the True Office
of the Military to Assist in the
Re-establishment of Civil Law*

It was soon apparent that occupation troops, including other units in the northern part of the state, would remain in Georgia for some time. Wilson therefore entered upon his duties as military governor of the Macon district with a determination to establish and maintain peace in his realm. His tactics brought swift results. Years later, the son of Howell Cobb recalled that only three days after the Federals occupied Macon, "the women and children were walking the streets as if nothing unusual had happened and the commercial business of the City was moving in its usual even channel."

Wilson did encounter some troubles; it would have been naive to think that the invaders and the invaded could quickly come to cordial terms. Many citizens refused to respect the Stars and Stripes, which now flew from flagpoles throughout the city. Some secessionists—including more than a few women—were elaborately disrespectful to Wilson's officers and troopers, whom they called "barbarians," and worse. And from street corners and church pulpits spokesmen conveyed anti-Unionist sentiments, directly or obliquely, to the townspeople.

But Wilson could be tolerant and tactful when he felt it beneficial. He solved such problems by prudent action—often by soft-spoken suggestions rather than overt force—and with a minimum of travail. Soon street gatherings dwindled, sermons moderated, and citizens came to regard the soldiers tolerantly if not warmly.

Wilson was particularly lenient, whenever possible, with citizens brought to him for making obvious display of their feelings toward Yankees. Rather than insist that townspeople immediately vow their love and undying devotion to the federal government, he allowed them time to recover from their bitterness. Soon he was writing the chief of staff of the Army of the Cumberland that "I have not harassed the people by any unnecessary restrictions whatever . . . assuming that liberality in this respect would have a good effect by contrast with the condition of affairs under rebel rule. The war having ended it is the true office of the military power of the government to assist in the re-establishment of civil law, not to replace it." His observations were so important that the Army referred them to President Johnson for his study.

In time, Wilson won the respect and trust of many of Macon's citizens. Howell Cobb came to regard him as an honest man concerned with the welfare of those under his rule. Thus, Cobb often gave him the benefit of his wide political experience, invaluable in promoting good public relations, and supported his views on how Reconstruction ought to proceed. Other people voiced approval of Wilson's program to detail guards to protect private property and noted that he refused no requests for such protection. Even churchmen—beginning with the local Presbyterian pastor, soon including clerics of the other denominations—began to warm to his rule and to insert in their sermons one of his favorite biblical verses, "Righteousness exalteth a nation, but sin is a reproach to any people," with special reference to the sin of disobeying lawful public authority.

In various other ways—such as by responding quickly to complaints against rowdy soldiers, by using troopers to make municipal improvements and to handle odd jobs (including setting type for a newspaper whose compositors had gone on strike, a newspaper he allowed to publish any material not defamatory to the federal government), and by distributing food supplies to impoverished families—Wilson indicated his intent to govern fairly and humanely.

However, not all citizens responded warmly to his regime. Many thought of him as the personification of Yankee tyranny and from the first were convinced that he looked upon Macon as a city of spoils. This opinion seemed to be confirmed when Wilson took over a magnificent Greek revival mansion as his private residence. From the house, which stood on a hill overlooking the city, Wilson could view the captured municipality, lying sprawled at his feet. A local historian wrote that Wilson "was not possessed of a single magnanimous quality or liberal sentiment" and won no true friends during his term of rule.

But Wilson was not a hard-hearted conqueror, as he demonstrated when tackling the problem of feeding and clothing the needy.

Although central Georgia had escaped devastation by the invading forces, the economic depression which accompanied the peace seriously afflicted its people. Menfolk called into the Confederate service had left fields and farms untilled, and many of these veterans, returning now to their homes, were physically unable to resume their prosperous prewar ways. Then, too, a great many new widows and orphans required sustenance which they could not provide for themselves. Assuming the responsibility of caring for such people, Wilson had General Sherman, at his earliest opportunity, send shipments of foodstuffs, clothing, and grain to his headquarters. He then doled out many of the surplus supplies to needy citizens.

One minor example furnishes tangible evidence of Wilson's belief that "too vigorous measures to prevent suffering cannot be inaugurated." Early in May an elderly widow living thirty miles from Macon wrote to ask him for "Some Assistance in regard to Provisions [.] i With my Family are Destitute of Necessaries Articles of life Such as Bacon flour and meal . . . and if you Will be So kind as to Send me Something to keep off Starvation I Shall be thankful to you. . . ." Although one of numerous requests to cross his desk, Wilson at once referred it to influential citizens, who arranged financial relief for the woman.

Another of his major concerns as military governor was the status of freed Negroes. Realizing the need for laws to guard their new-won freedom, he formulated a number of guidelines clarifying the position of former slaves under his regime. He made clear that "freedmen like all other men are amenable to civil and criminal law, and are liable to be punished for violations of law just the same as white citizens." But he also declared that "in no cases will brutality be allowed on the part of the former master. Thinking men will at once see that, with the end of slavery, all enactments and customs which were necessary for its preservation must cease to have effect." Under the new system ex-slaves had to be paid equitable wages for services rendered, and were allowed to travel and locate anywhere in the Macon district so long as under no obligation to guardians or parents. Wilson's regulations further declared: "The former masters of freedmen will not be permitted to turn away or drive from their plantations faithful hands who have helped to make the crops, when the crops are saved, without paying for the labor already performed."

Personally, Wilson was of two minds about the emancipation program which President Lincoln had inaugurated three years before. He believed the ex-slave ought to be thoroughly educated in the ways of modern civilization before the rights to vote and to hold public office were extended to him. His chief concern, therefore, was the degree of ignorance which the institution of slavery had inflicted upon most blacks. He believed that slavery had made Negroes "hopelessly ignorant" and by preparing them for no condition other than servitude had insured that, with the demise of the institution, they would resolve "to work no longer, but taste fully that liberty whose highest attribute in their dwarfed and benighted minds is a life of idleness and immunity from the lash."

On the other hand, he had faith in the freedman's potential. He wrote Badeau that "the race is capable of developments," which would come about when whites adhered fully to the ideals of Christian living, causing racial harmony to prevail. Wilson, however, still did not believe in the fundamental equality of the races. His views on this subject were well expressed by the following words contained in a letter which he wrote to Badeau later that year: "I hold that in this country substantially the white man will always rule—I hold the white men of *our* race to be the most *vital* race which has yet appeared. . . ."

Soon after occupying Macon, Wilson sent troops to hold other important cities, including Atlanta and Augusta, plus several small but strategically located towns. General Upton took Augusta on May 3 with part of his division; the rest of the unit, led by Colonel Winslow, occupied Atlanta shortly afterward. In both cities, as in Macon, the cavalry established a military governorship to administer civil affairs in behalf of the federal government. There, too, the occupation troops secured supplies sent by Sherman for the sustenance of soldiers and indigent townspeople.

As from Macon, parties rode out of Augusta and Atlanta to arrest politicians who had served prominently in the Confederate government. Such men included the former vice-president of the Confederacy, Alexander H. Stephens, whom some of Upton's men took into custody at Crawfordsville, Georgia; Robert Toombs, Jefferson Davis's secretary of state, whom Upton arrested at Washington, Georgia; and General Braxton Bragg, apprehended in the town of Monticello on May 10 and sent to report to Wilson's headquarters for parole.

Also arrested was Henry Wirz, jailer of the notorious Andersonville prison camp. On May 4 Wilson sent a detachment from Minty's division to the prison site, fifty miles southwest of Macon. When the soldiers arrived at the pen in which some 13,000 Federals had died, they found it deserted. But though the keepers had long since released the surviving prisoners, the camp still held a macabre fascination for the cavalrymen. They entered the stockade and stared at the deadlines, the stocks and chains, and the festering pools of filth. One trooper reported that within a short time each man in the party was covered with vermin and had to change his clothing.

Wirz was one of the few prison officials still at his post. The cavalrymen called at his headquarters, talked with him, looked through his records, but returned to Macon next day without taking him into custody. Nevertheless, alarmed by the likelihood of his eventual arrest, Wirz sent a letter to Wilson on the seventh, which revealed the extent of his anxiety. He called himself a foreigner who had been "carried away by the maelstrom of excitement and joined the Southern Army" but who had never sought such a post as had been given him. "The duties I had to perform were arduous and unpleasant," he continued, "and I am satisfied that no man can or will justly blame me for things that happened here and which were beyond my power to control. . . . Still I now bear the odium, and men who were prisoners here seem disposed to wreak their vengeance upon me for what they have suffered, who was the medium, or, I may better say, the tool in the hands of my superiors."

The letter was of no avail. As he had feared, cavalrymen soon returned. Despite Wirz's protestations of innocence, Captain Henry E. Noyes, one of Wilson's aides-de-camp, conducted him to Macon, where Wilson listened dully to his pleas for freedom. At first Wilson intended to try Wirz at his headquarters and set up a court for that purpose, but then he received word that the jailer was to be taken to Washington City for public trial. He sent Wirz north aboard a special train in custody of Captain Noyes and several troopers.

By far the most important fugitive Wilson captured during his stint in Macon was Jefferson Davis. The Confederate president was the target of a pursuit so energetic and precise as to justify Wilson's assertion that "I drew a net around Mr. Davis that would have reflected credit upon a detective policeman."

Word of Davis's flight had reached Wilson as early as April 11, when he came into possession of newspapers relating the story. Almost two weeks later, when in Macon, he heard a reliable report that Davis, still at large, was fleeing south through the Carolinas. Traveling with a large cavalry escort and some other Confederate officials, the president was thought to be heading either for the Trans-Mississippi Department or for Florida. Because his reported route would carry him into central Georgia, Wilson considered the glory and notoriety his capture would add to the already solid reputation of the Cavalry Corps, M.D.M.

Accordingly, he detached forces from Macon to watch for Davis's party in widely divergent areas. Within a few days 13,000 troopers were posted in and near such Georgia cities as Griffin, Jonesboro, West Point, Talledega, Cuthbert, Columbus, and Bainbridge, with others pushing into South Carolina. When all dispositions had been made, a cordon of troopers stretched for 350 miles, from a point northwest of Atlanta to the Gulf Coast near Tallahassee, Florida. Hearing of this, General George Thomas wrote from Nashville to an associate: "If Davis escapes . . . he will prove himself a better general than any of his subordinates."

Wilson went to great lengths to insure Davis's capture. Before April ended he was distributing to the people of Georgia copies of a notice offering a reward of $100,000 in gold for apprehending the president and handing him over to Federal authorities. The offer was in line with a reward which the War Department had officially authorized. Wilson also proclaimed: "Several million dollars of specie reported to be with him will become the property of the captors."

Leaving no stone unturned, he also selected some of General Upton's men to operate in unknown territory in an effort to locate Davis's band, infiltrate it, and deliver it to Federal forces. He chose a contingent of twenty scouts and placed them under a resourceful officer, Lieutenant Joseph A. Yeoman, of the First Ohio Cavalry.

Disguised as Confederates, Yeoman and his men left Macon on May 3 and after some hair-raising adventures and a great deal of traveling, learned that Davis was heading for Washington, Georgia and points farther south. Eventually the scouts succeeded in joining the fugitive band near Washington, accompanied it for a time before being forced to ride on or risk being unmasked, and reported its whereabouts to Wilson.

Armed with Yeoman's information, several other contingents set out from Macon to patrol the central Georgia district toward which Davis was moving. Two such bands—150 men of the First Wisconsin Cavalry under Lieutenant Colonel Henry Harnden, and a detachment of the Fourth Michigan, led by Lieutenant Colonel Benjamin D. Pritchard—finally closed in on the fugitives near Irwinville, Georgia on May 10. The two forces failed to cooperate properly, however, with the result that both located Davis's wagon camp early that day, advanced upon it from two directions, mistook each other in the morning gloom for enemy soldiers, and, opening fire, killed two and wounded four of their own number before discovering the mistake.

They apprehended the fugitive Confederate president under controversial circumstances, which Wilson publicized to the hilt without regard to fact or probability. The captors claimed they nabbed Davis in one of his wife's dresses, attempting by that disguise to escape at the last minute. Davis and his allies later insisted that the story had been concocted by enemies seeking to make a final mockery of the Confederate government. Davis claimed that he had mistakenly placed his wife's shawl over his shoulders when climbing from his dark wagon during the Federal attack. But Wilson—more willing to believe a story that would draw notoriety to himself, at Davis's expense—wired Secretary of War Stanton that the Confederate chief had worn a dress and bonnet and had carried a concealed weapon, a fierce-looking bowie knife.

Davis and his party—including his wife, his sister-in-law, his secretary, his aides-de-camp, the remnants of a disbanded cavalry escort, and John H. Reagan, Confederate postmaster-general—were taken by Colonels Harnden and Pritchard to Macon, where they arrived on the thirteenth. There Wilson honored Davis with a final recognition of his office; the troopers formed double lines facing inward and presented arms when the Rebel president passed between them.

At the Lanier House, Wilson met with Davis and chatted about the personalities and events of the late war, West Point matters, and such controversial topics as Lincoln's assassination. Davis expressed genuine sorrow over the murder, and disgust that Andrew Johnson— his enemy as well as Wilson's—was now in the White House. Davis also voiced his belief that a vengeful federal government would do its utmost to make him suffer for what it considered an act of treason. Throughout, he spoke lucidly, candidly, with a composure and a dignity that impressed his host and captor.

Wilson was somewhat saddened when it came time for Davis to

go. Late that afternoon the fugitives were sent to Atlanta. From there a guard, commanded by Colonel Pritchard, would convey them to Augusta, Savannah, and farther northward.

Eventually Davis would be imprisoned at Fort Monroe, Virginia. There, in casemated prison quarters, he would remain for two years. Then, when the North's desire for vengeance had subsided, he would be released and permitted to spend the rest of his life in peace and freedom among family, friends, and the last adherents of the Lost Cause.

Wilson had succeeded in apprehending Davis primarily because he commanded so many soldiers skilled in reconnaissance and intelligence work. But he had failed entirely in attempting to capture those southward-fleeing Confederate officials considered only slightly less important than Davis—Secretary of State Judah P. Benjamin and Secretary of War John C. Breckinridge. Even so, Wilson's reputation soared. Davis's capture won him the national prominence which had been denied him when his great Selma campaign was overshadowed by the more dramatic news stories which broke at the same time—Lee's and Johnston's surrender, Lincoln's murder, and Davis's flight from Richmond. By the close of May Wilson's name was splashed across the country's newspapers and his portrait appeared in leading periodicals such as *Harper's Weekly*. Unfortunately, this was in part owing to the colorful, but not strictly accurate and sometimes unabashedly sensational, statements which he gave the press. In the June 17 issue of *Harper's*, for instance, he was quoted thus: "The story of Davis' ignoble attempt at flight is even more ignoble than I told it. . . ."

As ever, he remained the dedicated pragmatist and opportunist.

AFTER HIS SUCCESSFUL CAMPAIGN TO entrap the Rebel chieftain, Wilson (who by now had been appointed to the full rank of major general of volunteers and had been named a brevet major general in the Regular Army) could give his undivided attention to other matters which concerned a military governor in Georgia. He recalled two of his divisions from scouting duty to resume occupation work in Macon, while parts of the third—Upton's—remained in Augusta and Atlanta.

One of his major concerns became the reconstruction of the railroad from Atlanta to Dalton and Chattanooga, which Sherman had destroyed before beginning his march but which had later become a vital supply line for the Federal occupation troops. To handle this giant chore he chose Colonel Winslow, who, though youthful, had experience

Wilson as Major General of Volunteers in 1865—*Photograph courtesy Library of Congress*

as a railroad contractor and was a soldier of resourcefulness and skill Winslow fully repaid his commander for his confidence. His brigade of troopers swiftly repaired tracks, ties, gradients, bridges, and depot buildings, and kept a careful account of the cost, with the expectation that the road company would reimburse the government for the work The cavalrymen refurbished the line to the point south of Dalton a which other Federal forces, under General Steedman, had halted thei labors after moving from the opposite direction. Within three weeks trains were carrying valuable supplies down the length of the line, "thu solving," as Wilson reported, "all of our difficulties."

Through the efforts of Colonel William J. Palmer, one of hi brigade commanders, Wilson also recovered a shipment of bonds securities, silver plate, script, and currency—more than seven millio dollars' worth—which die-hard Confederates had taken from the Ban of Macon before the cavalry arrived there. These valuables, containe in a wagon train which tried to slip through the network of Federal spanning central Georgia, were sent to General Upton in Augusta an by him distributed to their owners without loss of a single dollar.

A much different problem involved the Confederate governor c Georgia, Joseph Emerson Brown, a backwoods-born but suave an shrewd politician. In May, without consulting Wilson, the governo decided to summon the state legislature into session. This ran counte to the wishes of the War Department, which felt that "the restoration o peace and order cannot be entrusted to rebels and traitors who de stroyed the peace and trampled down the order. . . ." Brown's activitie eventually led to his arrest and imprisonment in Washington.

Before that, however, a personal confrontation occurred betwee Wilson and Brown. When receiving the governor to investigate th matter of the legislature, Wilson found him haughty and officious, confi dent that he could overawe the invaders of his state. At first he refuse to recognize Wilson's jurisdiction over him and insisted he would tele graph Washington for guidelines. But Wilson shattered his visitor' composure by displaying a pardon for Brown as commander in chief o the Georgia militia. He advised Brown to sign the document if h wished to be granted full citizen's rights under the federal government The governor read through the pardon and suddenly became grave. H stated that he could not possibly affix his signature, for the term Wilson had stipulated required him, as he felt, "to recant and abjure a the political acts and opinions of my life."

Wilson was aware of this. He also realized that the time had com to clearly establish his authority over the people in and near Macon, including all former officials.

Still Brown refused: "If I sign that paper it will destroy all my political prospects forever."

With that, Wilson lost his patience. He rose from the chair in which he had been sitting, gave Brown a dark look, and said: "My God! Governor, is it possible that you imagine, in the face of the part you have taken against the United States for the last four years, you have any prospect in this country but to be hanged?"

Brown hesitated. Then he said, softly, "That view of the matter had not occurred to me." Finally he took up his pen and endorsed the pardon, and Wilson's victory was complete. Thereafter, the governor posed no problem.

Generally speaking, Wilson's term of rule in middle Georgia was quite successful. Thanks to his work and to the efforts of former Confederate statesmen such as Howell Cobb, the people of the region were able to place themselves on a firm footing during their climb toward economic stability. The returning soldiers reworked their lands, carefully planned their harvest, and, as Wilson later noted, "although the season was late, made one of the best and most profitable crops the State ever raised." In fact, the harvest was so bountiful that Wilson considered becoming a local planter, on a small scale, once mustered out of the volunteer service. But in the end he found that he lacked the necessary funds to make his dream a reality.

Politically as well as economically, he strove to reconstruct the district. "I mingled much with the leading men," he wrote, "seeking their views and giving my own on every public question of interest. I counseled moderation in speech, abstention from public discussions, and a strict and studious devotion to the private duties of life." Such advice produced beneficial results; he found it unnecessary to raise a heavy hand against political dissidents.

However, not everyone in the North seemed pleased with his rule. When in June the government announced permanent assignments among the occupation forces in the conquered South, he found he had not been given command of the Department of Georgia, a post he felt eminently qualified to administer. Instead—primarily, it would seem, through the efforts of Andrew Johnson—General Steedman received the department, while Wilson retained control of a small portion of it, the District of Columbus, headquartered at Macon. As weeks passed, this position provided him with a dwindling volume of work and gave him plenty of time to wish he had not angered the president so much in the past.

After July, he had no corps of cavalry to command. For a time previous it had appeared that his force might be ordered south of the Rio Grande to battle French troops which had invaded Mexico. But when this course was not followed, Washington determined that so many troopers were no longer required to secure order in central Georgia. The corps was ordered to disband, and a few infantry regiments were detailed to take its place.

In short order the cavalry was mustered out and sent to depots for transportation north. Wilson's formal order announcing the dissolution of this huge command was dated July 2. Throughout the order Wilson used laudatory statements to describe the services of the command, but they were not exaggerations. Only superlatives could have properly cited the accomplishments of the Cavalry Corps of the Military Division of the Mississippi.

Once his officers and men had left Macon, Wilson found almost nothing to do. Because staff officers handled most of the administrative work relating to the few remaining regiments, their commander was personally employed only a few hours each day. He had never enjoyed the waiting game, and grew so bored that eventually he asked to be mustered out of the volunteer ranks and be given active duty in the Regular Army. His request, although approved by both the president and the adjutant general of the Army, later was countermanded by General Grant, who persuaded him to remain in Macon as long as any work at all was available. Since Grant had worked hard to gain Wilson's appointment to the post Steedman ultimately received and even now was trying to secure it for him, Wilson agreed to stay on the job a while longer.

But the volume of work did not increase, and not until August did he receive a special assignment, giving him the opportunity to participate in activity of national prominence. Henry Wirz was then being tried in Washington before a military tribunal which was also investigating conditions as they had existed at Andersonville. Since Wilson had arrested Wirz and later had personally examined the prison camp, he was ordered north to testify.

He spent several idle days in the capital, while the trial dragged on through sultry late-summer weather. When finally called on to describe Andersonville as he had found it, he painted a grim and hideous picture of the prison, its land, buildings, stockade, sanitary facilities, and water supply. As he spoke he continually referred to a large diagram of the prison complex, which had been drawn under his supervision.

Encouraged to provide personal commentary on his findings, he stated that one of Andersonville's major flaws was inadequate drainage and sewerage facilities, which must have caused thousands of deaths. He believed that the physical state of the prison was "intelligent enough for the purpose, but it did not exhibit any very humane engineering. It was simply an enclosure stockade, and made safe for men to go into, with no earthly preparation that I could see for their comfort; and if there ever were 30,000 men there, as I have been told there were, that would explain very readily the cause of the deaths. . . ."

His testimony, coupled with that of former prisoners and other officers who had examined the prison after its evacuation, sealed Henry Wirz's fate. Long before the trial ended, the Swiss immigrant's guilt seemed clearly established in the judges' minds. That November he was hanged in Washington, the only Confederate to be convicted and executed as a war criminal.

However, the testimony against Wirz had been greatly distorted, inflamed by the sensational reminiscences of bitter ex-prisoners. The charges against him—conspiracy to "destroy the lives" of prisoners and cold-blooded murder of several Federals—were never proven conclusively, and thus his execution was a travesty of justice. By implying that Wirz was inhumane in crowding prisoners into such a small enclosure (which he did pursuant to specific orders), Wilson played a culpable role in sending the jailer to an undeserved fate.

Wirz's trial, however, did furnish Wilson with other, more pleasant opportunities. While waiting to testify, he was able to visit old friends in Philadelphia, New York, and Washington. During his socializing he paid a visit to the Andrews's home, which altered the course of his future.

He had been in love with Ella Andrews, now a vivacious nineteen-year-old, for years. But because he had seen her only infrequently he had been unable to seriously consider an enduring relationship. Now, with the war at an end, and himself facing the prospect of leaving the Army for civilian life, he pressed a swift courtship, proposed marriage, and, to his surprise and joy, won her hand. On the night he proposed he noted in his diary that it was a doubly special occasion: "This is my 28th birthday—long to be remembered."

Later he wrote of his elation to Badeau. He was unable to describe his sweetheart, he said, because words were inadequate to convey an indication of her beauty and grace. Growing steadily sentimental, he continued: "I have watched her grow to girlhood—and womanhood—have seen her at rare intervals, and grown stronger in hope though I never spoke a word of love to her. . . . My visit north, accidental in itself, gave me an opportunity to see her. . . . She was good enough to listen to me and I am happy."

Again he tried to describe "Nelly," and this time felt he had succeeded: "She is a good girl—pure minded, innocent, child-like, but withal very different from me—a 'complement'—not 'counterpart.' She says she's a 'stupid, naughty, wayward and uncertain little girl'—but I see differently. . . ."

After Wirz's trial ended, Wilson took the opportunity to go west and visit Shawneetown. The homecoming, his first in two years, was made particularly pleasant by the news he carried with him—news of his engagement. He had a happy reunion with his mother and sister, rehashed the war with his recently discharged brothers, and basked once again in the glow of the townspeople's attention.

After spending a few days at home, he returned to duty via Louisville and Cincinnati, hoping to meet General Grant, who was visiting old friends and political officials in those cities. Due to a change in his schedule, Grant had to hurry east before Wilson could reach his side. Therefore Wilson went to Macon, where he attended to such work as had materialized during his absence, and made arrangements to obtain a furlough, during which he could marry and honeymoon.

Late in November he did have the chance to see Grant. With Badeau, Orville Babcock, and other members of his military family, the general was swinging through major cities in the occupied South to study the progress of Reconstruction. When in Georgia, he asked Wilson to travel to Atlanta to meet him, and Wilson did so without delay. Their meeting—the first in fourteen months—was warm and cordial, and their conversation, Wilson later recalled, was "one of the most interesting of my life."

They discussed a host of subjects, including the campaigns which had brought them fame; Lincoln's death and his vice-president's rise to power (Grant felt much the same as Wilson in regard to Andrew Johnson); and the problems that confronted the Reconstruction program. Grant emphasized, as Wilson wrote, "that we had had bloodshed and punishment enough, and that we of the North should now strive, without prejudice or passion, to protect those we had paroled, to close the wounds of war, and to start the South anew on the road to prosperity and fortune"—the same philosophy as had guided Wilson's military governorship. In more personal matters, Grant also congratulated Wilson on his engagement and accepted an invitation to attend the wedding, which was to be held in Wilmington early in January.

The two men talked deep into the night to close the great gap created by their long separation. At 1 A.M. they at last retired for the evening, but after thirty minutes found themselves still wide awake. Grant then came into Wilson's room with a lighted candle and said, "If you can't sleep, Wilson, let us get up and finish our conversation." Wilson agreed, and the friends chatted until called to breakfast in the morning.

Wilson would always remember that meeting as one of the most pleasant he ever held with the general-in-chief. But less than a month later, when he left Georgia and went northward to be wed, he suffered through one of the least cordial interviews of his life—with Andrew Johnson.

This was the first he had been in Johnson's presence since their clash in Nashville during the reorganization of the Tennessee cavalry. Wilson, of course, knew how the new president regarded him; Johnson had openly displayed his feelings by declining to give him the chief Reconstruction post in Georgia, despite Grant's recommendation. Nevertheless, since he was leaving his district command for an extended period, Wilson felt it his duty to pay his respects at the White House and, if Johnson deemed it proper, to discuss the Reconstruction picture as he saw it.

But Johnson did not deem it proper, and during the meeting displayed an austere manner and a scowling expression. He seemed not at all interested in Wilson's opinions on the rebuilding of the South; he appeared to take note only that Wilson had been retained in command of his district despite having expressed a desire to be relieved. After a few minutes, Johnson brought the visit to a close. Dismayed by the icy reception he had received, Wilson quickly left the Executive Mansion. He had completed his last official conference with Andy Johnson.

Traveling to Wilmington, he pushed the memory of the meeting out of his mind. Although being on bad terms with the president of the United States was enough to upset any soldier, Wilson managed to focus his thoughts on an entirely different subject—the responsibilities of a man soon to be married.

★XII★

*My Retirement
Is Only for
the Term of Peace*

The wedding of Major General James Harrison Wilson and Miss Ella Andrews was performed at the Andrews's estate, "Stockford," on the afternoon of January 3, 1866. In attendance were the families of both bride and groom, friends and relatives by the dozen, and a glittering array of the famous and near-famous. Guests included General Grant and several members of his staff such as Badeau and Babcock, plus Montgomery Meigs, the quarter-master-general of the Federal armies, Edward Hatch, who had been one of Wilson's most reliable subordinates for the last several months of the war, and two other cavalry cohorts, Generals Alfred Torbert and Ranald Mackenzie.

For their honeymoon Wilson and his bride went to New York City, where friends and acquaintances held a seemingly endless succession of dinners and balls in their honor. As a prelude to their long life together, the period was gaily auspicious. A few days later Wilson wrote Badeau from New York in a blissfully ironic vein: "The little lady says she's tired of me already, and I'm tired of her too, but don't tell her so. Ah, Badeau, Badeau, let well enough alone, don't get married, take the advice of a man of experience. . . ." Toward the close of the letter he grew very earnest: "We are having a splendid time. . . ."

The splendid time did not last long. On the sixth Wilson received a formal order from the White House, mustering him out of the volunteer service "at his own request" and directing him to report for duty, at the end of his leave, as a captain of engineers. The message stunned him. As he later wrote, the loss of rank was "without consequence or inconvenience," except that "the reduction of revenue from a major general's pay and allowances to those of a captain, with a wife to provide for, was a serious embarrassment."

And so Andrew Johnson had apparently taken his revenge at last. The demotion, of course, would have come sooner or later, for the volunteers' war, for all intents and purposes, had ended at Appomattox; and the Army was officer-heavy to boot. But Wilson had not expected to be dropped so far in rank so suddenly and without warning. He could not help but feel that Johnson, believing the reduction in rank and pay would particularly hurt him at this point in his life, had hastened it out of personal malice. Whether or not this belief was correct, Wilson would never alter it.

The situation was especially sobering because Wilson had managed to save very little from his general's salary while accumulating, through various means, a debt of several hundred dollars. As a military man, he could expect little via outside income; by this time he had found only a single possibility of private employment—as an executive in a newly formed corporation known as the National Express and Transportation Company. The enterprise, which had originated with a number of southern gentlemen including General Joseph Johnston, had been conceived as a southern-based competitor to the American Express and the Adams Transportation companies, the largest such agencies in the country. The position had been offered him through the auspices of General Grant, but the possibility of such a venture succeeding in the economically weakened South was chancy indeed.

Everything considered, the order directing his mustering out was a staggering blow. The newlyweds attempted to keep the news from ruining their first days together. But despite their efforts, the event cast a shadow over their honeymoon.

When the ten-day New York visit ended, the couple went south. In Richmond, still on leave, Captain Wilson met with the officials of the express company and completed arrangements to enter the agency as its "chief executive officer," at a salary of $12,000 a year. Had the enterprise survived its infancy, the income would have been a great aid. But within weeks, insufficient capital—the result of investors oversubscribing and then defaulting on their commitments—caused the venture's decline. Other problems, including exorbitant rates charged by railroads to ship freight, brought an end to the enterprise. When the agency went bankrupt in mid-March, Wilson resigned his position and sadly returned north.

Since he and Ella desired to remain in the East for a time, he tried to secure an engineering assignment in Washington. No work could be obtained there, however, and the situation placed him in a quandary. Colonel Delafield, his old superintendent at West Point, rescued him by providing him work, in late April, as an assistant engineer at a fort along the Delaware River, not far from Wilmington.

Service at Fort Delaware was neither exciting nor challenging, but Wilson remained there for three months, improving river defenses which had never been tested in battle. At least the work provided a steady income and enabled him and his wife to live in relative comfort.

When his tour of duty ended that summer, mutual friends influenced Grant to transfer him west, to work at improving the Mississippi River rapids, a project already in progress. Eventually, he and Ella settled in Davenport, Iowa, near which city he began to conduct land and water surveys for controlling the Rock Island and Des Moines rapids as well as for engineering a line of deep-water navigation from Green Bay, Wisconsin, via the Fox and Rock rivers, and also from Chicago, by the Illinois River, to the Mississippi. Here the work was more varied and stimulating than that on the Delaware; consequently it proved more enjoyable. However, he was required to travel a great deal and to be absent from home for long periods of time. Left in Davenport during such periods, his young wife found life quite lonely—not at all as it had been in the East. But Ella made a determined effort to adjust herself to the pace of life in Iowa and to assume the role of the model Army wife: adaptable, uncomplaining, willing to endure hardships to advance her husband's career.

Her life became less lonely in October. On the thirtieth their first child, Mary, was born, and she brought into the Wilson home a degree of happiness and delight not previously there. Her father was ecstatic, and as months passed his joy kept pace with her growth. Eventually he could write Badeau: "Mamie has two little bits of teeth and seems to take particular pleasure in trying them on my nose and ears whenever she can get a chance. She enjoys a romp with me immensely and no matter how much put out she is in regard to anything, she is put into a good humor at once by my turning her a couple of summer sets—which I am sure to do every chance I get and always to the special alarm of Mama. . . ." In a later letter he again turned quite serious when considering the contentment and stability his marriage had brought him, telling Badeau: "I'm sure my old boy if you could experience a tithe of the pleasure she is to me in a thousand ways that no man can describe, you would never rest till you had got a wife and were blessed with a real baby."

With passing time, nonetheless, Wilson encountered some problems. He was not the first young husband and father to discover that a growing family led to a scarcity of funds. "I find that a dollar is worth more to me now than it used to be, though it does not seem to go so far," he wrote less than a year after Mary's birth. To supplement his Army pay he investigated a number of projects, including one to extract peat from Iowa bogs for use in heating homes. But these did not materialize.

A welcome salary increase did come about through the continuing solicitude of General Grant. During the reorganization of the Army in 1866, Wilson was promoted to lieutenant colonel of the recently formed Thirty-fifth Infantry Regiment. The unit was then stationed in Texas, but through Grant's intercession Wilson was permitted to remain on engineering duty in Iowa while receiving the added rank and pay. Through the counterefforts of Andrew Johnson and other officials, however, his name was placed far down the list of lieutenant colonels, which made remote the possibility of a quick further increase in rank; but the promotion nevertheless gave a tremendous boost to his morale as well as a moderate lift to his economic status.

Another venture which earned him some small amount of profit originated with another old friend, Charles A. Dana, who after the war had left his government post to return to newspaper editing. Being well known in publishing circles, Dana had been offered a contract to write a biography of Grant. To help him do the job he called on Wilson, knowing that Wilson's intimacy with the general would provide fascinating insights into his character. Since Wilson then had some free time on his hands, his work load having temporarily diminished, and because writing had long intrigued him, he agreed to do most of the work himself. He put pen to paper in March, 1868, and—to have the manuscript ready for publication in time to boost Grant's chances for securing the presidency as the Republican candidate in the November election—he labored at a furious pace. Within two months he had completed 530 pages of script. Dana, who wrote only three of the book's forty-odd chapters, declared that "nothing like the rapidity with which it was written was ever known before." The book, an effusively laudatory study which boasted no prodigious literary talents, nevertheless gave Wilson his first experience in writing for publication, which in time became his great avocation. It is impossible, however, to determine to what degree, if any, the work contributed to Grant's victory that fall.

Wilson labored along the Mississippi for four years, removing the Rock Island rapids and neutralizing those at Keokuk, establishing a deep-water line from Lake Michigan to the Illinois River, building dams and locks to facilitate shipping, and promoting a venture for improving the mouth of the Mississippi by use of the jetty system. By mid-1870, however, he felt that he had served as an army engineer long enough. His work had given him a deep sense of accomplishment, for it had made possible a great increase in America's shipping capacity. But by this time he had made a number of moves toward establishing himself in private commercial life, which he hoped would prove more remunerative than a soldier's career.

Despite the urgings of President Grant and his secretary of war, William W. Belknap, both of whom considered him too valuable an officer to be lost to the service, Wilson submitted his resignation from the United States Army on July 15, effective the last day of the year. He stipulated that "my retirement from the service in which I have had more than my share of promotions, is only for the term of peace which seems to have settled so happily upon the country, and which every one should wish to be perpetuated." Should the country sound another call to arms, he wished to return to duty at once, to serve in any way he might. Yet at this time he had only mild reservations about quitting the service which had coordinated his energies for the past fifteen years. As he wrote Dana: "As a matter of course I feel some regrets at severing the pleasant social relations which connect me with the Service, but none which could for a moment deter me from the step I am taking."

The basic truth was that with a wife and child to support, he now thought of himself primarily as a breadwinner. The best way to pursue that role, he felt, was to pack away his blue uniform and to don the businessman's cutaway and top hat.

And so, when the New Year, 1871, dawned he and Ella and their four-year-old daughter left Iowa to take up residence in New York

City. There James Harrison Wilson planned to devote his time and energy to managing a railroad.

BY 1871, WILSON HAD BEEN INVOLVED IN rail enterprise for six years. He had acquired his first railroad stocks shortly after the close of the war, and by the time he settled in New York had accumulated a small but profitable portfolio.

He had been drawn into rail ownership during his work along the Mississippi, as a result of conversing with local promoters who prophesied a tremendous upsurge in rail travel in America during coming years. Interested, Wilson began to direct his attention to the obvious need for railroads in his home region of southern Illinois, which during the 1860s was served by only two roads.

He learned that a line running from Saint Louis through lower Illinois to his home village, Shawneetown, promised to be a lucrative venture. Quickly he formed a partnership with one of his former cavalry brigade commanders, Edward Winslow, an experienced railroad man. With several influential investors, Wilson and his partner secured from the state of Illinois on March 10, 1869 a charter to build and operate the so-called St. Louis & Southeastern Railway.

The term of Wilson's first ambitious postwar venture was relatively short. At first the Southeastern—with Winslow as its Saint Louis-based president and Wilson its vice-president with headquarters in Manhattan, near the nation's financial districts—did a thriving business. Subscribers and capital seemed plentiful and, as Wilson later commented, "The whole enterprise . . . grew into notice under our direction." But in the autumn of 1870 shareholders dwindled and capital shrank to a point at which Wilson and his associates were compelled to sell mortgage bonds on the road's property. The bonds moved slowly —even after Wilson sailed overseas to stimulate personally their sale in England and on the Continent—and finally they had to be released at prices so low as to be, in Winslow's view, catastrophic.

Although the road continued to do a thriving business by expanding into Indiana, Kentucky, Tennessee and, through connections with rival lines, into the Deep South, taxes and interest on loans consumed most of its profits. Again, in the summer of 1873, Wilson went abroad to stimulate bond sales, with little effect. Finally he had to compromise his principles by allowing associates to bribe rival agents in order that the Southeastern's tickets could be placed on sale throughout the cotton states. He justified the unethical practice by pointing to the ruthless and often unlawful tactics which competitors used against his line, including working in collusion to cut off the Southeastern's through traffic. Still, the idea of illegal dealing must have gnawed at Wilson's conscience, but once again he seemed willing to do almost anything to stave off personal ruin.

Early in 1873 a series of disasters—fires in uninsured rail shops, widely publicized accidents involving passenger deaths and injuries, court rulings holding municipalities not liable for payment of grants and subsidies allegedly promised the line—almost killed the Southeastern. Then, when the nationwide Panic of 1873 struck, the road's New York financial agents failed, and the Southeastern defaulted on bond payments several times. Late the next year, amidst the wailing of bondholders, the road finally passed into receivership, and Wilson conceded defeat.

Other reasons for his failure were overextension and imprudent investment. In February, 1872, as the Southeastern began its decline, Wilson and Winslow won a contract to complete work on General Ambrose Burnside's Cairo & Vincennes, whose right-of-way stretched from the Indiana-Illinois border to the Mississippi River. The partners completed the road according to specifications that December, whereupon Burnside offered it for lease to the Pennsylvania Railroad System. When that giant corporation later withdrew its interest from the line, Burnside found himself in dire straits. In war he had often been a thorn in Wilson's side; peace had not changed him. Now he refused to pay Wilson and his partner the sum they claimed for their completion work, and even added that, because he had tendered them some funds during their labors, they now stood "on the books of the company largely in its debt."

Court action, to which Wilson and Winslow at once resorted, proved slow and indecisive. Not even their chief counsel, Wilson's brother Bluford—the recently appointed district attorney for southern Illinois—could force the courts to pry money out of Burnside with alacrity.

Early in 1875, however, an Illinois judge finally ruled in the plaintiffs' favor, and Wilson's share of the judgments was fixed at $25,000 in cash, $97,000 in mortgage bonds, and $100,000 in common stock in the C & V. But the sum was never paid, for the road was later sold to British bondholders, who refused to assume responsibility for Burnside's debts. In later proceedings, Wilson and his partner had their claims dismissed by the Indianapolis courts—which left Wilson in debt and almost penniless. Winslow subsequently broke with him and resigned, and thus Wilson became the president of the in-receivership Southeastern. For the first time in his life, his future was ominous. At about this time he wrote a friend that he "must do something to keep out of the poor-house."

His family was an ever increasing concern. In March of 1873 Katharine Wilson—"Kitty," her father called her—had been born. Wilson was now pressed to provide sustenance for himself, his wife, and two young daughters.

A new opportunity for employment came as a result of his entrenchment in Republican-dominated New York City industrial circles. Shortly before Winslow and Wilson terminated their business relationship, Grant's secretary of the treasury, Benjamin H. Bristow, a close friend of Wilson, offered to make him his principal assistant. But after considering the salary which accompanied the position, Wilson decided to cast about for a more remunerative office.

Soon afterward he hit on such an enterprise. One of the businessmen with whom he had become associated in New York was George M. Pullman, inventor of railroad sleeping cars. In November, 1874 Pullman asked Wilson to aid him in introducing his "Palace Cars" into Europe. Enticed by a $250-per-month salary, Wilson quickly agreed, and went abroad with the entrepreneur on December 12.

At first Pullman's venture appeared successful, but eventually it died because of problems relating to the size of bond commissions to be charged in Europe. Upon his return to the United States, however, Wilson was asked "semi-officially" by Secretary Bristow if he wished to be considered for the post of commissioner of internal revenue. By now he was willing to accept almost any offer, but then he learned that for some reason never fully explained, President Grant did not favor his appointment. Thus, another opportunity for steady employment faded.

Through Pullman's help, he did find a position he could accept. In April, 1875 he became a consulting engineer for New York's Gilbert Elevated Railway Company, which Pullman's corporation controlled. The proffered salary was minuscule, but Wilson perceived the possibility of rapid advancement. His foresight was keen; by August he was both chief engineer and general manager of one of the firm's subsidiaries, the Rapid Transit Company. In January of the following year he became chief engineer of the Gilbert Company at a salary more than three times that at which he had started. Furthermore, his work was progressive and significant; it included supervising plans for the location and construction of the Sixth Avenue Elevated Railroad, between the Battery and Central Park.

Wilson as Rail Executive in the 1870s—*Engraving courtesy Nebraska State Historical Society*

But even his tenure with the Gilbert Company was of short duration. Late in 1876 he feuded with Pullman's vice-president, Horace Porter, the West Point-trained staff officer who had once been Wilson's close friend and then his bitter rival in the struggle to win General Grant's esteem.

By the time Wilson joined the Gilbert Company he was also at odds with Porter over political affairs relating to Grant's presidency. Their increasingly abrasive relationship prompted Pullman to ask for Wilson's resignation. This Wilson at first withheld, until learning that the Gilbert Company's directors would side with Pullman in any power struggle. On August 31 he left the company, noting his bitterness in a revealing diary entry: "I am 'set free from daily contact of *things* I loathe'."

Intermittent unemployment had now become a fact of life. In early September Wilson could gather only $475 in ready cash; yet he declared: "I would rather be myself than any scoundrel I know with all his fortune." To comfort him, he did have some investments, several influential associates, two lovely children, and a remarkable wife. "We are very happy," he wrote of his family, "and although not rich in this world's goods we may justly regard ourselves as fairly fortunate."

Again, he was not out of work for long. Shortly before he left the Gilbert Company, the St. Louis & Southeastern had become involved in foreclosure proceedings. During its court-ordered reorganization, Wilson sought and won the office of receiver. He then moved his family to Saint Louis, where he managed the bankrupt line until a new purchaser could be found. The new owner stepped forth in December, 1879, and so Wilson could again return to New York City with Ella and the girls. Upon the line's sale, his colorful and checkered ten-year association with the Southeastern came to a close.

Under new management, the road prospered. But because its sale negated prior stock and bond dealings, Wilson could not profit along with it. Yet his salary as receiver had helped him regain financial stability, and the work had returned to his reputation much of the luster which had been drained by his earlier troubles as the road's vice-president.

In later years he could take satisfaction also from observing that the St. Louis & Southeastern "constitutes the principal connection of that flourishing system to Chicago, St. Louis, and the Northwest, and for many years has earned and paid both interest and dividends on a much larger amount of money than it cost, thus fully justifying its construction and the hopes which we entertained of its usefulness and profit."

WHILE SERVING AS A RAILROAD EXECUTIVE, Wilson also devoted considerable attention to politics.

Because of his long and cordial relationship with Ulysses S. Grant, he developed a close association with national political affairs after Grant attained the presidency in 1868. But although the two men remained friends through Grant's first six years in office, they had a gradual falling-out during the close of his second term. One of the most crucial factors in this was the position assumed in the Grant Administration by Bluford Wilson, who became in June, 1874 the solicitor of the Treasury Department under James's friend, Secretary Bristow.

The major event which produced friction between Wilson and the president was the Whiskey Scandal of 1875. Bluford was one of the prime movers behind the much-publicized investigation, which boded ill for some of Grant's closest associates, including his personal secretary, Orville Babcock. Bluford found that Babcock and other officials were linked with Federal revenue officers who had accepted bribes from distillers wishing to evade taxation. Bluford was an earnest, conscientious prosecutor, but so far as Grant's allies were concerned, his enthusiasm carried him too far. They accused him of collaborating with anti-Administration forces to obtain evidence against the conspirators, thus embarrassing the president and wounding his feelings.

Because Secretary Bristow, a born reformer, was an ardent foe of the conspirators, he upheld Bluford's efforts and thereby lost Grant's friendship. When Grant discovered that James Wilson remained Bristow's friend, he began to withdraw his friendship from him as well.

The situation involved Bluford's older brother in a thorny conflict of loyalties. James Wilson had long admired and respected Grant and owed the major portion of his successful military career to his solicitude. However, by now he had become estranged from his former mentor; a host of new advisors and spokesmen had surrounded the president, precluding a continuation of the once intimate Wilson-Grant association. By now, too, Wilson had become critical of many of the politicians who served the president; the aura of corruption which some of them had given the Republican Party—characterized by a plethora of scandals, of which the whiskey fraud was but one—disgusted him.

New, stronger ties of friendship bound him to the reform-minded Bristow, who had offered him several political posts, while Grant had offered none; and fraternal loyalty caused him to champion Bluford's muckraking tactics.

Still he tried to retain the president's regard. On several occasions he met with him at the White House and tried to explain his reasons for backing his brother's investigation. But increasingly Grant displayed an unwillingness to listen to his words, and on some occasions excoriated Wilson for siding with political enemies. Hard words never won Wilson over to another man's thinking—not even when that man was Ulysses Grant. In the end, he decided Grant was so maliciously pig-headed as to deserve his loyalty no longer. Henceforth Wilson would not go out of his way to spare the president's feelings.

The troubles between the two men were not eased when Wilson became the recipient of several other offers tendered by Bristow. In April, 1875 the secretary tried to promote him for the chief post in the Department of the Interior, and the following March as successor to Secretary of War Belknap, another high official forced to resign his office through alleged complicity in a conspiracy to defraud the government. By this time Grant, having come to seriously doubt Wilson's loyalty, was far from keen about seeing the latter become a member of his cabinet.

By the start of the 1876 presidential campaign, the Wilson-Grant rift had widened substantially. Wilson's views on political reform and his friendship for Bristow caused him to urge the candidacy of the Treasury secretary. He was influential in persuading Bristow to enter the race, and then served as one of his advisors during the campaign. In so doing he further incurred Grant's animosity, for the president believed he was helping Bristow use the influence of the Treasury Department to further the secretary's candidacy. However, before the campaign was well under way, Bristow resigned his office under pressure from the president.

The campaign was particularly bitter and sordid, and both Bristow and his principal opponent for the Republican nomination, Congressman James G. Blaine of Maine, resorted to low tactics from the outset. Scandal-mongers, let loose by the Blaine forces, sought to discredit Bristow's honesty by publicizing several unfounded rumors about wrongdoing in the Treasury Department. Through the help of Wilson and other reform-minded associates, Bristow easily surmounted that obstacle. Wilson and his allies then launched a severe attack of their own. These included publishing a report that erstwhile rail executive

Blaine, when speaker of the House of Representatives, had given the Union Pacific Railroad practically worthless bonds on a smaller line as collateral for a "loan" of $64,000 which the Union Pacific, almost wholly dependent upon government favor, had never asked him to repay. The story came from a reliable source, and Wilson displayed a particular enthusiasm in spreading it through the Party. He was vastly displeased when Blaine later salvaged his candidacy by making an impassioned assertion of innocence before a congressional investigating committee.

But neither Bristow nor Blaine won the race, for at the Republican national convention that July, both fought so bitterly and so stubbornly refused to compromise that the convention deadlocked and a third candidate who had few political enemies, Ohio Governor Rutherford B. Hayes, gained the nomination. In November Hayes won the presidential election, succeeding Grant in the White House.

After the election, Wilson and the outgoing president severed their personal relationship. They remained apart and did not seek each other's company even at official Party gatherings. By 1880 Wilson had lost all respect for the general, even to the point of believing reports that after vacating the White House in 1876 Grant had placed himself in the hands of a corrupt syndicate which had groomed him for another attempt—a losing one—to gain the Party's nomination in 1880.

By 1881 Grant and Wilson, who had remained close in war and peace for almost two decades, could not tolerate each other's presence. A particularly vivid event told the story. That February, Grant entered a New York City restaurant with friends, found Wilson and others at a table, and, within sight of all, turned and went out. No amount of persuasion could induce the general to come back.

Wilson remembered the slight long after Grant's death, four years later.

WILSON BUSIED HIMSELF WITH THE FINAL details of his receivership until February, 1880. Then, the Southeastern having passed into the hands of the Nashville, Chattanooga & St. Louis Railroad, he was elected vice-president of the New York & New England system. He had been associated with that line, in various minor capacities, for more than a year.

Again the Wilson family was compelled to relocate, this time in Boston. There, in early October, a third daughter, Elinor, was born, and there Wilson once again occupied a front-desk office.

Soon after taking office, he promoted the long-planned completion of the road to Newburgh and Fishkill on the Hudson River. There it would connect with another system and would complete an east-west route from Boston to Lake Ontario.

Under his supervision, the extension work advanced economically and rapidly and the road gathered a comfortable amount of revenue; at the close of the first fiscal year following his election as vice-president, the New York & New England boasted an unusual 42 percent rise in net earnings. This was a significant factor in Wilson's promotion to road president on January 25, 1881.

A few months after assuming his new office, he saw storm clouds on the horizon when Jay Gould, the Erie Railroad magnate and one of the nation's most notorious "robber barons," made a power play to gain control of the line. Gould hoped to run the road in close competition with his arch-rival, Cornelius Vanderbilt, investor in several railroads in New York State and New England. Since Vanderbilt seemed an even greater menace than Gould, Wilson allowed the Erie crowd to take a large share in the line's operations in exchange for funds to finance its expansion, including its completion to the Hudson—a goal attained in November.

For a time the New York & New England continued to prosper, showing in 1882 a 33 percent increase in gross earnings over the previous year. But then major problems sprang up in profusion. A shortage of track and a too-heavy concentration on "through" business piled up empty boxcars. Government rail commissioners filed complaints about "unreasonable" traffic delays. A rash of road accidents attracted unfavorable publicity, and inefficient management on the part of the Erie men resulted in wasted capital and a personnel surplus. Noting the sad state of affairs, the *New York Times* took Gould and his partners to task for instituting policies which hurt their own road as much as they did the public.

By the mid months of 1883 the fortunes of the New York & New England were in sharp decline, and Wilson, seemingly helpless while Gould and his associates managed operations so poorly, learned that others in the front office were conspiring to oust him as president. The news depressed him terribly; once again, after initially successful efforts at management, he was administering a doomed enterprise. "I shall never run another railroad," he wrote that November.

Before the year was out he resigned, unable to convince the members of the road directorate that their future lay in leasing the New York & New England to the Erie system. As a result, the line passed into receivership early in 1884. By then Wilson had disposed of all his stock in the road and so took no loss when it went under. In truth, the stock sale had made him moderately wealthy.

Shunning any further direct contact with rail enterprise, he and his family moved from Boston to Wilmington, where they planned to spend the next several years.

Settling into domestic life, Wilson indulged a long-standing interest in writing by turning out articles, book reviews, and essays for various magazines, journals, and newspapers. Many of his themes related to Civil War exploits and to famous men he had known during his military, political, and business careers. A considerable amount of free time also enabled him to join various societies, such as those formed by veterans of the armies of the Potomac, the Tennessee, and the Cumberland. These and other civic and social organizations began to seek his services as speaker and toastmaster. Through such engagements he quickly established a reputation as an engaging and clear-speaking orator.

When he was not engaged in writing, speaking, or coordinating social activities, he indulged a fondness for traveling. In 1884 he visited Mexico and Central America, and early the next year a group of New York investors persuaded him to tour the Orient to study possibilities for building steam railroads in China and Japan. He sailed from San Francisco on October 19, 1885.

Wilson and a team of companions spent ten months in China, covering more than 15,000 miles on horseback and by cart and studying all aspects of Chinese life and culture. They traveled through numerous provinces, via guides and interpreters interviewed local landowners, and collected a wealth of information when visiting such cities as Tientsin, Peking, Kaiping, and Shan-hai-kwan.

In Tientsin, Wilson secured audiences with the first grand secretary of the Chinese Empire, Viceroy Li-Hung-chang, as well as with William M. Pethick, who doubled as Li's secretary and the U.S. viceconsul in Tientsin (and was a former Federal cavalryman who had served under Wilson). As the official who conducted foreign affairs for the Emperor, Li-Hung-chang was the man Wilson was most interested in meeting. From Li he learned that China needed railroads but lacked capital. Wilson voiced his belief that his country would willingly supply such funds.

From late December, 1885 to early March of the following year, Wilson explored rights-of-way between Tientsin and Canton via the Yellow and Yangtze rivers. The group traversed barren areas, averaging thirty miles per day, and gathered facts about the terrain, its natural resources, and its possible utility in rail enterprise. Afterward Wilson expressed the thought that rail trackage ought to be laid from Peking to the Yangtze River as a needed link between the capital and the central and southern provinces.

After further travel, which included a trip along the Great Wall of China and forays into Japan and Formosa, he returned to Tientsin for further conferences with Li-Hung-chang. The viceroy stated that by all indications the Chinese emperor would soon sanction massive railroad construction programs, but now he was pessimistic about opportunities for American investors. In August of 1886 Wilson returned to the United States with the opinion, derived from Li's statements, that his associates in New York would not be called upon to help finance Chinese industrial expansion.

After five months' preparation, a travel book emerged from his experiences. *China: Travels and Investigations in the "Middle Kingdom,"* a concise and interesting guide, appeared in print early in 1887. The book stressed Wilson's belief that by Western standards the Orient remained intellectually backward, lacked a progressive spirit, and was underdeveloped economically. However, he foresaw change in its near future, and fervently hoped that the trend toward national development would result in efforts to perfect civil administration, to bolster military resistance to the encroachments of foreign powers such as Russia, Germany, and France, to exploit abundant natural resources, and to strengthen industry—particularly the rail industry.

Although financially unsuccessful, the book was applauded by many critics. The *New York Times* called it "a remarkably fresh and entertaining book of travels, regarding the modern Chinaman from a natural and unbiased point of view and impressing one with the good sense and impartiality of the observer. . . ." The *Nation* found Wilson's statements "grave, judicial, and cautious" and his style "readable and pleasing."

The book's critical acclaim promoted further literary efforts. During the decade following his trips, Wilson remained in Wilmington, working on several manuscripts as well as investing in the New York stock market, advancing various promotional ventures, and engaging in political work.

Increasingly, politics claimed his attention. He threw himself into Republican Party affairs, consolidated his position in the G.O.P. organization in Delaware, and worked diligently for semipolitical organizations such as the Union veterans' societies. By 1889 his prominence in

Republican circles earned him consideration by President Benjamin Harrison for the office of secretary of war. But despite efforts in his behalf by several influential state and national politicians, the post was not tendered him. He hid his disappointment by working even more actively on the local level, and for five years served as chairman of the Republican Central Committee of Delaware. And as a delegate to the G.O.P national convention in July, 1892 he was instrumental in inserting several planks into the Party platform, including one which favored gold as the national monetary standard and another advocating political union between Canada and the United States.

His private interests were varied. He purchased and reorganized public utility companies and traded stocks through the R. Suydam Grant Company of New York. In the early 1890s he also sought to form banking firms in both America and England, and to establish an American ordnance company in association with the famed Krupp works of Germany. After promising beginnings, each of these ventures failed for lack of sufficient capital.

Transportation lines, especially railroads, continued to fascinate him. Despite his avowed intention to avoid management positions, he collaborated with associates in 1889 to organize a small line in Georgia. But, fearing that his partners were employing patently dishonest operating tactics, he soon left the company. In April, 1891 he became an executive in New York's Hudson Tunnel Company at a substantial salary, but before he could earn it he perceived that the venture was "a sinking boat," and so bailed out of it. In 1893 he secured a steady salary for the first time in nine years by joining the directorate of the Baltimore & Ohio Railroad, a post he relinquished the next year in order to co-receive, with his brother Bluford (now a prosperous attorney in Springfield, Illinois) the Louisville, Evansville & St. Louis, in which he had acquired an interest during a previous foreclosure. In mid-1896, while serving as receiver, he also figured in the formation of an American syndicate to finance construction of the Chinese-Russian Railway, whose beginnings he had observed during a trip to Russia five years before. But the project—like so many others in which he had become involved—died after a short life-span.

In February of 1898 he made a final attempt to regain a foothold in railroad management, but failed to secure the receivership of the Central Pacific Corporation, then in federal court. His interest in rail commerce never left him, but he came to recognize the futility of attempting to turn that interest into further profit.

He also continued his interest in political affairs but, except in

Photograph of Wilson in the 1890s from *Harper's Weekly—Courtesy Nebraska State Historical Society*

This photograph appeared shortly before Wilson's recall to duty in the Spanish-American War.

local politics, held no posts. Twice he had been considered for secretary of war and twice rejected. Various other national positions had eluded him, although men of less energy, political know-how, and integrity had succeeded to high office, including more than a few Civil War heroes. In December, 1896 he was for a third time a candidate for secretary of war, during President William McKinley's administration. Though widely recognized as a distinguished political figure and despite influential backers, he once again lost out—this time to Russell Alger, a former Civil War officer who Wilson deeply believed was not cabinet material. The new secretary had had a checkered military career, and Wilson did not hesitate to inform McKinley that he thought it "a disgrace to assign any man over the Army who had virtually been kicked out of the service during the Civil War."

Because of his knowledge of affairs in China, Japan, and Russia, he was called on by the McKinley Administration for information and advice about Asian culture and diplomacy; often he made suggestions for ambassadorial appointments. He himself was considered for the post of ambassador to Russia early in 1897, primarily because of his involvement in pending negotiations relating to the Chinese-Russian Railway. At first he appeared the front-runner, but when powerful congressmen who backed other candidates opposed him, he failed to win the position. Late that same year the president placed him in consideration for the Chinese ambassadorship, but within a short time Wilson discovered that McKinley was making only a token effort in his behalf. Soon he was out of contention.

Thus, political prizes continued to avoid his grasp, and he was forced to concentrate his efforts at other pursuits. He remained at home in Wilmington, laboring at his writing projects, handling a voluminous correspondence, arranging material for his memoirs, playing the stock market, maintaining his position in local politics, and vigorously enacting the role of Delaware's most distinguished soldier.

Despite the variety of his interests, life must have seemed rather lackluster and slow-paced, for he had passed most of his years at more colorful endeavors and in a more active style. But he was still a soldier, and with a soldier's patience he bided his time, awaiting an opportunity to return to the ways of old, hoping beyond hope for another call to duty.

★XIII★

*I Shall Cheerfully
Serve in Whatever
Position I Am Placed*

W hen in April of 1898 the United States declared war on the Spanish Empire, James Harrison Wilson was seven months beyond his sixtieth birthday. He was bald, his moustache had turned white, and hearty eating had given him more than a suggestion of a paunch. Despite his age, he carried himself erect and retained the vigor which had seen him through the Civil War and his business and political battles. He felt himself fit to retake the field against the country which for so many years had repressed the liberty of Cubans and Puerto Ricans and was now suspected of engineering the explosion which had sunk the American battleship *Maine* in Havana harbor. He was also caught fast by the expansionist enthusiasm then prevalent in America and was particularly anxious that his country win the opportunity to annex Cuba, which he considered the key to the Gulf of Mexico and the southern seaboard.

As the highest ranking Civil War officer below the age of mandatory retirement, he realized that he stood a strong chance of being able to again prove his ability in command. Even before the national clamor for war had achieved results, he had written from Delaware, offering his services to Secretary Alger in event of a national crisis. However, the War Department had replied: "It is hoped . . . that no such emergency will require your services," and had filed his letter for later consideration.

Once war became a reality, Wilson could not wait for the government to take action in his case. He wrote Delaware Senators Anthony Higgins and George Gray, asking their help in securing either the first available appointment as major general of volunteers or an assignment to active duty with the brevet rank of major general, United States Army. Still solicitous of his rank and prestige, he preferred the latter, hoping that the rank awarded him after the Civil War would be formally acknowledged. Because, as he had stipulated in his 1870 retirement request, he had never vacated that rank, he considered it to be yet in effect. He thought of himself as senior even to the general-in-chief of the Army, Major General Nelson A. Miles, whose Civil War commission postdated his own. But the officials who awarded command positions overwhelmingly rejected Wilson's claim for seniority because Miles had served in the Army since the close of the Rebellion whereas Wilson had not. When President McKinley personally upheld Miles's seniority, Wilson had to acknowledge that McKinley had the right to assign to command any major general he believed qualified, without reference to the date of his commission. Early in May, 1898, fearing that he had pressed his claim too vigorously, he informed Alger that "I shall cheerfully serve in whatever position I am placed."

Shortly thereafter he was invited to Washington for a conference. At the White House the president and the adjutant general of the Army, Henry C. Corbin, received him cordially and informed him that his name had been placed at the top of the list of volunteer major generals to be appointed from civil life. Perusing the list, Wilson demonstrated his generosity by offering the names of other qualified civilians with previous command experience, including a former Federal general, Adalbert Ames, as well as Basil Duke, who had been a brigadier under the famed Confederate cavalry leader, John Hunt Morgan.

On May 4, home again in Wilmington, Wilson formally received the commission for which he had hungered. His appointment as major general won quick confirmation by the Senate, in sharp contrast to the prolonged debate which had broken out over the confirmation of his first appointment as a general officer thirty-four years before. On the

Wilson as Major General of Volunteers in 1898—*Photograph courtesy National Archives*

present occasion two ex-Confederate soldiers, Senators Augustus Bacon of Georgia and William Lindsay of Kentucky, took the opportunity to praise the gentlemanly manners and patriotic bent which had characterized Wilson during his Civil War service.

Upon the outbreak of war, the army projected eight army corps to be filled predominantly by volunteers. Erstwhile Civil War generals won command of four of them—John R. Brooke, Fitzhugh Lee, Wesley Merritt, and Wilson, who in early May became the commander of the Sixth Army Corps, slated to assemble at Camp Thomas, on the old Civil War battlefield site at Chickamauga Park, Georgia.

On the fourteenth General Wilson donned the blue uniform which he had doffed almost three decades before. Amid vast publicity and official well-wishing he left Wilmington and, accompanied by some of the Regular Army officers assigned to duty on his staff, entrained for the South.

When he reached Georgia four days later, he found that initial steps had been taken to organize his corps. In camp was the remaining contingent of his staff officers, which included several soldiers upon whom he would rely heavily in coming months: Lieutenant Colonels Tasker H. Bliss, John Biddle, and Henry D. Borup and Major Clement Flagler. Wilson characterized each as "of the highest character and great experience."

Wilson and his aides busied themselves by organizing a school to tutor those staff officers to be selected from the volunteer ranks as well as by preparing their campsite to receive the thousands of recruits expected to congregate in the near future. But their expectations were not fulfilled. In subsequent weeks the other units organizing at Chickamauga Park, General Brooke's First and Major General James S. Wade's Third Corps, duly received their volunteers and began to train. But Wilson waited in vain for his troops.

Receiving not a single regiment or battery of artillery, he eventually realized that his corps was not going to be organized at all. He never deemed it prudent to mount an investigation to ascertain the cause, but he assumed that it was the spiteful work of Secretary Alger, who was keenly aware that Wilson considered him unsuited for his office. If Wilson was correct, it was not the first time that his animosity toward a high-ranking official had worked to his disadvantage.

The situation rankled him furiously. He stumped about Chickamauga Park, cursing the War Department and the Adjutant General's Office. To sympathetic listeners he expressed amazement that he, the only surviving general of the Civil War to have commanded a field army in independent operations, was apparently to be shuffled into the discard.

After a long and frustrating period of inactivity, he swallowed his pride and offered his services to General Brooke. Acknowledging Wilson's great experience, Brooke at once appointed him commander of his first division, which was composed largely of National Guard units.

Wilson cheerfully accepted the position and organized his new command with such a passion as had characterized his first days of service under Grant in Virginia. Through drills and exercises he worked hard to transform the Guardsmen into close facsimiles of Regular Army veterans, and the results were encouraging to even the most critical observers. Wilson greatly enjoyed the resumption of his military career: "It seemed to me as though I had merely returned from a short leave of absence. . . ."

While most of the Army drilled in camps in Georgia, Virginia, Alabama, and California, 20,000 soldiers assembled at Tampa, Florida, close to the point from which they were to embark on an overseas voyage. They had been placed under the command of Major General William Shafter, the white-haired, 300-pound Regular chosen by the War Department to conduct the invasion of Spanish-held Cuba. From late May to mid-June swarms of officers, eager to leave other duties and sail with the expeditionary force, hurried to Shafter's side. More than a few of the staff members originally detailed to the First Corps joined the rush, and this, as Wilson later remarked, "kept us more or less in a state of change and excitement." The rush also upset Wilson quite a bit, for once again it appeared that he was going to be held out of action—unable to participate in the first great campaign of the conflict. But there was no help for it, and he did his best to keep his mind from the events in Florida.

Because none of the military commanders at Tampa was experienced in launching such an invasion, the embarkation was a clumsy and confused process. In contrast, the organization of the First Division of the First Corps proceeded with order and precision, winning Wilson the unqualified acclaim of General Brooke.

On June 11, because of crowded conditions at Camp Thomas, Wilson's men were ordered to Miami. But when the directive later was countermanded, Wilson began to wonder if he would ever be able to leave Georgia for the seat of war. Finally, two weeks later, he received word that the whole of Brooke's command, plus Major General John J. Coppinger's Fourth Corps, then at Mobile, would soon sail overseas.

While Wilson readied his men for an expected trip to the coast,

General Shafter's troops sailed for Cuba. Because they took ever available transport, Wilson was forced to remain at Camp Thomas for a much longer period than he had anticipated—a development which caused him to curse War Department chaos.

On the twenty-second, Shafter landed at Daiquiri, on the south eastern coast of Cuba. Pushing westward across the island, he encour tered stubborn but not overwhelming resistance from Spanish troop: By July 1, after fighting successfully at Las Guasimas and El Caney, hi main army faced San Juan Heights and the nearby works which pro tected the great city of Santiago. At this juncture, the Americans, unac countably, began to falter. Not realizing that victory was within hi reach, Shafter informed Washington on July 3 that he intended t retreat to new positions five miles from Santiago.

Receiving the bad news and finding that further reports did no relieve the tense situation, the War Department anxiously telegraphe General Brooke on Independence Day to move his troops to the coas for embarkation as reinforcements. However, the only division Brook discovered immediately ready was Wilson's, comprising about 10,00(troops of all arms.

That morning Brooke discussed with the leader of his First Divi sion plans for a rapid movement to Charleston, South Carolina, wher Wilson could obtain transports. Then Wilson marched his men out o camp and off to war. They traveled on foot to Ringgold, Georgia where they boarded dirty and poorly ventilated cars for the trip to the Atlantic seaboard via Chattanooga and Atlanta.

During the journey Wilson peered from the train windows, study ing sites of some of his Civil War exploits. Not far away were fields or which almost 15,000 cavalrymen under his command had fought the final campaigns against the defenders of the Deep South. Those battle: had occurred during the zenith of Wilson's military career; at twenty seven, he had been in the prime of his young manhood—vigorous dynamic, facing an undeniably bright future. Later years had given him no higher or brighter moments, no greater successes. Now, undoubt edly, he wished that he could somehow return to those times of promise and fulfillment.

His division reached Charleston on the sixth. There Wilson foun(that the transports had been commandeered by other troops which ha(recently sailed for Cuba. Once again, the War Department had made a botch of things.

Knowing no other course to pursue, he placed his soldiers in camp outside the city and again drilled them. Mindful of the hostile reaction:

his blue-clad troops were likely to provoke among Charleston's old-line secessionists, he went out of his way to promote good civic relations. He enforced rigid discipline among his soldiers, elaborately displayed respect for local officials, and arranged band concerts, balls, breakfasts, teas, and luncheons for the citizenry. His wife and daughters, who joined him soon after he reached Charleston, hosted many of these functions.

On July 14, a week after arriving in South Carolina, Wilson learned that Santiago had surrendered. General Shafter had triumphed after all, without requiring reinforcements. But the war was not over, for although the great battle on San Juan Heights had won most of Cuba for the Americans, enemy ships reportedly menaced the seas, and Spanish soldiers still held Puerto Rico.

That same day Wilson heard from Adjutant General Corbin that "yellow fever is reported to be so bad at Santiago that no more troops will be sent there or to that neighborhood for the present. Your command will be a part of the Porto Rico expedition, which will sail in the near future. . . ."

Six days passed before the embarkation order arrived. Three transports finally reached Charleston, and at 7 P.M. on July 20, part of Wilson's command—a three-regiment, two-battery, one-troop brigade under the immediate command of Brigadier General Oswald H. Ernst —left for Puerto Rico. The 3,500 soldiers whom Wilson crowded onto the decks were all the ships could accommodate. Meanwhile, troops elsewhere in the South prepared to board other transports for the Puerto Rican journey, including 4,000 volunteers and Regulars under General Brooke.

Pursuant to orders, Wilson sailed for the port of Fajardo, on the northeastern shore of the island. The voyage was without incident, but when the transports came within sight of their destination on the morning of the twenty-sixth, they met a United States cruiser, whose captain transmitted orders from General Miles: Wilson was to join the general-in-chief at Guanica. Without delay the transports sailed around the island toward that small, almost landlocked harbor on its southwestern coast. The next morning they entered port and Wilson met Miles aboard his flagship. The commanding general had reached Puerto Rico with almost 12,000 troops; thousands of others were already on the island, and there to combat them were 17,000 Spaniards, who were outnumbered handily.

Despite Wilson's pique about Miles's seniority, he and the general-in-chief worked easily in tandem from the outset. A bond of Civil War fraternity drew them together, and Wilson was much impressed by his superior's intelligence, prudence, and strategic and tactical knowledge. Wilson granted him these talents even though Miles lacked what Wilson considered most desirable, perhaps indispensable, in a high-echelon commander—a West Point education.

After conferring with Wilson and other subordinates, Miles determined to move sixteen miles eastward to the port of Ponce, where roads leading inland were of much better quality than those at Guanica. Arriving at Ponce on the twenty-eighth, the Americans found it empty of Spaniards, for the hostile troops had abandoned the town that morning. Porto de Ponce was now guarded by a detachment of American marines from ships blockading the harbor.

The disembarkation was a tedious operation; scows and motorboats, which would have quickly transported men and equipment onto the beach one half-mile away, had not been supplied, and only the ships' lifeboats could be used. Nevertheless, with the assistance of the Navy, Wilson got his soldiers ashore as rapidly as possible. At 7 A.M. he set foot on the harbor wharf, assembled his staff, and moved inland. He had reached Puerto Rico at last.

QUICKLY HE SET TO WORK TO MAINTAIN a firm hold on the island's southwestern coast. In Porto de Ponce he formed his units—the Sixteenth Pennsylvania and the Second and Third Wisconsin infantry regiments, two batteries of Regular artillery, and a troop of New York cavalrymen—and marched them toward Ponce proper, second largest city in Puerto Rico, which lay three miles inland. His soldiers trooped to the cheers of "Viva los Americanos! Viva Porto Rico libre!" When the brigade marched through the port village, native bands played Sousa airs and the "Star-Spangled Banner," and merchants threw open their stores to the liberators, offering all wares for free. Wilson had not expected so demonstrative a welcome.

The reception continued in like manner when General Miles reached shore, joined Wilson, and rode with him in a carriage to the town proper. There they met the Spanish consul general, who, on behalf of his country, formally surrendered Ponce to the United States Army. Later Miles and Wilson appeared to an immense crowd of natives on the balcony of the municipal hall, the Casa del Rey, and drew a thunderous round of applause. One observer noted: "All that afternoon the Porto Ricans continued to arrive in carriage, on bicycles and on foot to cheer the generals and the troops. . . ."

Before Wilson could push farther north and engage the Spanish troops, there was much to be done. When General Miles departed from the town and returned to his ship, Wilson set up camp, distributed rations to his men, made dispositions to secure the surrounding area, and reconnoitered along the broad road which led northeastward through steep mountains to another large city, Coamo. When he found the opportunity, he formulated a plan to capture that city, which was garrisoned by some 350 well-fortified Spaniards.

He was also saddled with a heavy load of municipal administrative chores. Having been appointed by Miles the military governor of the Ponce district, he had to invent oaths of allegiance, tranquilize the foreign consuls, protect local Spaniards from vengeance-seeking natives, adopt a new monetary standard for the city, appoint court officials, free political prisoners, jail opponents of the new regime, inform parish priests that the occupation forces would make no appropriations for religious organizations, and oversee the publication of all local newspapers and journals.

By August 7 he was at last able to move ahead with his plan to take Coamo. By this time he had determined to throw part of his force at the rear of the Spanish garrison and thus avoid a perhaps disastrous frontal assault. General Miles met with him and approved the plan, but cautioned him about proceeding too swiftly in such a delicate undertaking. This was a mild criticism but, characteristically, Wilson took offense and huffed: "You are commanding general in the island, and if you are not willing to trust my discretion, you have only to give your specific orders and they will be literally obeyed." General Miles, a most tactful commander, assured his sensitive subordinate that he had faith in his prudence and know-how.

On the afternoon of the eighth Wilson pushed his advance force from its forward position outside Ponce to within three miles of Coamo. While the Wisconsin regiments, the cavalry, and the artillery took the direct road into the city, Colonel Willis J. Hulings's Sixteenth Pennsylvania, guided by Wilson's chief engineer officer, Lieutenant Colonel Biddle, made a night march over mountains and across valleys to turn the Spaniards' right flank and reach their rear. The Pennsylvanians were to strike the garrison from that direction at the same time that the rest of the brigade—which was being directed into place by another of Wilson's staff members, Major Flagler—would make a limited direct assault along the main highway.

Because of the rocky terrain it encountered, the Sixteenth Pennsylvania was almost an hour late in deploying for its attack. But precisely on time, six o'clock the next morning, the rest of General Ernst's men moved out. A covering fire from the artillery enabled the foot soldiers and horsemen to drive back the Spanish troops. At first the enemy gave ground slowly, but when Hulings's men fired in their rear and came on with a martial precision that belied their lack of experience under fire, the Spaniards' tenacity began to fade. After only a half-hour of fighting, the garrison turned to flee. But even as they retreated, their ranks were shredded by rifle fire pouring down upon them from hills in the rear of Coamo. Many of Hulings's men, still perched there, enjoyed a vantage point from which they could menace the full extent of the retreat route.

When the fighting ceased, the Spanish commander lay dead beside four of his soldiers; forty others had been wounded, and 167 officers and men had become prisoners. Only four Americans had been injured, none seriously, although many of the attackers—particularly Hulings's Pennsylvanians—had been threatened by a heavy artillery barrage.

While his cavalry, infantry, and artillery pressed the retreating survivors, Wilson—who had personally directed the main attack at General Ernst's side—accepted the congratulations of his subordinates. His plan had worked almost flawlessly; apparently his 33-year sabbatical from active duty had not at all diminished his tactical skill.

The few Spaniards who escaped from Coamo fled ten miles to the north toward the city of Aibonito, where one of the largest Spanish contingents on the island—2,000 strong—awaited Wilson's advance. Other Spanish forces held several large cities at other points throughout Puerto Rico, including San Juan, in the northernmost central region. There, in the capital city, 7,000 soldiers had assembled.

General Miles's plan for the campaign called for four independent movements by the forces under his command, and by now all operations were well advanced. On the western part of the island, two of these forces, under Brigadier Generals Theodore Schwan and Guy Henry, were moving north from the coast, aiming to liberate several sizable towns. Farther to the east, Wilson was marching along a path which would carry him to Aibonito, near which he would link with the fourth large column, led by General Brooke, also moving north. After taking Aibonito, Wilson and Brooke were to move on to San Juan, hopefully to end the conflict entirely.

On the twelfth Wilson prepared to move out of Coamo toward Aibonito. He would be rather glad to leave Coamo behind, for his reception there had not been so warm as that which the people of Ponce had given him. In part, this was due to the misbehavior of his troops; before he could stop them, some of the soldiers had taken all manner of goods from stores and restaurants without offering payment. Quickly the merchants had closed their shops and the citizens locked their homes in anger and fright.

Aibonito, surrounded by steep and treacherous mountains, could be reached only by winding trails. With the aid of native guides, however, Wilson located passes by which his command might once again gain the enemy's rear. He decided to send Ernst's infantry and cavalry up the slopes to turn the enemy's flank. Beforehand, to develop the Spanish positions, a battery, personally commanded by Wilson's chief of artillery, Major J. M. Lancaster, would shell the works in front of the town.

At 1 P.M. on August 12 the battery galloped into position along the main road into Aibonito. Immediately it came under fire from Spaniards in rifle pits along neighboring ridges. Spanish cannon also blasted away, killing and wounding a few of Wilson's gunners.

When the U.S. battery unlimbered, its five guns so accurately returned fire that after thirty minutes only a single enemy cannon was still operating. But when the Spaniards subsequently pulled back to another line of hilltop trenches, Wilson saw that only his projected turning movement could dislodge them.

Before dispatching Ernst's men through the mountain passes, he sent his chief of staff, Lieutenant Colonel Bliss, to deliver a surrender demand to the garrison. Reports of pending negotiations to end the fighting on the island had recently reached headquarters, and Bliss added this information to his demand. Wilson did not believe that such news would of itself cause the town to capitulate, but "I had long years before learned that it was no mistake in war to ask for what you would like to have, even if you should be forced to accept only what you could get away with."

He was right to hope for little; Bliss's information was telegraphed to San Juan and the next morning brought a curt refusal from the Spanish general-in-chief.

By now, Ernst's movement had begun, but although the enemy was not willing to capitulate, Wilson called Ernst back, suspecting from the Spanish commander's terms of refusal that he "was well informed as to the progress of peace negotiations" and might receive further information from his superiors in the Spanish Empire at any time. After waiting a few hours and hearing no further word from the enemy garrison, Wilson prepared to resume operations. But before he could get word to Ernst, a courier from General Miles galloped up to his command post with news that an armistice had been concluded. All hostile operations were suspended, and both Americans and Spaniards were to hold their positions until they received further orders.

And so the war was over in Puerto Rico as well as in Cuba. With peace in force, Wilson could assess the results of his operations with great pride. In Cuba the campaigning had been needlessly long and rather sloppy, but here the work had moved swiftly and precisely— thanks largely to the Americans' overwhelming numerical advantage. During nineteen days of operations, the United States forces had moved almost at will over Puerto Rico, and had suffered only three killed and forty wounded, while inflicting several times as many casualties upon the enemy. Without great hardships, Wilson and his associates had acquired a precious island possession for their nation.

WITH THE COMING OF PEACE, WILSON ceased to be an active field commander and devoted all time and effort to his duties as military governor of the district including and surrounding Ponce. While the Spanish troops remained at certain points on the island pending a formal surrender agreement, Wilson took all precautions to maintain order and discipline in his realm. He assured the populace that he would make no attempt to interfere with local laws and customs except when necessary to protect his soldiers and to preserve peace.

He kept his word. He maintained most aspects of local government and commerce, keeping the *alcaldes*—the mayors—in office, and allowing the police, the markets, and the railroads to resume their affairs. The Army did take over the operations of the post office and the customs house but only to relieve the chaotic conditions which beset them; much to the islanders' delight, the troops administered both with great efficiency. Sensing a need to initiate good relations with the population, Wilson duplicated his work in Charleston by providing free band concerts, plus bazaars and luncheons, for the public. In a short time, many of the inhabitants of the region were whistling one of the Army's favorite ditties, "A Hot Time in the Old Town Tonight."

On one occasion at this time, speaking before a large group of influential citizens, Wilson emphasized his intention to promote the well-being of all the people in the district. He advised his audience to turn their backs upon the events of the past and to look hopefully to the future. Warning of the evils of bigotry and intolerance, he asked them to think in friendly terms even of the Spanish people. He stressed that citizens ought to manage only their private affairs, eschewing politics and narrow-mindedness; a spirit of national tranquility would result. Then, summing up his desire to spread charity and tolerance, he quoted the motto of an American missionary, a former Federal soldier, who had founded a well-known aid society, the Helping Hand: "I shall pass through this world but once; therefore, whatever good thing I may do for any human creature, let me do it now; let me not postpone or delay it, for I shall not come this way again."

Each member of the audience stated his approval of Wilson's proposals and pledged his support in attaining such goals as he had outlined. One of the listeners asked Wilson to transcribe his remarks, which he did gladly. Soon his words were circulating about the island via the local newspapers, and later throughout America, evoking an overwhelmingly favorable response.

Wilson's peaceful regime as military governor lasted but a month. He then received orders relieving him from duty and returning him to the mainland. Despite General Miles's hope of seeing Wilson confirmed as governor general of Puerto Rico, the officials in Washington decided to tender the honor to Brooke. They wished Miles to return home, and Miles, in turn, decided that Wilson's troops ought to accompany their commander to America for mustering out.

And so Wilson's command boarded ships for New York and landed at their destination a few days later. Miles had intended that the troops should march through the streets in review and to the cheers of the citizens, but a War Department decision—rendered without public explanation—meant, as Wilson wrote, that "the only organization that came back from the war in better condition than when it entered it was disbanded and sent home without any public recognition or ceremony whatever."

After spending some days in Wilmington with family and friends, Wilson received further orders. He was to succeed Brooke in command of the First Army Corps, most of whose men were again in southern camps. The order was dated October 13, and precisely a week later, Wilson reported to the corps' new campsite near Lexington, Kentucky.

The bulk of the command was still on active duty because an important overseas assignment was upcoming. Within a few weeks of Wilson's arrival in Kentucky, orders came designating the First Corps as part of a 50,000-man force to be sent to Cuba as occupation troops following the Spaniards' departure. The call to duty fell sweetly on Wilson's ears.

To facilitate movement to the coast, the troops were again transferred to Georgia, this time to the Macon area, where on November 8 Wilson established his headquarters. Familiar sites brought back a wealth of memories which recalled the period he had spent in Macon following the close of the Civil War. This link with the past was strengthened when he set up offices in the same rooms in the Lanier House hotel in which he had conducted his military governorship more than thirty-three years before.

However, Macon was hardly the same as it had been in 1865. Its population had trebled, its area had increased proportionately, and the city had regained in full volume the bustle and hum of prosperity which the Civil War had nearly silenced.

Drills and reviews occupied the newly arrived soldiers while they awaited orders to sail for Cuba. At the same time, Wilson held conferences with a bevy of congressmen and cabinet members who came south to brief him on his course of rule on the island. In free moments, he busied himself as he had that summer, by planning teas, dinners, and balls. Again Ella joined him, bringing Kitty with her, and they served as his hostesses. Wilson enjoyed the sociability of the local people, whom he found entirely willing to forget the unhappy conflict of three decades ago. In mid-December he wrote a friend of the generosity the citizens had displayed in opening their homes to him and his family, and he acclaimed the functions which the local board of trade conducted in his honor.

His most distinguished visitor in Macon was President McKinley, who arrived during the third week in December while on a speaking tour of the South. After reviewing Wilson's soldiers, the president delivered a speech before a large crowd of citizens. He received especially large rounds of applause by frequently referring to the nation's recent triumphs overseas. Sitting upon the speaker's platform, Wilson believed he heard "world power" allusions in McKinley's speech.

After the president resumed his seat, Wilson was called upon for a few words. At first surprised by the invitation, he met the occasion with a stirring off-the-cuff speech which elaborated upon many of the president's remarks. Wilson was so excited by the enthusiastic reception his words produced that he entered a controversial area of discussion. Referring to his long-active interest in continental union—an interest of which he believed McKinley fully approved—he declared that the United States was too powerful a nation to share North America with lands such as Canada and Mexico. The next day local newspapers reported him as having said: "I hope to see the day when our starry flag shall float everywhere, from the frozen north to the sunny clime of

Central America. We are too big and powerful and progressive to have neighbors on this continent, and I trust that before the next administration of the President closes the flag will fly over every foot on the continent from the northern extremity of the Dominion of Canada to the Gulf of Mexico. . . ."

It may have been an eloquent speech, but it did not please McKinley one bit. When Wilson later became aware of this, he felt the president's reaction had been triggered by newsmen, whom Wilson accused of condensing his remarks "into a spread-eagle intimation to all the world, and especially to Great Britain, that she must not only withdraw from the Western Hemisphere, but leave it to the exclusive control of the American people." This had not been his meaning, for Wilson wished that a peaceful, "equal and honorable" union of America and Canada might one day come to pass by mutual consent. But McKinley, fearing that the publicity might cause unwished-for troubles with England and other nations, thereafter nursed a grudge against Wilson. Soon afterward, the issue of continental union was discreetly dropped from the Republican Party platform.

Even before he made his speech, Wilson had not always found it easy to serve in harmony with Administration policy, and this may have been an underlying cause of his failure to receive chief command during the Cuban occupation. From the outset he had been a prime candidate for the post of governor general, as he had in Puerto Rico, although he was opposed by such distinguished contenders as Generals Fitzhugh Lee and James Wade. Dozens of newspapers across the nation endorsed him. Prominent politicians also advanced his candidacy, avowing (in the phrase of Iowa Senator William B. Allison) their "high personal regard for & good opinion of Genl James H. Wilson as a man & soldier." Elihu Root, the recently appointed successor to Secretary of War Alger, wrote one of Wilson's backers that "there are, however, other officers of high distinction and service to be considered, and the determination must of course be made upon a view of the whole field."

Wilson was disappointed when General Brooke, reportedly dissatisfied with his command in Puerto Rico, was named chief military governor of Cuba on December 13, three days after a peace treaty was finally concluded between the United States and Spain. Seventeen days later Wilson learned that he himself was to head one of the six large departments of occupation, as military governor of the Matanzas district. This was considered a less prestigious department than the province of Havana. Although Brooke would have liked him to have the latter post, it eluded Wilson's grasp; the president personally decreed that General Lee, the former U.S. consul general in Havana, should take it.

Originally it was intended that Wilson and one of his divisions would sail for Cuba late in December, but lack of transportation postponed the operation till January 7, 1899. Three days later, as the last of the Spanish troops prepared to leave Cuba, Wilson arrived on the island upon which the balance of the late war had been fought. At once he distributed his men through the Matanzas district, in the central part of the island.

Parts of Wilson's department were densely populated; the district contained about one-third of Cuba's people and one-third of its total area. Natives of the region—which produced 80 percent of the island's principal crop, sugar, and half of its tobacco—had long been poor and had suffered most severely during the war.

Soon after settling into Matanzas and raising the Stars and Stripes, Wilson began to improve conditions. He revamped the civil government by dividing it into four departments and appointed a local official of probity to head each. Under his supervision the officials assumed and perfected the administration of affairs as formerly conducted under Spanish colonial rule.

Wilson soon discovered, however, that General Brooke was not acting within the guidelines of a specific occupation policy, for the United States government had drawn up no such policy. Brooke had been told only to pacify the island and to establish its commercial prosperity, goals that looked neat and simple on paper but whose details were frightfully complicated.

But Wilson formulated his own policies quickly enough. Three weeks after landing in Cuba he wrote a friend in the states that he considered his duties "maintaining public tranquility, relieving the indigent, finding work for the unemployed and cultivating good relations with the Cuban people." He remarked that "I am glad to say that one and all, Cuban officers and soldiers, Cuban citizens and Spanish citizens, are conducting themselves in an orderly, dignified and reassuring manner."

Despite this spirit of cooperation, Wilson's job in Cuba, because of the lack of government instructions, was quite possibly the toughest assignment he had ever faced during his military career; few battlefield campaigns could have been more demanding. Soon after assuming his post, he poured over all available statutes, acts of Congress, treaties and regulations, to ascertain the state of law under which he and his men might be said to be acting in Cuba. The results were discouraging, for he found that few such guidelines existed on paper at all. To enhance his knowledge, he traveled to distant points by rail and on horseback, seeking out *alcaldes* and other officials. To them he explained his ambitions as military governor and from them gathered advice about the most efficient manner in which to reach his goals.

That spring he commenced a particularly extensive trip. He spent several months touring all points in the two districts now within the sphere of his authority (in June he was also given command of the extensive region which bordered Matanzas, the Department of Santa Clara). Talking to small landowners as well as to municipal authorities, he thoroughly acquainted himself with the economic, legal, political, sanitary, and military conditions of the area. He was amazed at the extent of his jurisdiction: it encompassed about 12,000 square miles, several large cities and villages, and approximately 560,000 Cubans.

Other discoveries gave him great concern. His two districts were marked by symptoms of the most miserable poverty and the deepest distress. Repairs to roads and public buildings had not been made for years, many of the people who had been driven from their farms into the cities by the "reconcentration" policy of the Spaniards were dispossessed and were wandering in search of sustenance, and everywhere fields lay barren. Many of the large sugar plantations had been ravaged by war; only the wealthiest had been able to continue crop production. Signs of starvation were to be found everywhere, and from this Wilson grew convinced that had Spanish rule continued for another year, the major portion of the island's population would have been wiped out by famine.

Cuba's mild climate and fertile soil offered hope for a fairly rapid economic recovery if programs to that end could be initiated quickly and properly. After his return to Matanzas in the summer, Wilson began to formulate plans which he hoped to put into practice with the aid of his subordinate officers and local officials. After jotting down his ideas, he sent a series of reports to his superiors, explaining the conditions in his department and recommending that allotments from the insular treasury—primarily customs revenues—be made toward the purchase of farm equipment, animals, seed, and other desperately needed goods, to be sold to farmers under long-term, low-interest contracts. He also advocated a program whereby homeowners would be granted loans to rebuild their property and to retill their lands. Repayment on such loans, he noted, should be added to the capital of an agricultural bank, an agency which every island official agreed was a necessity.

Unfortunately, his recommendations were not put into practice on a large scale. Rumors led him to believe that General Brooke was responsible for quashing his plans because he felt they smacked too much of paternalism. Brooke doled out only a few thousand dollars for agricultural reform; the rest of the insular treasury went toward sanitation, transportation, and educational needs.

With what funds he could get, Wilson put two agricultural programs into effect. They produced quick and gratifying results. The first, originally begun near the city of Sangua la Grande, involved the appropriation of money to buy wagons, plows, oxen, and other farm equipment, which was placed in the hands of salaried representatives of the government. The representatives then distributed the goods among families who had been placed upon property provided by the more prosperous people of the city. The farm families were then divided into groups and given land surrounding central stations which housed other animals, seeds, and implements. A Cuban correspondent for *Harper's Weekly* explained the process then put into effect: "Each central station would, in succession, plough and prepare for planting a small part of the land belonging to each family, and after thus serving each group would start at ploughing more land, and so on until enough of the land had been prepared for each family to plant crops sufficient to support them. . . ."

The other system Wilson instituted supplied islanders with animals and tools to the limit of $250 per family. The recipients signed contracts with their representative municipalities, promising to pay for the goods within two years, the terms being those upon which the government had originally purchased the items.

In still other ways, Wilson helped return a measure of prosperity to central Cuba. Through his efforts public buildings, roads, and communication facilities were repaired; the system which maintained municipal schools, asylums, and hospitals was restructured, and destitute citizens were settled in homes and provided with employment. He improved sanitary conditions in rural, suburban, and urban districts through innovative efforts (no less than $100,000 was spent on sanitation during the first six months of his regime), reorganized the court system and increased the number of courts, bolstered the municipal police force to better maintain peace and order, and entrusted the office of civil governor in Matanzas and Santa Clara to hard-working, honest, and dedicated officials.

In a later report to his superiors, Wilson stated proudly that "a condition of complete tranquility continues to prevail in the provinces under my command. The disorders are no greater than might occur in any well-governed country."

In this report he also asserted: "So far as I can discover the Cuban people in the provinces of this department are now as ready for self government as they are likely to be at any time in the near future." With this in mind, he repeatedly advocated convening a constitutional convention to establish a local government free from United States domination. "A government having been inaugurated," he believed, "a treaty of alliance and friendship, covering all subjects of common interests between the United States and Cuba, would naturally follow. . . ."

This report indicated a considerable shift of opinion from the position Wilson had held prior to the Spanish-American War. Then he had considered annexation Cuba's proper destiny; now he shared the island's wish for local self-government. He believed Cuban statesmen to be unusually sober, judicious, prudent, and honest—entirely capable of ruling their own land without foreign intervention. Then, too, Wilson feared that imposed American rule might unwittingly perpetuate many of the evils of Spanish domination.

His genuine sympathy for the islanders' wish to become politically independent won him the gratitude of thousands of Cubans, and his statements on the subject were so influential that they constituted the basis for policies which the United States eventually formulated for its Caribbean possessions.

At the time Wilson first voiced his opinions, they ran counter to the views of President McKinley and many of the other generals in occupied Cuba, a few of whom believed the island would not be ready for self-government for many years. In truth, the army remained on the island until late in 1900. But the Platt Amendment, which in March, 1901 authorized the United States to return the government and control of Cuba to its people, directly evolved from ideas propounded by Wilson and a few other insular officials.

Some of Wilson's efforts in behalf of Cuban self-rule embarrassed the Administration, and of course the President still recalled Wilson's controversial speech at Macon. When General Brooke was relieved from command in Havana in December of 1899 and when he himself was not appointed to the position, Wilson attributed his misfortune to either or both factors. Because he had so logically appeared in line for Brooke's post, the Administration's selection of General Leonard Wood, formerly in command of the famed Rough Riders, certainly seemed an intentional slight.

But when he was recalled to the States for top-level conferences late that month, Wilson did not grumble about his treatment. He was too familiar with the often unappetizing intrigues which underlay political and military affairs to bewail his situation.

In Washington he spoke of Cuban affairs with Secretary of War Root, who continually alluded to the chagrin which some of Wilson's policy statements had caused the president. After a week of discussions at the War Department, Wilson went to see McKinley himself, to whom he reported the complete pacification of Cuba. Despite the president's earlier views on the subject, Wilson even found an opportunity to voice his advocacy of Cuban self-rule. To his surprise, McKinley seemed in agreement, favoring insular policy "substantially" along the lines Wilson advocated.

Concluding his business in Washington, Wilson sailed again for Cuba, accompanied by Ella and two of their daughters, who had originally joined him in Matanzas two months before and had returned to Wilmington while he conducted his official business in the capital. By this point in time, much of his crucial work had been accomplished, and the Cubans under his jurisdiction were taking their first steps along the road to economic stability. But he felt that he could not afford to relax his efforts; so much remained to be done to consolidate the advances already made.

When he returned to the island, he found to his pleasant surprise that he could work quite easily with the new governor general (although Wood was far from being his close friend); and troop reductions had left him a force of infantry and cavalry which was easily manageable. He found himself with time for socializing as well as for working in his office. With wife and daughters by his side, he entertained civil and military officials at his private residence, the Quinta Felix Torres, which soon became the cultural and entertainment center of the district.

Then the gaiety of life at the Quinta was shattered by the most painful personal tragedy of Wilson's life. On the morning of April 28, 1900, Ella, while riding to the local beaches, was horribly burned. A friction match, tossed into her carriage by a careless passer-by, set her skirts ablaze. Called from his headquarters by a panic-stricken orderly, Wilson rushed to the beach, where he found his wife in agony, townspeople having finally extinguished the flames. He drove her back to the Quinta, where their daughters and the staff surgeon tried to ease her suffering. Little could be done, however, and within a few hours she died in great pain. "Like a bolt out of the clear sky," Wilson remembered a decade later, "it overwhelmed us with consternation and grief."

For a time he could not be comforted and he threw aside his administrative duties. Then he tried manfully to bear the burden of grief, and accepted the condolences of friends and numerous officials in both the United States and Cuba. But his sorrow lasted long after Ella's body was returned home for burial in the Andrews family plot in the churchyard of Old Swedes, Wilmington.

For the remainder of his term in Matanzas, Wilson went about his work in an abstracted calm, sending in reports which detailed the effectiveness of his efforts to restore the island economically. That summer, perceiving that his most vital work was nearing completion, he so informed Secretary Root and placed himself at his disposal.

By that time his daughters had left Cuba to return to the States, and he wished to follow them. After so long a period in a foreign land, he cherished the thought of settling at home among old friends and neighbors. There, too, he could again be close to Ella.

★XIV★

*The Man Who Gets
Ahead of Me Will Have
to Move with Great Celerity*

N o rest period was immediately available to General Wilson. Although by the summer of 1900 he was thinking seriously of settling down in Wilmington, the nation decided that it required his presence elsewhere.

In fact, Wilson sensed that he might be called on for further service, and his sense of duty, coupled with a still potent desire to win military laurels, impelled him to declare himself available. In the middle of June, when he wired the secretary of war to place himself at the government's disposal, he added a reference to the Boxer Rebellion, then in progress in the Orient: "If I can be of service in connection with China you are quite at liberty to use me."

Two weeks after telegraphing Root, he wrote an army friend that " 'God knows I have no desire to go to China again,' but I should have felt guilty of neglecting my duty if I had failed to place myself at the disposal of the Secretary in such an important matter, especially in one where I might be supposed to possess special knowledge and qualifications. . . ."

The fighting in China had been precipitated by nationalists who feared the complete domination of their land by foreign nations who in recent years had displayed explicit designs on her wealth. The uprising was tacitly supported by the Empress Dowager at Peking, a strong-willed monarch who focused her concern on the several countries which maintained large diplomatic legations in the capital city. These included Great Britain, the United States, Germany, Russia, France, Italy, and Japan. Emigrants from these nations, as well as Chinese Christians—converts to a foreign religion—were killed by the score when the so-called Boxer terrorists roamed the countryside, plundering the homes of missionaries and diplomats. In the walled city of Peking the legations barricaded themselves in their compounds to withstand a terrorist siege.

Through that summer, the eyes of the Western world turned upon China, whose Imperial Army, in a token attempt to end the marauding, clashed with the Boxer bands. Then, when it appeared that the Imperial troops could or would not prevent the fanatics from crashing into Peking and annihilating the foreign diplomats, nations with embassies there became violently alarmed. Their fear increased when a relief expedition composed of forces from all countries involved in the crisis failed to fight its way through to Peking and rescue the diplomats.

Wilson followed the progress of the crisis as best he could from his island headquarters. For a time it appeared that his request for consideration as a commander in China would go unanswered. Then he received word that another expeditionary force, including a large contingent of American troops drawn from the Philippine Islands, would try to rescue the legations. Three weeks after this news arrived, the adjutant general informed Wilson that he might join the expedition if he so chose. Major General Adna R. Chaffee, who had won renown in the Cuban campaigning, had already received command of the American contingent. If agreeable, Wilson would be assigned to duty as Chaffee's executive officer.

The offer did not overwhelm Wilson, for he considered himself wholly qualified to fill the top position. Chaffee was a younger man, had no experience in Chinese affairs, and had won his second star only recently and solely for the purpose of leading the relief force. Even so, this meant that he ranked Wilson, for because of a War Department decree affecting the status of occupation officers, Wilson, as military governor of Matanzas and Santa Clara, had lost his commission as a major general of volunteers and had been reappointed a brigadier.

Wilson did acknowledge Chaffee's ability as a field commander. Therefore, believing himself acting in the best interests of the service, he again overlooked his pride and wired his acceptance of the adjutant general's offer. He was then ordered to proceed at once to the United States for the trip to China. He would have to catch Chaffee's force, however, for the Americans would have sailed from their station by the time Wilson left Cuba.

On July 23 he disposed of the last of his affairs as military governor, a post at which he had served so well for a year and a half. After dispatching final reports, he turned his records over to General Fitzhugh Lee, who would now administer his own and Wilson's departments. Soon afterward Wilson sent his horses via Galveston to the California coast (he would embark for China from San Francisco), then gathered up the staff officers who were to accompany him, and left Cuba on the twenty-fourth.

On the way to his new post of duty, he took the time to write Colonel Bliss, formerly his chief of staff and now collector of customs in Havana. He stated that he could see many reasons why the government officials might have placed him above Chaffee "but that is their affair and not mine." In the same letter he restated an attitude which had characterized his military service through two previous wars: "All I have to say is that if I am allowed any kind of a free hand, and there remains any work to be done . . . the man who gets ahead of me will have to move with great celerity."

The long voyage—via New York, San Francisco, Hawaii, Yokohama, and Nagasaki, to Taku, northeastern China—consumed thirty-seven days. Given the travel facilities of the age, Wilson confidently believed it to be "the quickest trip ever made" between Cuba and the Orient. But long before he reached the interior of China he learned, to his great dismay, that other soldiers had relieved the legations without requiring his help. Wilson's attitude was much akin to the hardly admirable disappointment he had expressed in August of 1861, believing that the Civil War had ended before he could get into the fighting.

Three weeks before Wilson's arrival in China, allied forces had smashed down the gates at the entrance to the inner districts of the capital, where the diplomats had stood besieged. Boxers, ringing the walls around the embassy precincts, fled upon the soldiers' approach, unable to mount a final attack which might have swept them inside the grounds and over the legation forces. After almost two months of siege and desperate valor, the diplomats had been rescued; and their deliverers had then secured all important districts, insuring that the Boxers would not return. By this point, in fact, the only remaining troubles seemed to stem from the friction existing among the several allied commanders, who were at odds as to whom should be given primary credit for the diplomats' salvation, and which sectors of Peking each nation should occupy.

Wilson completed his 12,000-mile journey from Cuba when he entered Peking on September 6. All was quiet there; the fighting was a dim echo of the past. Escorted by a detachment from the Sixth U.S. Cavalry, he rode through the battle-scarred inner districts and sought out General Chaffee. The dignified and usually solemn commander greeted him warmly, showing great respect for Wilson's military fame. Wilson later met the members of the various legations and soon formed an especial regard for the British minister, Sir Claude Macdonald, and his American counterpart, Edwin H. Conger, both of whom had worked hard to inspire and encourage the besieged commands. In the American compound Wilson also saw two familiar faces: an old friend and Army colleague, Herbert Squiers, Conger's secretary; and William Pethick, the diplomat and scholar whom he had met during his China tour of 1885–86. Squiers and Pethick had rendered valuable assistance to the U.S. legation guard, a detachment of Marines, during the desperate fighting.

General Chaffee gave Wilson field command of one of the two brigades of American troops which had arrived with the relief force. Placed under him were the Ninth and Fourteenth Regular Infantry, a battery of artillery, and a squadron from the Sixth Cavalry. Additionally, he received special charge over the southern entrance to the Forbidden City, the district which housed religious shrines and temples. In another district, the Chinese City, most of the various relief forces were quartered; and Wilson was also assigned command of the American contingent there. Still another precinct placed in his charge was the land near the imperial palaces, across which the Empress's court had fled after the Boxers' retreat.

With Pethick's aid, Wilson drew up notices which proclaimed his intent to enforce safety of life and property within the American quarter, and posted them in public areas. "In a few days," he afterward recalled, "the streets had been policed, the markets and shops were reopened, and the people of all classes had apparently resumed their daily occupations as though no foreign soldiers were at hand."

From his headquarters in the Temple of Agriculture, on the edge of an ancient cedar grove, Wilson assigned his men various duties, such as clearing rubble-filled streets, breaking up gatherings of political dissidents, and in general preserving order and tranquility. To help accomplish the latter, he strictly charged his soldiers to refrain from looting nearby palaces and temples, a practice in which some of the other occupation troops had indulged on a grand scale. Emphatic about protecting Chinese property, Wilson especially denounced the European troops, many of whom seemed to consider wholesale plunder a favorite pastime.

A short time after assuming his duties in Peking, Wilson heard reports that the Boxers, having retreated from the capital, had established new headquarters on a steep hill about a dozen miles to the northwest. Atop the hill rose Pa-ta-chow, the "Eight Temples," on land which had formerly served as a resort for missionaries and diplomats from the capital. An observer described the ground as "a vast landscape garden, with winding stone walks to the very summit."

Ascertaining the validity of the rumors, the commanders of the relief troops decided to send an expedition to capture the stronghold, scatter the Boxers, and destroy their nearby arsenal. British and American soldiers were told off for the expedition, and Wilson, to his pleasant surprise, was honored by being appointed to the overall command. He supposed that his selection came about because he had visited the Eight Temples in 1885, giving him an understanding of the local topography.

His troops moved toward the hills on September 16. Wilson led 2,200 men—detachments from each of the units he directly commanded, plus Welsh fusileers and contingents of Hindu troops. To mislead the enemy, he at first marched his command to the southwest and then, on the seventeenth, toward the north. Before daylight that morning his men were in the vicinity of their objective. Dividing his column, Wilson sent a flanking column to perform a maneuver which he had carried out with great success in Puerto Rico. Guided by Americans from the legation in Peking, including Squiers, a battalion of the Fourteenth U.S. Infantry and some of the Hindu soldiers climbed neighboring Mount Bruce and came up in the rear of the Boxers' position.

As it reached the summit of the mountain, the flanking force heard heavy firing coming from below. Minutes before, the main column had rushed through an opening in the foothills of the slopes on which the temples stood, and had encountered Chinese riflemen. The Americans in the flanking party now descended into the valley and struck the enemy's rear, scattering most of them, capturing their headquarters, and moving into position to cut off their retreat. By 8 A.M. the main Boxer force had been cut to pieces, and most of its survivors had surrendered; others had fled up hillsides to the northeast and the wide-open country beyond. Twenty Boxers had died in the fighting; the attackers had suffered no casualties at all.

A short time after the fighting ended, the British adjutant general brought Wilson the warm congratulations of the allied command in Peking. Soon afterward General Chaffee telegraphed word of Wilson's success to Washington, speaking of the victorious commander in highly complimentary terms.

His accomplishment at first placed Wilson in a lofty mood. But he was shocked when the British decided to destroy one of the shrines on the captured hill, a lovely white porcelain pagoda which had been standing for hundreds of years. Although Wilson thought the idea outrageous, its proponents wished to demonstrate that they did not fear the Chinese gods in whose honor the shrine had been erected. Thus, when the American soldiers withdrew from the Eight Temples the next day, the British exploded a charge of gunpowder which they had planted inside the pagoda. They then burned the Boxer arsenal at San-kia-tien.

Ever afterward Wilson considered the act of apparently wanton destruction proof that a barbaric streak marked the English people. The incident added fuel to an already heated anti-Anglo bias, which he had indulged for many years and which had probably been intensified by his failure to raise needed railroad funds in England during the 1870s.

His criticism was specific. In June of 1890 he had been one of several eminent persons to reply to the question, "Do Americans Hate England?" as asked by the *North American Review*. His answer was a decided "yes." However: "The most abiding and deeply-rooted aversion felt by Americans is to the English government and to the class by which it has always been controlled," not to the great majority of the country's populace. Later in life he left little doubt that he had been speaking for himself and indicated the basis for his Anglophobia, when writing of the English government's sympathy for the Confederate cause: "Damn her, I shall never forgive England for her attitude towards the United States throughout the entire war for the Union."

Later expeditions left Peking to run down Boxer bands, and a few were commanded by Wilson; but small forces conducted them and achieved less spectacular results than the troops who had fought at the Eight Temples. Now the duties of the U.S. forces consisted chiefly of rescuing Chinese Christians who lived outside the capital, prime targets for small Boxer raids. Increasingly, Imperial troops regained control of the provinces, and General Chaffee notified Washington: "Surrounding countryside daily growing less hostile. . . ."

By early October the continuing pacification of the country had made Wilson restive. To a friend he wrote that "there is no adequate command left for me, and I expect to receive orders before a great while to return to the States." Talk of a troop reduction was widespread.

A week after Wilson wrote this letter, Field Marshal Count von Waldersee arrived to accept the proferred command of all relief forces in Peking. In due course Wilson came to form a high opinion of the sixty-eight-year-old German commander, and the two long-time soldiers became firm friends. Wilson spent the remainder of his term in Peking by parading his troops for Waldersee; attending conferences and social receptions with him and diplomats, officers, and legation attachées and their families; and by handling routine administrative matters.

Late in October, following America's decision to cut its military strength in China, Wilson was relieved of his command. He left Chaffee, Waldersee, friends and colleagues—many of whom would remain in China for five months more—and on the eleventh of November boarded a transport at Nagasaki. In the midst of December he reached Wilmington, able to enjoy for the first time in two and a half years the prospect of a lengthy stay.

Soon after reaching the United States, however, he was called to the White House, where President McKinley thanked him for his services in Cuba and Peking, and informed him of a pleasant circumstance: he intended to ask Congress for authority to transfer Wilson and two other generals who had seen service both in the Civil War and against the Spanish—ex-Confederates Fitzhugh Lee and "Fightin' Joe" Wheeler—to the Regular Army and thereafter to retire them with the rank of brigadier general. Wilson was cheered to learn that he could receive that status even though not eligible for retirement by virtue of age, continuous service, or infirmity.

Congress would duly grant the president's request, and by special enactment Wilson would retire from the service thirty days later, on March 2, 1901, at the age of sixty-three.

When in Washington, Wilson also saw Secretary Root, who respectfully inquired if he wished any further duty pending his retirement. Promptly Wilson said no. He had come back into the service in 1898, he added, only because he felt his services were needed in war, and had remained on duty until the establishment of order in Cuba. War in China had then called him, but now that he was free at last from active campaigning he wished to resume a business career.

Root understood fully. Wishing him good fortune, he shook Wilson's hand.

UPON HIS RETIREMENT, JAMES HARRISON WILSON settled into domestic life with no intention of again leaving it. He took up residence at Stockford and in subsequent weeks received friends and acquaintances who wished to welcome him home and to congratulate him on his successful exploits in foreign lands.

Wilson's eldest daughter, Mary, had married in 1891, but his other girls, Katharine and Elinor, remained at Stockford with him. Even so, he must have keenly felt Ella's absence. Perhaps as an anodyne for his sorrow, he threw himself into oratory, civic improvement, and politics.

Short weeks after returning to Wilmington, he was on the speaker's circuit. He spoke to community, political, and fraternal organizations regarding his war service, his opinions on the great issues of the day, and his pet projects. That May, at a dinner at Delmonico's Restaurant in New York City, he addressed a veterans' association, the Military Order of the Loyal Legion of the United States, New York Commandery, and made some lighthearted observations on the American fighting man as he had come to know him in Puerto Rico and Peking. "We mustn't be vainglorious about the American soldier," he told the Legionnaires. "He isn't a great disciplinarian. His collar doesn't always fit just right, and his leggings may lack a few loops of being fastened. But when it comes to fighting, he gets there. . . . He's a good deal like those fighters in South Africa [then fighting in the Boer War], who are not very much to look at, but are hell on fighting. . . ." The speech was of the sort he especially favored—custom-made to the interests of a military-minded audience. The Legionnaires received it enthusiastically.

Other subjects which he often worked into his speeches included free trade with Cuba and the need for a Panama Canal. He spoke on the former topic when addressing economic organizations in New York, Boston, and other eastern cities, and it formed the basis of a pamphlet, *An Address on Our Trade Relations with the Tropics*, published in 1901, and also of a small book, *Our Relations with Cuba,* which he published in Wilmington the following year. The Panama Canal issue was in large measure the outgrowth of the interest in water navigation which he had acquired while working along the Mississippi after the Civil War. Long before the Canal became a reality under President Theodore Roosevelt, Wilson pushed vigorously for its construction, although quick to point out that "I have not the remotest personal or pecuniary interest in it above that of any other citizen of the United States."

In mid-1902 he was coaxed out of private life for the final time. Following the death of Queen Victoria, her son, Edward, Prince of Wales, stood ready to accept the crown of the British Empire. In assembling a contingent to represent the United States at the coronation, President Roosevelt named Wilson, one of the nation's most esteemed soldiers, to appear in behalf of the Army. His feelings toward British monarchy having by this time moderated, Wilson accepted the honor with alacrity.

Because of the Prince's illness, the ceremony was delayed for two months, but that summer Wilson sailed for England with daughters Katharine and Elinor, his private secretary, an orderly, two aides-de-camp (one being Lieutenant Colonel Biddle, his chief engineer during the Spanish-American War), the representative of the Navy, Captain Charles E. Clark, and a diplomatic detachment headed by Special Ambassador Whitelaw Reid. In due course the travelers reached London, where they lodged in a sumptuous house, and later appeared at court amidst such pomp and ceremony as captivated not only Wilson's unmarried daughters but their father as well.

After performing his official duties, Wilson accompanied the girls on a tour of the city, visiting historic sites, including Queen Victoria's tomb at Windsor Castle, upon which he placed a wreath. They all returned to America a few weeks later, immensely delighted by their trip. Wilson's enjoyment diminished, however, when he found it difficult to persuade the government to reimburse him for expenses which he had paid out of his own pocketbook. Not until April, 1903 did the War Department send him a check for $1,430 in repayment.

Back home, General Wilson re-established himself in the Republican Party in Delaware and was soon waging a relentless struggle to foil the designs of John E. Addicks, a local businessman-turned-politician. For years Addicks had ruthlessly sought to buy a U.S. Senate seat, spending money lavishly to secure the votes of the Delaware state legislators, who elected the state's national senators. Thanks partially to Wilson's efforts, Addicks was continually frustrated and, eventually, in 1906, was compelled to withdraw from the leadership of his so-called Union Republican Party. However, Wilson was unable to realize the dream of gaining the office denied to Addicks. The Legislature gave it to another reform candidate with credentials even more gleaming than Wilson's, Colonel Henry A. du Pont, who with Wilson had served under Sheridan in the 1864 Shenandoah Valley campaign.

Yet Wilson remained keenly attuned to politics on the national level, and cherished his position as one of America's most influential military advisors. When called upon for opinion, he rarely remained silent. In December of 1903, for example, he appeared, by invitation, before the Senate Committee on Military Affairs, chaired by Redfield Proctor of Vermont. Senator Proctor's committee was delving into the qualifications of Leonard Wood, the former governor general of Cuba, whose recent promotion to major general in the Regular Army had come up for confirmation. Wilson was outraged by the situation, for in the space of two years Wood had received promotions from captain to general "over the heads of some 600 other officers, his seniors in service, rank, and military merit." Undoubtedly personal animus prompted Wilson's anger to some extent, as did jealousy over Wood's unprecedented rise in the service. Wilson was also influenced by his high regard for West Point training, which Wood lacked.

Appearing before the committee in mid-January, Wilson stated his belief that Wood's promotion would be "the severest blow to the discipline and sense of fairness of the army ever administered in my day." Later the promotion was confirmed by the Senate, but at least Wilson had been able to voice his opinion. Although sixty-six, he remained as staunch in his animosity toward some men as in his friendship for others.

While he advised the government about military affairs, Wilson's business career continued to be varied. Although long ago he had bowed out of his last executive position, he still played the stock market, which assured him a comfortable income, and served as a trustee of New York City's Mutual Life Insurance Corporation. In the first decade of the new century he investigated various other commercial opportunities, including the possibility of building a gun and ship factory in partnership with the Bethlehem Steel Company and some English investors. But little came of it—as of a more promising-looking foray into the tin can production business.

In 1903–1904 he teamed with investment analyst R. Suydam

Grant in financing the development of a device which, according to its inventor, would revolutionize tin can manufacturing. They were able to raise the necessary funds and at the outset it appeared that the venture would prove a great success; Wilson and Grant had visions of selling the rights to their machine to the giant American Can Company. They went so far as to plan a small corporation of their own before learning that the cost of feeding necessary amounts of raw material into the machine would be prohibitive. American Can wanted no part of so expensive a contraption, and thus Grant informed his partner that the only tangible result of their investment was "a very interesting and curious machine. . . . but we can abandon all hope of making money by it."

More profitable, in terms of pleasure derived, were his travels. By now a voyager of considerable experience, he had no desire to repress his wanderlust. His trips included a tour of Cuba early in 1903, during which he visited Matanzas and Santa Clara and found their people "doing very well" under self-rule; two trips to Europe, in 1909 (which included stopovers in London, Paris, Venice, Budapest, and Vienna) and again two years later; a journey through Alaska in mid-1910; and a tour of Alabama and other scenes of his Civil War campaigning, in 1911.

Still another abiding pastime was his writing. During a sixteen-year period following his return from the Boxer war, he published a wide array of books, articles, and sketches, many of them dealing with people and events of the Civil War. His books included memoirs of such respected comrades-in-arms as General William Farrar Smith (published in 1904), Charles A. Dana (1907), and John A. Rawlins (1916)—the latter the product of his efforts as Rawlins's literary executor, a task which Rawlins, shortly before his death in 1869, had asked Wilson to undertake. Wilson handled most of his subjects with a fair degree of objectivity and accuracy. But he could regard none of them dispassionately and in some cases, as General Smith's, was bound by the wishes of the subject's family to paint a more favorable portrait than he might otherwise have desired to create. Yet he accepted such restrictions willingly enough.

In at least one case, however, he did a great disservice to the memory of a historical figure. His deep friendship with Rawlins and his checkered association with Grant caused him to paint a less than wholly accurate picture of those men's relationships. Specifically, he helped perpetuate the myth of a commanding general almost totally dependent on his adjutant's temperance, prudence, and probity to stabilize and strengthen his character. Later historians, failing to recognize the bias in Wilson's viewpoint, accepted such assertions as fact.

The work to which Wilson devoted his most strenuous efforts and the greatest amount of time was, quite naturally, his own memoirs. He began to re-create his career shortly before the turn of the century, working from official records, his diaries, correspondence, interviews with men who had shaped his life and career, and from memory. The culmination of his work was the publication in 1912 of a two-volume set, *Under the Old Flag: Recollections of Military Operations in the War for the Union, The Spanish War, The Boxer Rebellion, Etc.*

Upon its appearance, the work was hailed by many historians and literary critics for its dramatic style, its clear, polished prose, and its enlightening observations on dozens of military and civilian notables. In later years, however, knowledgeable readers came to recognize that in writing it Wilson allowed his memory to work to his great advantage and at the expense of the reputations of former superiors and subordinates. Although generally reliable in his accounts of military operations, Wilson studiously avoided making statements about difficulties he encountered in command. His troubles during such episodes of his Civil War career as the Wilderness Campaign, the Petersburg railroads raid, and the battle of Spring Hill—when he acknowledged their existence at all—he attributed to the errors of others. And he drew highly questionable portraits of some commanders with whom he was, at one time or another, in conflict—including Grant, Sheridan, Meade, and Schofield.

Nevertheless, if these and related points are kept in mind, the latter-day reader can gain from the work a great amount of factual information about James Harrison Wilson and can catch more than a glimpse of his character and personality. By careful study of official documents and consideration of opinions expressed by qualified historians of a later period, one ought to be able to discover the book's truths, errors, exaggerations, and omissions easily enough.

An interesting and perceptive manuscript upon which Wilson worked for a lengthy period was never published. In "Heroes of the Great Rebellion" he comments upon Generals Grant, Thomas, and McClellan as they revealed themselves in personal association with him. Grant the soldier wins his high regard, although again Wilson gives undue consideration to Rawlins's solicitude as an invaluable factor in Grant's success. As politician, Grant comes in for much less praise, which, given the extent of his postwar difficulties with Wilson, is understandable: "As a statesman, his career must be regarded as a disappointment, if not as a signal failure." Yet he also views Grant as a tool in the hands of unscrupulous politicians and businessmen who took advantage of Grant's simple good nature and naive faith in the sacredness of friendship.

In contrast, Wilson portrays George H. Thomas as "the peer of any other General in the army" as well as "a proud, self-respecting, honorable man, full of dignity and authority. . . ." And he characterizes McClellan as an egotistical braggart elevated to a position he did not merit and in which he could not properly coordinate those military talents he did possess. Here Wilson seems directly on target with his analyses, although it must be said that with the exception of his portrait of Thomas, Wilson's views were largely derived from retrospective analysis rather than from his contemporaneous opinion. He could not perceive in contemporary associates many of the flaws and limitations which he believed he saw in later years but which were often suggested to him by the writings of other historians. If nothing else, however, it can be said that in many cases Wilson possessed twenty-twenty hindsight.

Most of his writing and commercial investigating were done at home, which, during the last several years of his life, was at 1305 Rodney Street, Wilmington. His business affairs and his personal interests consumed so great a portion of his time that it is unlikely he had much opportunity to grow very lonely, despite the fact that Katharine and Elinor married, in 1904 and 1908 respectively. Often he had "Kitty" by his side, for even after her marriage she kept house for him. Sometimes his grandchildren would visit, and, more often still, old friends and associates would stop by to chat with the man who was still Delaware's favorite soldier and one of the country's greatest.

When he was not at home or on world travels, he enjoyed appearing at the Wilmington Country Club, of which he was a distinguished member. When in other cities such as Philadelphia and New York, he often stayed at the Union, Philadelphia, University and Army and Navy clubs. There he could bask in the esteem of other members and find a ready audience for his most cherished anecdotes and reminiscences. However, some of the younger members felt that he too blithely considered respect his due, moving through the lounges, game rooms, and dining halls with an air of self-importance. Such observers were essentially correct, for humility had never been one of the general's most enduring traits, and forty years after achieving his most notable military feats he was still self-assured and self-esteemed—more than a little vain.

Yet he also exhibited more admirable characteristics. From his home, for example, he wrote philanthropists and charitable organizations, soliciting contributions to worthy causes ranging from aid to Cuban orphans to the construction of a Young Men's Christian Association quarters in Wilmington.

For the last decade and a half of his life he remained quietly on Rodney Street, tending to his business affairs, conducting a massive correspondence, writing, socializing, and riding about the environs of Wilmington. Whereas in earlier times he had taken his exercise upon horseback, he now made his rounds from the seat of his Locomobile touring car.

During these years he remained remarkably healthy and vigorous, apparently defying the effects of time. Vastly proud of his military experience, he stood ready for active duty whenever a national crisis developed. In 1914 he placed himself at the disposal of President Woodrow Wilson when the possibility of conflict with Mexico attracted widespread attention, but he was not called on to serve. The next year he advanced to the rank of major general, United States Army (retired), and sought to drop the "retired" designation when the United States went to war against the Central Powers in 1917. Although nearing his eightieth birthday, he considered himself fit to campaign, and viewed the conflict as "a battle between democracy and small armies on one side and autocracy and great armies on the other. . . ." He was certain that America had sided with democracy.

He tried to his determined best to enter the war, assaulting the adjutant general with requests to serve in any capacity. When the Army matched his stubbornness by countering with refusal upon refusal, he gave up the fight at last. But he did recommend the names of several officers whom he felt deserved high rank and important command assignments. Late in the war he toured training bases and compared notes with officers whose grandfathers had campaigned with him on the battlefields of the past.

He survived World War I by seven years. These, finally, were the lonely years, made especially so when his close companion, Kitty, died during the influenza epidemic which swept the country in 1918. Now he was alone for a great deal of time, except during occasional visits by relatives and friends. The country all but completely forgot him as it moved through the Roaring Twenties, pausing only briefly every year to note that the last surviving Civil War corps commander had celebrated another birthday. By 1924 only he and three other Federal soldiers who had held the rank of general officer during the War—Brooke, Miles, and Adalbert Ames—still lived.

Late that year Wilson's health began to fail from the encroachments of age. He was confined to bed until early in 1925, when for a time he seemed to be improving—once again displaying the soldier's determination to fight long odds. But by now he had lived eighty-seven years, and the overpowering strength of time made this battle the last one he would ever wage. On the twenty-third of February, while shaving in his home, he suffered a heart attack, which proved fatal.

FEW CONTEMPORARIES could match the variety of James Harrison Wilson's lifetime endeavors. Few men stamped their image on the military, political, and commercial history of the nineteenth century with so much color and drama and with such a strong faith in the rightness of their own ideals. And few men as dynamic and controversial as he have been so largely neglected by those responsible for recording human achievements for posterity.

Wilson's contributions to history were made possible by a long-standing urge to succeed at all costs. From his earliest years he single-mindedly charted his future: he perceived that a military career would enable him to attain all of the possessions he craved—rank, power, influence, notability. When at last he had the opportunity to carry out his plan, he saw that his belief had been entirely correct.

His fame rests chiefly upon several notable, specific contributions to American military science. Almost without exception, they have reference to one of the most important service arms of the nineteenth-century army, the cavalry. As Chief of the Cavalry Bureau he enjoyed his most complete success, for through his energy and youthful idealism he reorganized and rejuvenated the mounted service and also foiled unscrupulous businessmen who sought to defraud the United States government. By his efforts in the Bureau—particularly by his determination to see the Spencer carbine adopted as the standard cavalry weapon—and later through his organizational and command activities in the field, he enabled mounted soldiers to contribute their fair share toward the winning of America's most crucial conflict. However, his Selma campaign of 1865 was his most valuable legacy to latter-day practitioners of the art of warfare. On this expedition he demonstrated for the first time that a massive, highly mobile strike force—the forerunner of the mechanized battalions of the twentieth century—could be used to overwhelming effect.

Wilson made his mark not only in uniform. In private commercial life he contributed significantly to the effectiveness of national water and rail travel. By his efforts to build transportation lines across the country, he opened the American Middle West to settlement and thereby increased national prosperity. In New York State and New England, as well, he gave a tremendous impetus to rail commerce and promoted transportation agencies in still other regions.

He was less successful in his political endeavors, finding that the great fund of talent he had developed in the military could not be brought to effective use in the wide-open market of the political arena. Despite a towering ambition to win elective or appointive office, he lost every opportunity to come his way, largely as the result of an unenviable combination of conditions which could not be controlled by the advantages of military rank—many enemies, a tendency to be outspoken and uncompromising on subjects of national import, ill fortune, and simple bad timing.

Wilson's military services occurred during a period of more than forty years. Though elderly and comfortably settled in civilian life, he re-entered the service in 1898 and remained on active duty for almost three years, demonstrating that he was never too old or too weary to serve when he believed his country was threatened. His military training never ceased to influence him although for many years he remained out of uniform. Even when wearing cutaway coat and top hat, he carried himself erect and with dignity, mindful that he had once served under such great commanders as Grant, Thomas, and Sheridan.

He made one of his most admirable contributions to international well-being during his stint as a military governor in Cuba. There he went to great lengths to ease the misery of the people under his jurisdiction by helping to stamp out poverty and providing food, shelter, and clothing to the indigent. His methods received the unalloyed approval of the Cuban people, as did his great desire to see self-rule conferred upon the island. Although for a time his policies ran counter to the official views of his superiors in Washington, they greatly influenced later American diplomacy toward Caribbean lands.

In addition to these many achievements, Wilson was a biographer and historian of more than a little influence, publishing books, articles, and pamphlets on a variety of subjects relating to national and international affairs as well as to his personal experiences in war and peace.

However, his occasional narrow-mindedness and his tendency to show prejudice against many of his contemporaries have hindered latter-day historical interpretation.

Notwithstanding his many contributions to military, political, and industrial life, James Harrison Wilson was far from being the outstanding humanitarian of his age. He possessed more ambition and vanity than many of the successful men of his time; often he seemed to place his own personal concerns above the best interests of his country. He was driven by a massive compulsion to succeed and an obsession with divesting himself of all vestiges of culpability for failures great and trivial, by which he alienated numerous associates; and many times he was arbitrary in his evaluation of others and in his assessments of events in which he took part. His flaws of character posed great problems in interpersonal relationships; it can be said with certainty that he made at least as many avid enemies as close friends during his lifetime —often to his disadvantage, as graphically demonstrated by his failure to attain national office, one of the greatest disappointments he ever experienced.

Wilson's saving grace, apropos to the advancement of his career, was his refusal to recognize such flaws and failings as crippling handicaps. Instead, he utilized them to promote a military and civilian career of singular renown. In the last analysis, his life story illustrates that a man of supreme self-confidence, determination, and organizational talent—even if unable to win national office—can significantly influence the political and social life of his era.

Notes

Note: Rather than burden this book—already weighted by a lengthy bibliography—with an additional fifty-odd pages of notes, the author has decided to cite only references to unpublished and therefore not easily accessible source materials.

CHAPTER I

Information on Wilson's early life in Illinois: Thesis, "James Harrison Wilson: a Partial Biography," by Paul C. Pehrson, ll* 1–7, Southern Illinois University Library, Carbondale, Illinois.

Free-soil beliefs of the Wilson family: Wilson to Morris Schaff, March 22, 1906, in Wilson Papers, Library of Congress (hereinafter cited as *WP*).

Wilson's term at McKendree College: See the following entries in his diary, Delaware State Historical Society, Wilmington, Del. (hereinafter cited as *WD*) for 1855: Subjects: entries for Jan. 1–3, 18; Church: Jan. 14,

---

* l and ll are the symbols standing, respectively, for "leaf" and "leaves."

Feb. 4, Mar. 18, 25; Books read: Feb. 14, Mar. 11; His departure for home: Mar. 24, 30.

Nomination for West Point cadetship: Wilson's cadet application files, National Archives Microfilm Series 688, Roll 200.

Journey from home to West Point: *WD* for June 9, 11, 12, 1855.

Quote about determination to succeed: *WD* for Sept. 7, 1855.

Fight with Cadet McCreery and Hardee's punishment of Wilson: Wilson to Morris Schaff, March 22, 1906, *WP*.

Wilson's academic record: Grades and demerits list furnished the author by the U.S.M.A. Archives.

General service at Fort Vancouver: Files of the Topographical Engineer Department, 1860–61, National Archives Microfilm Series 66, Roll 22.

Wilson's fear for the stability of the Union: *WD* for Jan. 5, Feb. 1, Mar. 23, 1861.

CHAPTER II

Wilson's illness and his stopover in Wilmington: *WD* for Aug. 24–25, 1861.

His first impressions of Miss Andrews, as he recalled them four years later: Wilson to Adam Badeau, November 20, 1865, *WP*.

Lack of employment in Washington: *WD* for Sept. 3, 6, 1861.

Troubles with Navy in Georgia: *WD* for Jan. 18, 19, 20, 28, 1862.

Venus Point Battery: Letter from Horace Porter to his father, February 16, 1862, Porter Papers, Library of Congress.

Reconnaissance and skirmish on Wilmington Island: *WD* for Apr. 17, 1862.

Boredom during lull in operations in Georgia: *WD* for Apr. 25, May 4, 1862.

Socializing in New York City and Wilmington: *WD* for Oct. 8–9, 1862.

CHAPTER III

Wilson's first audience with Grant: *WD* for Nov. 8, 1862.

Desolation of upper Mississippi: *WD* for Dec. 4, 1862.

Wilson's first war victim: Pehrson thesis, ll 51–53.

Wilson's feelings about Grant's parole decision and about the need for a vigorous siege: Pehrson, l 45.

CHAPTER IV

Nationalized Army plan: Pehrson, ll 42–43; *WD* for Dec. 31, 1862; and Wilson to Gen. William F. Smith, July 9, 1864, *WP*.

Typescript copies of telegrams sent from Assistant Secretary of War Dana to Secretary Stanton are contained in *WP*.

Wilson's "pretty Rebel": *WD* for Oct. 10, 1863; and Pehrson, ll 22, 53.

Shawneetown homecoming: *WD* for Aug. 24, 1863.
Inspection tour: *WD* for Sept. 18, 1863; and Pehrson, ll 54–55.

CHAPTER V

Cavalry Bureau reforms, including establishment of new inspection boards: Wilson to the commander of the St. Louis Cavalry Depot, February 6, 1864, War Department Records in the National Archives, Record Group 108, Entry 69.
Defaulting contractors: Wilson to Stanton, March 22, 26, April 6, 1864, National Archives RG-108, E-69.
Jailing of contractors: Unsigned biographical sketch of Wilson, *WP*.
Battle over Wilson's confirmation as general: Wilson to Gen. William F. Smith, April 25, 1864, *WP*.
Troubles at Giesboro Point: Wilson to Col. C. R. Lowell, February 18, 1864, National Archives RG-108, E-69.
Filling up ranks of veteran units: Wilson to Stanton, February 9, 1864, National Archives RG-108, E-69.
Governor Johnson's regiments: Wilson to Stanton, February 9, 1864; Wilson to Johnson, March 31, 1864; and Wilson to Gen. H. W. Halleck, April 5, 1864; all, National Archives RG-108, E-69.
Contractors upping price of horseflesh: Wilson to Stanton, February 29, 1864, National Archives RG-108, E-74.
Bureau carbine survey: 1863 "Report of Arms," National Archives RG-108, E-75.
Wilson "getting along admirably": Wilson to Gen. William F. Smith, February 10, 1864, *WP*.
Wilson as administrator: "Reminiscences" of Gen. August V. Kautz, l 62, in Kautz Papers, Library of Congress (hereinafter cited as *KR*).
Problems with Quartermaster's and Ordnance departments: *KR*, l 62; and Wilson to the commander of the St. Louis Cavalry Depot, March 11, 1864, National Archives RG-108, E-69.
Wilson and the Lincolns: *WD* for Feb. 9, 1864; Wilson to Gen. William F. Smith, February 10, 1864, *WP*; and Pehrson, l 79.
Grant as lieutenant general: Wilson to Gen. William F. Smith, February 14, 1864, *WP*.

CHAPTER VI

Wilson's first day in field command: *WD* for Apr. 17, 1864.
Quote about Wilson's bad bookkeeping: entry for Dec. 11, 1863, in Cyrus B. Comstock's diary, Comstock Papers, Library of Congress.
Reforming the Third Cavalry Division: *WD* for Apr. 19, 30, 1864.
Crossing the Rapidan River: *WD* for May 4, 1864.

Col. Bryan's removal during Richmond Raid: Wilson to Gen. T. F. Rodenbough, October 14, 1908, *WP*.

CHAPTER VII

Wilson's railroad raid orders: *WD* for June 21, 1864.
Fight at the Staunton River bridge: *KR*, l 80.
Battle at Reams's Station: Entry for June 29, 1864 in Kautz's diary, Kautz Papers, Library of Congress.
Retreat from Reams's Station and Kautz's vision: *KR,* l 82.
Wilson's anger over pillaging: *KR,* l 81.
Wilson's "disaster": Gen. George G. Meade to his wife, June 30, 1864, in Meade Papers, Manuscripts Department, The Historical Society of Pennsylvania, Philadelphia, Pa.
Orders relating to Wilson's transfer to the Shenandoah: Maj. Elmer Otis, Chief Inspector of Cavalry, to Capt. William R. Price, Assistant Inspector-General, Cavalry Bureau, August 5, 1864, National Archives RG-108, E-74; and *WD* for Aug. 1, 1864.
Eluding Merritt's "trap": Wilson to Gen. Sir Thomas Fraser, September 22, 1910, *WP*.
Third Cavalry Division at Winchester: Wilson to Gen. T. F. Rodenbough, October 14, 1908, *WP*.
Wilson's transfer to Sherman: *WD* for Sept. 30, 1864.
Possible reason for transfer: Bluford Wilson to James Harrison Wilson, May 20, 1913, *WP*.

CHAPTER VIII

Wilson's transfer "no disgrace": Wilson to Gen. William F. Smith, October 29, 1864, *WP*.
A table of organization for Sherman's cavalry at the time of Wilson's arrival in the western theater can be found in Wilson's Speech, Article and Book File, *WP*.
Call to Cavalry Bureau for mounts and supplies: Wilson to Maj. William R. Price, October 18, 25, 1864, National Archives RG-108, E-74.

CHAPTER IX

Thomas's excitement after the victory at Nashville: Wilson's "Heroes of the Great Rebellion," l 246, MS. in *WP*.
Stretching five days' rations during pursuit of Hood: Pehrson, l 112.

CHAPTER X

Wilson's hopes for spring campaign: Wilson to Gen. William D. Whipple, December 30, 1864, National Archives RG-108, E-74.
General A. J. Smith and outpost duty: *WD* for Jan. 13, 1865.
"If we get Montgomery . . .": Wilson to Adam Badeau, February 27, 1865, *WP*.
Wilson's worry over delays: Wilson to Badeau, March 7, 1865, *WP*.
Wilson's command in magnificent condition: Wilson to Badeau, March 20, 1865, *WP*.
Meeting with Forrest at Cahaba: Wilson to Gen. E. W. Rucker, July 17, 1915, *WP*; and *WD* for Apr. 8, 1865.
Capture of Montgomery: *WD* for Apr. 11, 12, 1865.
Wilson on Lincoln's death: Wilson to Badeau, April 29, 1865, *WP*.
Wilson's men "invincible": Wilson to Badeau, May 27, 1865, *WP*.

CHAPTER XI

Macon's return to normalcy: Letter of John A. Cobb to President William McKinley, December 10, 1898, *WP*.
Wilson's policies regarding Georgia Reconstruction: Wilson to the Chief of Staff of the Army of the Cumberland, June 15, 1865, in the Andrew Johnson Papers (microfilm), Library of Congress.
Wilson on education of Negroes: Wilson to Badeau, June 30, August 2, 1865, *WP*.
Wilson's audience with Jefferson Davis in Macon: Wilson to Charles F. Adams, February 22, 1908, *WP*.
Wilson's request for muster-out: Wilson to the adjutant general of the Army, November 19, 1865, Appointments, Commissions and Personnel File of James H. Wilson (hereinafter referred to as "Wilson's A.C.P. File"), National Archives.
Engagement to Ella Andrews: *WD* for Sept. 2, 1865.
Description of his fiancée: Wilson to Badeau, Nov. 20, 1865, *WP*.

CHAPTER XII

Wedding at Stockford: Wilson to Badeau, Dec. 28, 1865, *WP*; and *WD* for Jan. 3, 1866.
New York honeymoon: Wilson to Badeau, Jan. 8, 1866, *WP*.
Resignation from National Express Company: *WD* for Mar. 18, 1866.
Opportunity for duty at Fort Delaware: Wilson to Badeau, Apr. 22, 1866, *WP*.

Listless period at Fort Delaware: Wilson to Badeau, Apr. 28, 1866, *WP*.

Transfer to Iowa: *WD* for June 30, 1866, Mar. 25, 1867.

Wilson's first child: Wilson to Badeau, July 5, 6, 1867, *WP*.

Dwindling finances: Wilson to Badeau, Aug. 12, 1867, *WP*.

Lt. Col., 35th Infantry: Letter from president of board for examining officers to the adjutant general, Oct. 23, 1866; and Wilson to adjutant general, Mar. 25, 1867; both in Wilson's A.C.P. File, National Archives.

Wilson-Dana book on Grant: *WD* for May 5, 1868.

Grant and Belknap on Wilson's retirement: Secretary of War Belknap to the adjutant general, Aug. 29, 1870, Wilson's A.C.P. File, National Archives.

Wilson's letter of resignation: Wilson to the adjutant general, Sept. 2, 1870, Wilson's A.C.P. File, National Archives.

Few regrets over leaving service: Wilson to Charles A. Dana, Sept. 19, 1870, *WP*.

Entrance into civil life: *WD* for Jan. 1, 1871.

Initial endeavors with the Southeastern: *WD* for Mar. 25, 1869.

General information on Wilson's association with the Southeastern: Thesis, "Post-Civil War Career of James Harrison Wilson," by Samuel W. Newman, ll 24–46, 50–58, in Baylor University Library, Waco, Tex.

Letter-books containing voluminous correspondence between Wilson and Edward F. Winslow are contained in *WP*.

Wilson's association with the Cairo & Vincennes: Newman thesis, ll 61–72.

Opportunity to become Assistant Secretary of the Treasury: Wilson to Badeau, December 5, 1874, *WP*.

Wilson-Pullman venture in Europe: *WD* for Nov. 30, Dec. 1, 12, 1874.

I.R.S. offer: *WD* for Mar. 2, Apr. 7, 1875.

Wilson vs. Pullman and Porter: *WD* for Aug. 24, 31, Sept. 1, 1876.

"I would rather be myself . . .": *WD* for Sept. 2, 1876.

"Although not rich in this world's goods . . .": *WD* for Jan. 3, 1876.

Bluford Wilson as solicitor of the Treasury: *WD* for June 20, 22, 1874, July 28, 1876.

Grant's snub of Wilson in restaurant: *WD* for Feb. 16, 1881.

Joining the New York & New England: *WD* for Jan. 25, 1881.

Wilson's association with the New York & New England: Newman thesis, ll 75–93.

Leaving the line: *WD* for Jan. 13, 1883.

Trip to the Orient: Newman thesis, ll 94–107.

Hudson Tunnel Company venture: *WD* for Apr. 9, May 1, 9, 1891; and Wilson to Board of Directors of Hudson Tunnel Railroad Company, May 20, 1891, *WP*.

Russian ambassadorship opportunity: *WD* for Aug. 17, 1897.

Wilson's commercial interests following his China tour: Newman thesis, ll 107–22.

CHAPTER XIII

Wilson's offer to serve in Spanish-American War: adjutant general to James H. Wilson, April 6, 1898, *WP*.

Wilson's attempt to secure first appointment as major general: Wilson to Sens. Gray and Higgins, Apr. 15, 1898, Wilson's A.C.P. File, National Archives.

Attempt to attain military seniority: Wilson to Secretary of War Alger, May 7, 1898, Wilson's A.C.P. File, National Archives.

Senate speeches by Bacon and Lindsay: *WD* for May 4, 1898.

Wilson's departure for Camp Thomas: *WD* for May 14, 1898.

Ella and daughters in Charleston: *WD* for July 6, 1898.

Wilson's headquarters in Macon: *WD* for Nov. 8, 1898.

Warm reception by people of Macon: Wilson to H. W. Biddle, Dec. 17, 1898, *WP*.

Wilson's speech during McKinley's tour: Newspaper clipping in *WD* for Dec. 1898.

Allison's endorsement of Wilson as governor-general in Cuba: Sen. William B. Allison to James H. Wilson, Oct. 3, 1898, *WP*.

Root's reply to Wilson backer: Secretary of War Elihu Root to Col. Le Grand B. Cannon, Nov. 14, 1898, *WP*.

Population and area of Wilson's department in Cuba: Speech by Wilson, "Cuba Revisited," Speech, Article and Book File, *WP*.

Wilson's aims in Cuba: Wilson to Prof. Goldwin Smith, Jan. 19, 1899, *WP*.

Wilson's discharge as major general and appointment as brigadier, Apr. 1899: Record and Pension Office statement of Mar. 15, 1902, Wilson's A.C.P. File, National Archives.

CHAPTER XIV

Wilson's letter tendering services for China: Wilson to Secretary of War Root, June 17, 1900, Wilson's A.C.P. File, National Archives.

"I have no desire to go to China again, but . . .": Wilson to Gen. William Ludlow, June 30, 1900, *WP*.

"The man who gets ahead of me . . .": Wilson to Col. Tasker H. Bliss, July 25, 1900, *WP*.

Trip from Cuba to China: Newman thesis, ll 149–50.

Eight Temples expedition: Newman thesis, l 156.

Wilson's Anglophobia with reference to Civil War: Wilson to Charles F. Adams, Dec. 15, 1911, *WP*.

"No adequate command" remaining in China: Wilson to Manuel L. Diaz, Oct. 9, 1900, *WP*.

Wilson's final discharge from duty: Circular from the office of the adjutant general, Mar. 2, 1901, *WP*.

Views on the Panama Canal: Wilson to Gen. O. H. Ernst, July 26, 1901, *WP*.

Trip to London for coronation of Edward VII: Wilson to the adjutant general, Feb. 11, Mar. 8, Sept. 11, 1902, *WP*; and *New York Tribune* clipping dated Jan. 15, 1902, contained in the Adam Badeau Papers, Princeton University Library.

Reimbursement for funds spent in London: Secretary of War Root to James H. Wilson, April 11, 1903, *WP*.

Wilson vs. Addicks: Wilson to Charles F. Adams, Feb. 11, Oct. 6, 1903, *WP*; Wilson to Theodore Roosevelt, Mar. 9, 1901, Nov. 8, 1902, *WP*; and *WD* for Jan. 1, 1901.

Appearance at Senate hearings on Gen. Wood: Acting adjutant general to James H. Wilson, Dec. 7, 1903, Wilson's A.C.P. File, National Archives; and Wilson to Isaac R. Pennypacker, Jan. 16, 1904, *WP*.

Steel factory venture with Bethlehem Company: Wilson to Col. Le Grand B. Cannon, Apr. 4, 1901, *WP*.

Wilson's foray into tin-can manufacturing: R. Suydam Grant to James H. Wilson, June 29, 1903, Feb. 8, Apr. 15, 1904, *WP*; and Wilson to R. Suydam Grant, Jan. 16, 1905, *WP*.

Wilson's 1903 trip to Cuba: Wilson to Col. John Biddle, Mar. 16, 1903, *WP*.

Wilson's 1909 trip to Europe: Wilson to William B. Allison, July 14, 1909, *WP*.

Wilson's 1911 trip to Alabama: Wilson to Gen. George B. Rodney, Jan. 27, 1911, *WP*.

Writings about Grant and Rawlins: "Heroes of the Great Rebellion," ll 85, 90, MS. in *WP*.

Writings about Thomas: "Heroes of the Great Rebellion," l 245.

Writings about McClellan: "Heroes of the Great Rebellion," ll 286–87.

Attempt to re-enter Service, 1914: Wilson to President Woodrow Wilson, Apr. 27, 1914, *WP*.

Bibliography

I. Manuscripts:

Carbondale, Ill. Southern Illinois University Library. Thesis: "James Harrison Wilson: A Partial Biography" by Paul C. Pehrson.

Philadelphia, Pa. Manuscripts Department, Historical Society of Pennsylvania. George Gordon Meade papers.

Princeton, N.J. Princeton University Library. Adam Badeau papers.

Waco, Tex. Baylor University Library. Thesis: "Post-Civil War Career of James Harrison Wilson" by Samuel W. Newman.

Washington, D.C. Library of Congress. Andrew Johnson papers.

Washington, D.C. Library of Congress. August V. Kautz diary (1861–65) and "Reminiscences," in Kautz papers.

Washington, D.C. Library of Congress. Cyrus B. Comstock diary (1863–67), in Comstock papers.

Washington, D.C. Library of Congress. Horace Porter diary (1861–65) and papers.

Washington, D.C. Library of Congress. James Harrison Wilson papers.
Washington, D.C. Library of Congress. Ulysses S. Grant papers.
Wilmington, Del. Delaware State Historical Society. Ella Andrews Wilson diaries (1859–82).
Wilmington, Del. Delaware State Historical Society. James Harrison Wilson diaries (1855–1921).

II. Government Documents:

Academic Record of James Harrison Wilson, Class of July 1860. Department of the Army, United States Military Academy, West Point, N.Y.
Annual Report of the Major-General Commanding the Army, to the Secretary of War. Washington, D.C., 1898–99.
Appointments, Commissions and Personnel File of James Harrison Wilson. National Archives, Washington, D.C.
Cadet Application File of James Harrison Wilson. Microfilm Series 688, Roll 200, National Archives, Washington, D.C.
Civil Report of Major-General John R. Brooke, U.S. Army, Military Governor, Island of Cuba. Washington, D.C., 1900.
Correspondence Relating to the War with Spain . . . Including the China Relief Expedition . . . Washington, D.C., 1902.
Files of the Topographical Engineer Department (1860–65). Microfilm Series 66, Rolls 22 and 23. National Archives, Washington, D.C.
Files of the U.S. Cavalry Bureau (1863–65). Record Group 108, Entries 69, 74, and 75, National Archives, Washington, D.C.
Maps Prepared By or Under the Direction of James Harrison Wilson (1862–65). Cartographic Division, National Archives, Washington, D.C.
Official Records of the Union and Confederate Navies in the War of the Rebellion. Washington, D.C., 1894–1922.
Post Returns, Fort Vancouver (1860–61). National Archives, Washington, D.C.
War of the Rebellion: A Compilation of the Official Records of the Union and Confederate Armies. Washington, D.C., 1880–1901.

III. Newspapers and Magazines:

Augusta (Ga.) *Daily Chronicle and Sentinel* (1864–65).
Daily Richmond Enquirer (1864–65).
Daily Richmond Examiner (1864–65).
Frank Leslie's Illustrated Newspaper (1864–65).
Harper's Weekly (1861–1901).
Montgomery Advertiser (1864–65).
Nashville Daily Times and True Union (1864–65).
Nashville Dispatch (1864–65).

New York Times (1861–1925).
New York Tribune (1864–65).
North China Herald and Supreme Court and Consular Gazette (Shanghai, July–November, 1900).
Philadelphia Daily Evening Bulletin (1864–65).
Philadelphia Inquirer (1861–65).
Savannah Republican (1864–65).
Washington Daily National Intelligencer (1862–65).

IV. Personal Narratives, Reminiscences, and Regimental Histories:

Agassiz, George R. (ed.). *Meade's Headquarters, 1863–1865: Letters of Colonel Theodore Lyman from the Wilderness to Appomattox.* Boston, 1922.

Annals of the War, Written by Leading Participants, North and South, The. Philadelphia, 1879.

Bennett, L. G., and Haigh, William M. *History of the Thirty-Sixth Regiment Illinois Volunteers during the War of the Rebellion.* Aurora, Ill., 1876.

Boudrye, Louis N. *Historic Records of the Fifth New York Cavalry.* Albany, 1865.

Carter, W. R. *History of the First Regiment of Tennessee Volunteer Cavalry in the Great War of the Rebellion.* Knoxville, 1902.

Cox, Jacob D. *Military Reminiscences of the Civil War* (Volume 2). New York, 1900.

Crofts, Thomas (comp.). *History of the Service of the Third Ohio Veteran Volunteer Cavalry in the War for the Preservation of the Union from 1861–1865.* Toledo and Columbus, 1910.

Curry, W. L. (comp.). *Four Years in the Saddle: History of the First Regiment Ohio Volunteer Cavalry, War of the Rebellion—1861–1865.* Columbus, 1898.

Dana, Charles A. *Recollections of the Civil War: With the Leaders at Washington and in the Field in the Sixties.* New York, 1898.

Davenport, Edward A. (ed.). *History of the Ninth Regiment Illinois Cavalry Volunteers.* Chicago, 1888.

Davis, Richard Harding. *The Cuban and Porto Rican Campaigns.* New York, 1898.

Farrar, Samuel Clarke (comp.). *The Twenty-Second Pennsylvania Cavalry and the Ringgold Battalion, 1861–1865.* Pittsburgh, 1911.

Grant, Ulysses S. *Personal Memoirs* (Volumes 1 and 2). New York, 1885–86.

Hagemann, E. R. (ed.). *Fighting Rebels and Redskins: Experiences in Army Life of Colonel George B. Sanford, 1861–1892.* Norman, Okla., 1969.

Harwell, Richard B. (ed.). *Destruction and Reconstruction: Personal Experiences of the Late War,* by Richard Taylor. New York, 1955.

History of the Eighteenth Regiment of Cavalry, Pennsylvania Volunteers, 1862–1865. New York, 1909.

Hood, John Bell. *Advance and Retreat: Personal Experiences in the United States & Confederate States Armies* (Reprint). Bloomington, Ind., 1959.

Johnston, Joseph E. *Narrative of Military Operations* (Reprint). Bloomington, Ind., 1959.

Kidd, J. H. *Personal Recollections of a Cavalryman with Custer's Michigan Cavalry Brigade in the Civil War.* Ionia, Mich., 1908.

Kirk, Charles H. (comp.). *History of the Fifteenth Pennsylvania Cavalry.* Philadelphia, 1906.

McGee, B. F., and Jewell, William R. *History of the Seventy-Second Indiana Volunteer Infantry of the Mounted Lightning Brigade.* LaFayette, Ind., 1882.

Merington, Marguerite (ed.). *The Custer Story: The Life and Intimate Letters of George A. Custer and His Wife Elizabeth.* New York, 1950.

Miles, Nelson A. *Serving the Republic.* New York, 1911.

Moyer, H. P. (comp.). *History of the Seventeenth Regiment Pennsylvania Volunteer Cavalry.* Lebanon, Pa., 1911.

Nevins, Allan (ed.). *A Diary of Battle: The Personal Journals of Colonel Charles S. Wainwright, 1861–1865.* New York, 1962.

Norton, Henry. *Deeds of Daring, or History of the Eighth N.Y. Volunteer Cavalry.* Norwich, N.Y., 1889.

Pickerill, W. N. *History of the Third Indiana Cavalry.* Indianapolis, 1906.

Pierce, Lyman B. *History of the Second Iowa Cavalry.* Burlington, Iowa, 1865.

Private and Official Correspondence of Gen. Benjamin F. Butler during the Period of the Civil War (Volume 4). Norwood, Mass., 1917.

Pyne, Henry R. *The History of the First New Jersey Cavalry.* Trenton, 1871.

Sanford, W. L. (comp.). *History of the Fourteenth Illinois Cavalry and the Brigades to Which It Belonged.* Chicago, 1898.

Schofield, John M. *Forty-Six Years in the Army.* New York, 1897.

Scott, William Forse. *The Story of a Cavalry Regiment: The Career of the Fourth Iowa Veteran Volunteers.* New York, 1893.

Sheridan, Philip H. *Personal Memoirs* (Volumes 1 and 2). New York, 1888.

Sherman, William T. *Memoirs of General William T. Sherman* (Reprint). Bloomington, Ind., 1957.

Sipes, William B. *The Seventh Pennsylvania Veteran Volunteer Cavalry: Its Record, Reminiscences and Roster.* Pottsville, Pa., 1905.

Sparks, David S. (ed.). *Inside Lincoln's Army: The Diary of Marsena Rudolph Patrick, Provost Marshal General, Army of the Potomac.* New York, 1964.

Temple, Wayne C. (ed.). *Campaigning with Grant*, by Horace Porter (Reprint). Bloomington, Ind., 1961.

Thatcher, Marshall P. *A Hundred Battles in the West, St. Louis to Atlanta, 1861–65: The Second Michigan Cavalry.* Detroit, 1884.

Thomas, Benjamin P. (ed.). *Three Years with Grant, as Recalled by War Correspondent Sylvanus Cadwallader.* New York, 1955.
The Wilderness Campaign, May–June, 1864 (Papers of the Military Historical Society of Massachusetts, Volume 4). Boston, 1905.
Wilson, James Harrison. *Under the Old Flag* (Volumes 1 and 2). New York, 1912.

V. General Sources:

a. Articles:

Ambrose, Stephen E. "A Theorist Fights: Emory Upton in the Civil War." *Civil War History,* Volume 9, Number 4 (December 1963), pp. 341–64.
———. "West Point in the Fifties: The Letters of Henry A. du Pont." *Civil War History,* Volume 10, Number 3 (September 1964), pp. 291–308.
Athearn, Robert G. (ed.). "The Civil War Diary of John Wilson Phillips." *Virginia Magazine of History and Biography,* Volume 62, Number 1 (January 1954), pp. 95–123.
Barton, John V. "The Procurement of Horses." *Civil War Times Illustrated,* Volume 6, Number 8 (December 1967), pp. 17–24.
Carpenter, Louis H. "Sheridan's Expedition Around Richmond, May 9–25, 1864." *Journal of the U.S. Cavalry Association,* Volume 1, Number 3 (November 1888), pp. 300–324.
Chaffee, Adna R. "James Harrison Wilson, Cavalryman." *Cavalry Journal,* Volume 34, Number 140 (July 1925), pp. 271–89.
Colby, Elbridge. "Wilson's Cavalry Campaign of 1865." *Journal of the American Military History Foundation,* Volume 2, Number 4 (Winter 1938), pp. 204–21.
Dickman, J. T. *Experiences in China.* Pamphlet of the Kansas Commandery, Military Order of the Loyal Legion of the United States, 1901.
Gilpin, E. N. "The Last Campaign—A Cavalryman's Journal." *Journal of the U.S. Cavalry Association,* Volume 18, Number 68 (April 1908), pp. 617–75.
Hay, Thomas Robson. "The Cavalry at Spring Hill." *Tennessee Historical Magazine,* Volume 8, Number 1 (April 1924), pp. 7–23.
Hay, William H. "James Harrison Wilson." *Annual Report of the Association of Graduates of the United States Military Academy,* 1931, pp. 75–83.
Jones, James P. (ed). " 'Your Left Arm': James H. Wilson's Letters to Adam Badeau." *Civil War History,* Volume 12, Number 3 (September 1966), pp. 230–45.
Julian, Allen P. "Fort Pulaski." *Civil War Times Illustrated,* Volume 9, Number 2 (May 1970), pp. 8–21.
Keenan, Jerry. "Wilson's Selma Raid." *Civil War Times Illustrated,* Volume 1, Number 9 (January 1963), pp. 37–44.
King, Spencer B., Jr. "A Poor Widow Asks for Food, 1865." *Georgia His-*

torical Quarterly, Volume 52, Number 4 (December 1968), pp. 449–50.

———. "April in Macon." *Georgia Review*, Volume 14, Number 2 (Summer 1960), pp. 143–55.

Longacre, Edward G. "Wilson-Kautz Raid." *Civil War Times Illustrated*, Volume 9, Number 2 (May 1970), pp. 32–42.

Luvaas, Jay. "Cavalry Lessons of the Civil War." *Civil War Times Illustrated*, Volume 6, Number 9 (January 1968), pp. 20–31.

Lynne, Donald M. "Wilson's Cavalry at Nashville." *Civil War History*, Volume 1, Number 2 (June 1955), pp. 141–59.

Mayo, William H. "Wilson's Cavalry Raid." *Maine Bugle*, Campaign 5, Call 4 (October 1898), pp. 391–96.

Miles, Nelson A. "The War with Spain—III." *North American Review*, Volume 169, Number 1 (July 1899), pp. 125–37.

Nye, Wilbur S. "James H. Wilson—A Profile." *Civil War Times Illustrated*, Volume 1, Number 2 (May 1962), pp. 40–41.

Stockham, Richard J. "Alabama Iron for the Confederacy: The Selma Works." *Alabama Review*, Volume 21, Number 3 (July 1968), pp. 163–72.

Thompson, E. Bruce. "The Bristow Presidential Boom of 1876." *Mississippi Valley Historical Review*, Volume 32, Number 1 (June 1945), pp. 3–30.

West, Richard S., Jr. "Gunboats in the Swamps: The Yazoo Pass Expedition." *Civil War History*, Volume 9, Number 2 (June 1963), pp. 157–66.

Wigginton, Thomas A. "Cavalry Operations in the Nashville Campaign." *Civil War Times Illustrated*, Volume 3, Number 8 (December 1964), pp. 40–43.

Wilson, James Harrison. "America's Interests in China." *North American Review*, Volume 166, Number 495 (February 1898), pp. 129–41.

———. "Do Americans Hate England?" *North American Review*, Volume 150, Number 303 (June 1890), pp. 771–75.

———. "A Staff-Officer's Journal of the Vicksburg Campaign, April 30 to July 4, 1863." *Journal of the Military Service Institution of the United States*, Volume 43, Number 154 (July–August 1908), pp. 93–109 and Volume 43, Number 155 (September–October 1908), pp. 261–75.

"Wilson's China." *Nation*, September 8, 1887, p. 196.

b. Books:

Alger, Russell A. *The Spanish-American War*. New York, 1901.

Ambrose, Stephen E. *Upton and the Army*. Baton Rouge, 1964.

Bache, Richard M. *Life of General George Gordon Meade, Commander of the Army of the Potomac*. Philadelphia, 1897.

Bearss, Edwin C. *Decision in Mississippi: Mississippi's Important Role in the War Between the States*. Jackson, 1962.

Boatner, Mark M., III. *The Civil War Dictionary*. New York, 1959.

Bowman, S. M., and Irwin, R. B. *Sherman and His Campaigns: A Military Biography.* New York, 1865.

Boynton, Henry V. *Was General Thomas Slow at Nashville? With a Description of the Greatest Cavalry Movement of the War, and General James H. Wilson's Cavalry Operations in Tennessee, Alabama, and Georgia.* New York, 1896.

Brackett, Albert G. *History of the United States Cavalry, from the Formation of the Federal Government to the 1st of June, 1863.* New York, 1865.

Bruce, Robert V. *Lincoln and the Tools of War.* Indianapolis, 1956.

Buckeridge, J. O. *Lincoln's Choice.* Harrisburg, Pa., 1956.

Carter, William Harding. *The Life of Lieutenant General Chaffee.* Chicago, 1917.

Catton, Bruce. *Grant Moves South.* Boston, 1960.

———. *Grant Takes Command.* Boston, 1969.

Chadwick, French E. *The Relations of the United States and Spain: The Spanish-American War* (Volume 2). New York, 1911.

Chipman, N. P. *The Tragedy of Andersonville: Trial of Captain Henry Wirz, the Prison Keeper.* Sacramento, 1911.

Civil War Sketches and Incidents: Papers Read by Companions of the Commandery of the State of Nebraska, Military Order of the Loyal Legion of the United States (Volume 1). Omaha, 1902.

Cleaves, Freeman. *Meade of Gettysburg.* Norman, Okla., 1960.

———. *Rock of Chickamauga: The Life of General George H. Thomas.* Norman, Okla., 1948.

Coolidge, Louis A. *Ulysses S. Grant.* Boston, 1922.

Coppée, Henry. *General Thomas.* New York, 1893.

Cox, Jacob D. *The March to the Sea, Franklin and Nashville.* New York, 1886.

Cullum, G. W. *Biographical Register of the Officers and Graduates of the United States Military Academy, at West Point, N.Y. from Its Establishment in 1802, to 1890.* Boston, 1891.

Dana, Charles A., and Wilson, James Harrison. *The Life of Ulysses S. Grant, General of the Armies of the United States.* Springfield, Mass., 1868.

Davies, Henry E. *General Sheridan.* New York, 1899.

Draper, John W. *History of the American Civil War* (Volume 3). New York, 1870.

Farley, Joseph Pearson. *West Point in the Early Sixties.* Troy, N.Y., 1902.

Flinn, Frank M. *Campaigning with Banks in Louisiana, '63 and '64, and with Sheridan in the Shenandoah Valley in '64 and '65.* Boston. 1889.

Foote, Shelby. *The Civil War: A Narrative* (Volume 2). New York, 1963.

Gillmore, Q. A. *Official Report . . . of the Siege and Reduction of Fort Pulaski, Georgia.* New York, 1862.

Glimpses of the Nation's Struggle: A Series of Papers Read before the Minnesota Commandery of the Military Order of the Loyal Legion of the United States (Volume 6). Minneapolis, 1909.

Greeley, Horace. *The American Conflict: A History of the Great Rebellion in the United States of America, 1860–'65*. Hartford, 1867.

Hay, Thomas Robson. *Hood's Tennessee Campaign*. New York, 1929.

Henry, Robert Selph. *"First with the Most" Forrest*. Indianapolis, 1944.

Herr, John K., and Wallace, Edward S. *The Story of the U.S. Cavalry, 1775–1942*. Boston, 1953.

Hicken, Victor. *Illinois in the Civil War*. Urbana, Ill., 1966.

Horn, Stanley F. *The Army of Tennessee: A Military History*. Indianapolis, 1941.

———. *The Decisive Battle of Nashville*. Baton Rouge, 1956.

Humphreys, Andrew A. *The Virginia Campaign of '64 and '65: The Army of the Potomac and the Army of the James*. New York, 1883.

Johnson, Richard W. *Memoir of Maj.-Gen. George H. Thomas*. Philadelphia, 1881.

Johnson, Robert Underwood, and Buel, C. C. (eds.). *Battles and Leaders of the Civil War* (Volumes 2, 3, and 4). New York, 1884–88.

Johnson, Rossiter (ed.). *The Twentieth Century Biographical Dictionary of Notable Americans* (Volume 10). Boston, 1904.

Johnson, Virginia W. *The Unregimented General: A Biography of Nelson A. Miles*. Boston, 1962.

Johnston, Angus James, II. *Virginia Railroads in the Civil War*. Chapel Hill, N.C., 1961.

Jordan, Thomas, and Pryor, J. P. *The Campaigns of Lieut.-Gen. N. B. Forrest and of Forrest's Cavalry*. New Orleans, Memphis, and New York, 1868.

Kettell, Thomas P. *History of the Great Rebellion*. Hartford, 1865.

Lawrence, Alexander A. *A Present for Mr. Lincoln: The Story of Savannah from Secession to Sherman*. Macon, Ga., 1961.

Lodge, Henry Cabot. *The War with Spain*. New York, 1899.

Lossing, Benson J. *Pictorial History of the Civil War in the United States of America* (Volume 3). Hartford, 1877.

Lytle, Andrew N. *Bedford Forrest and His Critter Company*. New York, 1931.

Macartney, Clarence E. *Grant and His Generals*. New York, 1953.

———. *Little Mac: The Life of General George B. McClellan*. Philadelphia, 1940.

McElroy, Robert. *Jefferson Davis: The Unreal and the Real* (Volume 2) (Reprint). New York, 1969.

McKinney, Francis F. *Education in Violence: The Life of George H. Thomas and the History of the Army of the Cumberland*. Detroit, 1961.

Malone, Dumas (ed.). *Dictionary of American Biography* (Volume 20). New York, 1943.

March, Alden. *The History and Conquest of the Philippines and Our Other Island Possessions*. Philadelphia, 1899.

Marquis, Albert N. (ed.). *Who's Who in America* (Volumes 1–13). Chicago, 1899–1925.

Marshall-Cornwall, James. *Grant as Military Commander.* New York, 1970.

Martin, John H. (comp.). *Columbus, Geo., From Its Selection as a "Trading Town" in 1827, to Its Partial Destruction by Wilson's Raid, in 1865.* Columbus, Ga., 1874.

Mathes, J. Harvey. *General Forrest.* New York, 1902.

Michie, Peter S. *The Life and Letters of Emory Upton.* New York, 1885.

Miers, Earl Schenck. *The General Who Marched to Hell: William Tecumseh Sherman and His March to Fame and Infamy.* New York, 1951.

———. *The Web of Victory: Grant at Vicksburg.* New York, 1955.

Military Essays and Recollections: Papers Read before the Commandery of the State of Illinois, Military Order of the Loyal Legion of the United States (Volumes 2, 3, and 4). Chicago, 1894–1907.

Miller, Francis Trevelyan (ed.). *The Photographic History of the Civil War* (Volumes 3, 4, and 9). New York, 1911.

Millis, Walter. *The Martial Spirit: A Study of Our War with Spain.* Boston, 1931.

Monaghan, Jay. *Custer: The Life of General George Armstrong Custer.* Boston, 1959.

Moore, Frank (ed.). *The Rebellion Record: A Diary of American Events* (Volumes 4, 8, and 11). New York, 1862–68.

Moore, James. *Kilpatrick and Our Cavalry.* New York, 1865.

Nields, John P. *James Harrison Wilson: Delaware's Greatest Soldier.* Wilmington, 1929.

O'Connor, Richard. *Sheridan the Inevitable.* Indianapolis, 1953.

Pennypacker, Isaac R. *General Meade.* New York, 1901.

Personal Recollections of the War of the Rebellion: Addresses Delivered before the Commandery of the State of New York, Military Order of the Loyal Legion of the United States (Volume 3). New York, 1907.

Pollard, Edward A. *The Lost Cause: A New Southern History of the War of the Confederates.* New York, 1867.

Pond, George E. *The Shenandoah Valley in 1864.* New York, 1883.

Pratt, Fletcher. *Eleven Generals: Studies in American Command.* New York, 1949.

Regulations for the U.S. Military Academy, at West Point, New-York. New York, 1853.

Rhodes, Charles D. *History of the Cavalry of the Army of the Potomac.* Kansas City, Mo., 1900.

Robinson, Albert G. *Cuba and the Intervention.* New York, 1905.

Schaff, Morris, *The Battle of the Wilderness.* Boston, 1910.

———. *The Spirit of Old West Point, 1858–1862.* Boston, 1908.

Shannon, Fred A. *The Organization and Administration of the Union Army, 1861–1865* (Volumes 1 and 2). Cleveland, 1928.

Shellenberger, John K. *The Battle of Spring Hill, Tennessee, November 29, 1864.* Cleveland, 1913.

Sketches of War History, 1861–1865: Papers Read Before the Ohio Commandery of the Military Order of the Loyal Legion of the United States (Volumes 1 and 2). Cincinnati, 1888.

Society of the Army of the Cumberland: Twenty-Seventh Reunion, Columbus, Ohio, 1897. Cincinnati, 1898.

Southern Historical Society Papers (Volume 5). Richmond, 1878.

Stackpole, Edward J. *Sheridan in the Shenandoah: Jubal Early's Nemesis.* Harrisburg, Pa., 1961.

Steele, Matthew Forney. *American Campaigns* (Volume 1). Washington, D.C., 1922.

Steere, Edward. *The Wilderness Campaign.* Harrisburg, Pa., 1960.

Stine, J. H. *History of the Army of the Potomac.* Philadelphia, 1892.

Stribling, Robert M. *Gettysburg Campaign and Campaigns of 1864 and 1865 in Virginia.* Petersburg, Va., 1905.

Swinton, William. *Campaigns of the Army of the Potomac.* New York, 1866.

Thomas, Benjamin P., and Hyman, Harold M. *Stanton: The Life and Times of Lincoln's Secretary of War.* New York, 1962.

Vale, Joseph G. *Minty and the Cavalry: A History of Cavalry Campaigns in the Western Armies.* Harrisburg, Pa., 1886.

Van Horne, Thomas B. *History of the Army of the Cumberland: Its Organization, Campaigns, and Battles* (Volume 2). Cincinnati, 1875.

———. *The Life of Major-General George H. Thomas.* New York, 1882.

Warner, Ezra J. *Generals in Blue: Lives of the Union Commanders.* Baton Rouge, 1964.

———. *Generals in Gray: Lives of the Confederate Commanders.* Baton Rouge, 1959.

War Papers: Read before the Commandery of the State of Wisconsin, Military Order of the Loyal Legion of the United States (Volumes 1 and 3). Milwaukee, 1891–1903.

Webb, Ross A. *Benjamin Helm Bristow, Border State Politician.* Lexington, Ky., 1969.

Williams, Kenneth P. *Lincoln Finds a General* (Volumes 1, 3, and 4). New York, 1949–56.

Wilson, James Harrison. *An Address on Our Trade Relations with the Tropics.* Boston, 1901.

———. *Annual Report of Brigadier General James H. Wilson, U.S.V., Commanding the Department of Matanzas and Santa Clara.* Matanzas, Cuba, 1899.

———. *China: Travel and Investigations in the "Middle Kingdom"* . . . *with a Glance at Japan.* New York, 1887.

———. *Life and Services of William Farrar Smith, Major General, United States Volunteers, in the Civil War.* Wilmington, Del., 1904.

———. *The Life of Charles A. Dana.* New York, 1907.

——. *The Life of John A. Rawlins.* New York, 1916.
——. *Our Relations with Cuba.* Wilmington, Del., 1902.
Wyeth, John Allan. *Life of General Nathan Bedford Forrest.* New York, 1899.

VI. Maps:

Esposito, Vincent J. (ed.). *The West Point Atlas of American Wars* (Volume 1). New York, 1959.
The Official Atlas of the Civil War (Reprint). New York, 1958.

Index